MAYHEW'S CHARACTERS

The Crippled Street Bird-Seller

MAYHEW'S CHARACTERS

Edited with a note on the English character
by PETER QUENNELL

selected from
'London Labour and the London Poor'
by HENRY MAYHEW

SPRING BOOKS

Published by The Hamlyn Publishing Group Limited
London · New York · Sydney · Toronto
Hamlyn House, Feltham, Middlesex, England
Printed in Czechoslovakia by TISK Brno
T 2055

CONTENTS

Contents

LIST OF ILLUSTRATIONS

Frontispiece: THE CRIPPLED STREET BIRD-SELLER

A NOTE ON THE ENGLISH CHARACTER

By Peter Quennell

The English character is like the English landscape — a pattern of incongruities, a tissue of contrast, composed in different moods, full of fragmentary survivals and odd anachronisms. A few steps from the tarmac arterial road runs a narrow lane tunnelled under the elder bushes. The air is heavy and sticky with the scent of elder flowers: and presently the path opens into a tangled clearing where a moorhen jigs desperately out of sight at the noise of an intruder, leaving a dark trail through the duckweed of a stagnant pond, and an ancient cottage glowers stolidly from beneath its brows of thatch. The weed on the pond is as green and dense-looking as the top of a billiard-table: the cottage comes from Rowlandson's or Morland's sketch-book: we are home again in a pastoral vignette of the eighteenth century.

Similar reminiscences of the past are still to be distinguished in the character of the present-day Englishman. A thousand years of accretion have made him what he is; but we must not forget that, during the process of development, the attributes that he has shed are almost as numerous as the attributes he has taken on. Some of his early changefulness may perhaps be accounted for by his racial origins:

> *"The Romans first with Julius Caesar came,*
> *Including all the nations of that name,*
> *Gauls, Greek, and Lombards; and, by computation,*
> *Auxiliaries and slaves of ev'ry nation...*
> *Thus from a mixture of all kinds began*
> *That heterogeneous thing, an Englishman:*
> *In eager rapes and furious lusts begot*
> *Between a painted Briton and a Scot;*
> *Where gendering offspring quickly learnt to bow*
> *And yoke their heifers to the Roman plough;*

From whence a mongrel halfbred race there came
With neither name nor nation, speech nor fame.
This nauseous brood directly did contain
The well-extracted blood of Englishmen."

And, although as early as the writing of the *Canterbury Tales,* we
seem to recognise the gradual evolution of a specifically English
temperament, it has undergone many and curious vicissitudes
between Chaucer's and our own period. To look back only as
far as the early sixteenth century, Erasmus, whose testimony,
however, is somewhat difficult to reconcile with Holbein's alarming portaits of the Tudor ruling class, their tightly folded lips,
angular reptilian jaws and pouched suspicious eyes) commented
on the flightiness and effusiveness of our national manners which
caused English persons of both sexes to kiss and embrace the
timid foreigner in and out of season. Equally strange to us seem
Elizabethan habits. Eloquence is no longer a particularly English
trait; but never has the human race been more in love with
language than were our ancestors in this bustling, aggressive and
vainglorious epoch. Shakespeare's clowns are as wordy as his
lovers and courtiers—they too have their conceits, their euphu-
isms, their attempts at high-sounding phraseology—and the
Puritans themselves were as verbose as the manufacturers of
"sugared" sonnets, magniloquent stage plays and rhetorical prose
romances. From the dreary monotone of moral reproof, the Puritan pamphleteer soon rises to the level of poetic declamation
sometimes with literary results that are extremely striking.

It is hard to believe that, gentle or simple, pagan or Puritan,
our sixteenth-century ancestors were ever slow or tongue-tied;
and, judging by all we know of their tastes and customs, the
groundlings who filled the bear-gardens, and packed the London
inn-yards to applaud or pelt the players, must have been as talk-
ative, as capricious and excitable, as any Neapolitan crowd. Just
as dissimilar from our own existence were the habits and pre-
occupations of the individual. Out of the semi-darkness that covers the life of a Shakespeare, a Marlowe or a Tourneur spring odd
glimpses of scholarly but dissipated bohemians who were frequently political agents first and poets afterwards. Most Eliza-

bethans had a touch of the gangster, and the legal records they have left behind them reverberate with passionate quarrels — stabbing affrays and duels between rival poets (such as the affair from which Jonson escaped only by pleading "benefit of clergy"), drunken rows in midnight streets and ignominious fisticuffs exchanged by landlady and lodger. If the character of the Elizabethan poet is often mysterious, so is the personality of the Elizabethan nobleman. Harnessed in a suit stiff with several thousands pounds' worth of orient pearls, heavily musk-scented against the stench of unwashed bodies, moving an elaborate train from house to house as the dirt accumulated in successive presence-chambers became at length intolerable, selfseeking politician student of the Latin classics and euphuistic author of English verses, he may sometimes be admired: we cannot claim that we understand him.

With the seventeenth century we cross the threshold of the modern universe. Seldom in so brief a period has any country produced so many admirable poets of the second rank side by side with poets and prose-writers of heroic magnitude. But, throughout the century, most educated Englishmen had certain points in common: a strain of mysticism, now and then, as in the works of Donne and Crashaw, inseparable from perfervid sensuality: a delight in witty conceits and profound analogies: a passionate love of music. Just why the English, from being an exceedingly harmonious race, should have become possibly the least musical in the entire contemporary world is a problem that no social historian has yet attempted to solve. The English love and knowledge of music did not die out till the opening of the industrial age: and during the seventeenth century poets as different in temperament as Milton, Crashaw and Dryden, men as diverse in character and outlook as Pepys and Evelyn, were alike in their sensitiveness to the power of harmony. Particularly during its latter decades the seventeenth century bore a considerable resemblance to the world we live in; but, although Pepys (even to the touch of *bourgeois* humbug that characterised his account of his rather squalid bar-parlour and back-room dissipations) shared many traits with a modern Englishman of the equivalent social class, his tastes were more eclectic and his pastimes on the whole considerably less uncivilised. With the interests of a born careerist he combined a thirst for knowledge, a liking for eloquence and a natural inclination towards the nobler products of the life around him — splendid books and good music, dignified houses among well-planned gardens and fine plantations, ingenious scientific treatises and the masterpieces, new and old, of the English poetic drama.

Comparatively, Georgian prospects seem flat and humdrum. The amazing versatility of earlier lyric writers has dwindled into the insipid poetising of Gay and Prior: speculation is replaced by conformity, invention by the worship of tame correctitude: and it required the genius of a Pope to be correct yet passionate. After the eager, troubled faces of the preceding epoch appear the smooth expressionless contenances of the early Augustan age. But if one side of the period emerges in the portraits, letters and memoirs of Lady Suffolk and her circle, Sir Robert Walpole illustrates its complementary aspect. On an equally massive scale were his talents and his shortcomings. It is the strength of eighteenth-century England that Sir Robert personifies, the cynicism, the sensuality, the exuberant good humour, before Gothic fantasy had begun to prevail over a classical love of form. He is the England of the cultured middle class and the lettered squirearchy, who quoted Cicero, Virgil and Horace on the benches of the House of Commons. Walpole's magnitude was acknowledged even by his bitterest enemies. Typical of our compatriots is their affection for the man who contrives to get most done when he affects to be least busy: for the statesman who, like Walpole, opens a letter from his gamekeeper before he breaks the seal of important state despatches, and defends his leisure and his private life against all intruders. Only once, during his last crisis, did Walpole allow himself to be deprived of a good night's sleep; and his courage at the moment of defeat bewildered all his adversaries. He remained imperturbable in triumph, and rose philosophic and undejected from the depths of failure.

It was during the age of Walpole, and a little later in the period covered by Hogarth, Fielding, Smollett, that the specific "Englishness" of Englishmen would seem first of all to have been exploited. From Hogarth's coarse abundant genius sprang a vision of bluff, rotund, smiling, red-cheeked Englishmen, reared on sides of roast beef frothing porter-pots, and of a France peopled by fat priests and cadaverous dancing-masters. The growth of insular pride coincided both with our acquisition of a lucrative Empire beyond the seas, and with the rise at home of a powerful and opinionated middle-class. Among the aristocracy there still prevailed a more liberal point of view. Chesterfield and Horace Walpole were as much at their ease in Parisian or Roman as in London drawing-rooms: they congratulated themselves on their elegant fluency in the French and Italian idiom: "polite society" was as acceptable wherever they found it—with Madame du Deffand in her conventual lodgings or with Lady Suffolk in her dignified retirement at Marble Hill, at St. James's or Saint Cloud, in Bath or Venice. The world they shared did not admit of territorial boundaries: their intimacies and acquaintanceships covered the whole of Europe.

In the narrower sense, both of them were "un-English" charracters, though their letters are among the chief glories of the English language: for they had none of the angularity that was to become a by-product of the idea of patriotism. Thus Gibbon's sympathies were as well-rounded as his physical framework: and the man who had fretted at English country life, and groaned under the dull restrictions of English military service, found himself, and worked out his genius, beside the Lake of Geneva, on international soil, in a neutral climate. Yet simultaneously the prodigious but distorted talents of Samuel Johnson were reaching full expansion. That combination of great gifts and small views, of vigorous intellect and violent prejudices, was to appear again and again in the years that followed—in the age of incomplete *colossi* and crippled giants, when it was one of the signs of literary genius to be a trifle cranky and the most exuberant and prolific writers were often the most irrational. In theory Johnson's thirst for knowledge comprehended the universe—did he not urge Boswell to visit the Wall of China and expatiate on the credit and satisfaction of ranging so far afield?—but in practice he clung tenaciously to Streatham and Fleet Street.

The dream of a homogenous international culture, as it had existed in the society of More and Erasmus, and still flourished, through a different language and with very different moral and political objects, in the society of Hume and Voltaire and Gibbon, was gradually losing its hold on the English intellect. The dawn of romanticism was accompanied by the birth of patriotism. For a few months, during the year 1789, English intellectuals enjoyed a dazzling vision of human brotherhood and warmed to the conception of general political freedom: but they shrank hurriedly into their insular shells as the Terror darkened. Some, like Wordsworth, Southey and, to a lesser degree, Coleridge, seem never quite to have recovered from their disappointment. Wordsworth retreated into conservatism of the most crabbed and graceless kind: Southey "sold out" to the Tory government, earning thereby the ferocious execrations of Shelley and Byron: Coleridge cut his losses, sublimated his sense of guilt and drifted off into the regions of nebulous opium fantasy. In fact, by the accident of the Napoleonic Wars, and by the long separation from the Continent those wars entailed, the navel-cord that bound England to Europe was slowly severed. Henceforth, Great Britain was to be the realm of mystery: its inhabitants, whether admired or disliked, to be regarded as scarcely human.

In any study of the Victorian Englishman (whom the Industrial Revolution and the Napoleonic Wars had now finally established as a being entirely distinct from his Continental, neighbours) attention must be paid to the great work of Henry Mayhew, *London Labour and the London Poor,* which first reached the English reading public exactly a hundred years ago. Mayhew dealt only with the poor, and with that section of the poor whose livelihood was most precarious; but he throws important light on the whole Victorian background. Nowhere, observed our foreign visitors, was the division between wealth and poverty more horrifying and more dramatic than in Europe's wealthiest capital: and from such contrasts they felt obliged to conclude that English prosperity was founded on a solid basis of national hypocrisy. Foreign criticism was obviously far-fetched; but it is certainly true that the Victorian middle- and upper-middle classes, conscious of a great formless, rootless proletariat, without traditions, loyalties or political privileges, immediately beneath their feet, because they felt constantly insecure, took refuge in some of the grosser forms of social snobbery and moral humbug. Podsnap's respectability was, in part, a façade, concealing fears that, since the year of revolutions, 1848, had never quite abated...

In two earlier volumes, *Mayhew's London* and *London's Underworld*, extracts have already been made from Mayhew's weighty masterpiece. The former depicted the London scene, and the extraordinary diversity of trades by which the urban poor subsisted; the latter explored the criminal depths underlying the world of honest, ill-paid daily work. But, besides being a social historian, Mayhew had a keen eye for individual oddities; and this collection of his *Characters* includes a number of the personal portraits for which space could not be found in either of the previous volumes. Among Englishmen or Englishwomen illustrated here are a flower-girl, a blind bootlace-seller, a vendor of ballads, a crippled bird-seller, a "Cheap-John", a beggar, a cesspool-sewerman. Mayhew gives us their life-stories as they were told to him in their own words; and those untutored autobiographies have, even today, a remarkably English and contemporary flavour. The social conditions they describe have long ago vanished; but the Cockney voices are still clearly recognisable. For instance, the street-seller who lived by hawking broad-sheet reports of notorious murder-trials:

"Greenacre didn't sell so well as might have been expected, for such a diabolical out-and-out crime as he committed; but you see he came close after Pegsworth, and that took the beauty off him. Two murders together is never no good to nobody..."

Or the contented cesspool-sewerman:

"Then I'listed into the Marines. *Oh, I hardly known what made me;* men does foolish things and don't known why; it's human nature... I was ... put on board the *Thunderer* man-of-war. ... She sailed through the Straits ... and was three years blockading the Dardanelles and cruising among the islands. ... They called them Greek islands, but I fancy as how it was Turks near the Dardanelles. O yes, the men on the islands was civil enough to us; they never spoke to us, and we never spoke to them. ... After that I was eight years and a quarter a gentleman's servant ... and then got tired of that and came to London... and have been on the sewers about five years. Yes, I prefer the sewers to the Greek islands."

While the crowds with money to spend thronged through the doors of the brand-new glittering Crystal Palace, and journalists spoke of Prince Albert's achievement as the crowning manifestation of British wealth and strength and industry, such were the voices that came from slums and street-corners — the voice of the ordinary unlettered Englishman, tough, stoical, insular, who remains unimpressed by the drama of history as it sweeps across his head. Today those voices have a vote behind them. But, in spite of revolutionary political changes, the accent has not greatly changed.

HENRY MAYHEW'S *PREFACE* TO *LONDON LABOUR AND THE LONDON POOR*

THE PRESENT volume* is the first of an intended series, which it is hoped will form, when complete, a cyclopaedia of the industry, the want, and the vice of the great Metropolis.

It is believed that the book is curious for many reasons:

It surely may be considered curious as being the first attempt to publish the history of a people, from the lips of the people themselves — giving a literal description of their labour, their earnings, their trials, and their sufferings, in their own "unvarnished" language; and to portray the condition of their homes and their families by personal observation of the places, and direct communion with the individuals.

It may be considered curious also as being the first commission of inquiry into the state of the people, undertaken by a private individual, and the first "blue book" ever published in twopenny numbers.

It is curious, moreover, as supplying information concerning a large body of persons, of whom the public had less knowledge than of the most distant tribes of the earth — the government population returns not even numbering them among the inhabitants of the kingdom; and as adducing facts so extraordinary, that the traveller in the undiscovered country of the poor must, like Bruce, until his stories are corroborated by after investigators, be content to lie under the imputation of telling such tales, as travellers are generally supposed to delight in.

Be the faults of the present volume what they may, assuredly they are rather short-comings than exaggerations, for in every instance the author and his coadjutors have sought to understate, and most assuredly never to exceed the truth. For the omissions,

---

* This Preface appeared in the first volume of *London Labour and the London Poor*. Two further volumes completed Mayhew's original plan, but in 1862 a fourth volume was added dealing with thieves, prostitutes and swindlers. *Mayhew's Characters* and *Mayhew's London* are compiled from the first three volumes, while *London's Underworld* is a selection from the fourth. [Publisher's note.]

the author would merely remind the reader of the entire novelty of the task—there being no other similar work in the language by which to guide or check his enquiries. When the following leaves are turned over, and the two or three pages of information derived from books contrasted with the hundreds of pages of facts obtained by positive observation and investigation, surely some allowance will be made for the details which may still be left for others to supply. Within the last two years some thousands of the humbler classes of society must have been seen and visited with the especial view of noticing their condition and learning their histories; and it is but right that the truthfulness of the poor generally should be made known; for though checks have been usually adopted, the people have been mostly found to be astonishingly correct in their statements—so much so indeed, that the attempts at deception are certainly the exceptions rather than the rule. Those persons who, from an ignorance of the simplicity of the honest poor, might be inclined to think otherwise, have, in order to be convinced of the justice of the above remarks, only to consult the details given in the present volume, and to perceive the extraordinary agreement in the statements of all the vast number of individuals who have been seen at different times, and who cannot possibly have been supposed to have been acting in concert.

The larger statistics, such as those of the quantities of fish and fruit, &c., sold in London, have been collected from tradesmen connected with the several markets, or from the wholesale merchants belonging to the trade specified—gentlemen to whose courtesy and co-operation I am indebted for much valuable information, and whose names, were I at liberty to publish them, would be an indisputable guarantee for the facts advanced. The other statistics have been obtained in the same manner—the best authorities having been invariably consulted on the subject treated of.

It is right that I should make special mention of the assistance I have received in the compilation of the present volume from Mr. HENRY WOOD and Mr. RICHARD KNIGHT (late of the City Mission), gentlemen who have been engaged with me from nearly the commencement of my inquiries, and to whose hearty co-operation both myself and the public are indebted for a large increase of knowledge. Mr. Wood, indeed, has contributed so large a proportion of the contents of the present volume that he may fairly be considered as one of its authors.

The subject of the Street-Folk will still require another volume, in order to complete it in that comprehensive manner in which I am desirous of executing the modern history of this and every other portion of the people. There still remain — the *Street-Buyers,* the *Street-Finders,* the *Street-Performers,* the *Street-Artizans,* and the *Street-Labourers,* to be done, among the several classes of street-people; and the *Street Jews,* the *Street Italians and Foreigners,* and the *Street Mechanics,* to be treated of as varieties of the order. The present volume refers more particularly to the *Street-Sellers,* and includes special accounts of the *Costermongers* and the *Patterers* (the two broadly-marked varieties of street tradesmen), the *Street Irish,* the *Female Street-Sellers,* and the *Children Street-Sellers* of the metropolis.

My earnest hope is that the book may serve to give the rich a more intimate knowledge of the sufferings, and the frequent heroism under those sufferings, of the poor — that it may teach those who are beyond temptation to look with charity on the frailties of their less fortunate brethren — and cause those who are in "high places," and those of whom much is expected, to bestir themselves to improve the condition of a class of people whose misery, ignorance, and vice, amidst all the immense wealth and great knowledge of "the first city in the world," is, to say the very least, a national disgrace to us.

A RUNNING PATTERER

FEW OF THE residents in London – but chiefly those in the quieter
streets – have not been aroused, and most frequently in the evening, by a hurly-burly on each side of the street. An attentive
listening will not lead anyone to an accurate knowledge of what
the clamour is about. It is from a "mob" or "school" of the
running patterers (for both those words are used), and consists of
two, three, or four men. All these men state that the greater the
noise they make, the better is the chance of sale, and better still
when the noise is on each side of a street, for it appears as if the
vendors were proclaiming such interesting or important intelli-
gence, that they were vieing with one another who should supply
the demand which must ensue. It is not possible to ascertain with
any certitude what the patterers are so anxious to sell, for only
a few leading words are audible. One of the cleverest of running
patterers repeated to me, in a subdued tone, his announcements
of murders. The words "Murder," "Horrible," "Barbarous,"
"Love," "Mysterious," "Former Crimes," and the like, could only
be caught by the ear, but there was no announcement of anything
like "particulars".

If, however, the "paper" relate to any well-known criminal,
such as Rush, the name is given distinctly enough, and so is any
new or pretended fact. The running patterers describe, or profess
to describe, the contents of their papers as they go rapidly along,
and they seldom or ever stand still. They usually deal in murders,
seductions, "crim.-cons.," explosions, alarming accidents, "assas-
sinations," deaths of public characters, duels, and love-letters.
But popular, or notorious, murders are the "great goes". The
running patterer cares less than other street-sellers for bad
weather, for if he "work" on a wet and gloomy evening, and if the
work be "a cock," which is a fictitious statement or even a pretended fictious statement, there is the less chance of anyone detect-
ing the *ruse*. But of late years no new "cocks" have been printed,
excepting for temporary purposes. Among the old stereotyped

"cocks" are love-letters. One is well-known as "The Husband caught in a Trap," and being in an epistolary form subserves any purpose: whether it be the patterer's aim to sell the "Love-Letters" of any well-known person, such as Lola Montes, or to fit them for a local (pretended) scandal, as the "Letters from a Lady in this neighbourhood to a Gentleman not 100 miles off."

Of running patterers there are now in London from 80 to 100. They reside—some in their own rooms, but the majority in lodging-houses—in or near Westminster, St. Giles's, Whitechapel, Stratford, Deptford, Wandsworth, and the Seven Dials. The "Dials," however, is their chief locality, being the residence of the longest-established printers, and is the "head meet" of the fraternity.

It is not easy to specify with exactitude the number of running or flying patterers at any one time in London. Some of these men become, occasionally, standing patterers, chaunters, or ballad-singers—classes I shall subsequently describe—and all of them resort at intervals to country rounds. I heard, also, many complaints of boys having of late "taken to the running patter" when anything attractive was before the public, and of ignorant fellows —that wouldn't have thought of it at one time—"trying their hands at it." Waiving these exceptional augmentations of the number, I will take the body of running patterers, generally employed in their peculiar craft in London, at 90. To ascertain their earnings presents about the same difficulties as to ascertain their number; for as all they earn is spent—no patterer ever saving money—they themselves are hardly able to tell their incomes. If any new and exciting fact be before the public, these men may each clear 20s. a week; when there is no such fact, they may not earn 5s. The profit is contingent, moreover, upon their being able to obtain 1d. or only ¹/₂d., for their paper. Some represented their average weekly earnings at 12s. 6d. the year through; some at 10s. 6d.; and others at less than half of 12s. Reckoning, however, that only 9s. weekly is an average profit per individual, and that 14s. be taken to realise that profit, we find £3,276 expended yearly on running patterers in London; but in that sum the takings of the chaunters must be included, as they are members of the same fraternity, and work with the patterers.

The capital required to commence as a running patterer is but the price of a few papers — from 2*d*. to 1*s*. The men have no distinctive dress: "our togs," said one of them, "is in the latest fashion of Petticoat-lane;" unless on the very rare occasions, when some character has to be personated, and then coloured papers and glazed calicoes are made available. But this is only a venture of the old hands.

From a running patterer, who has been familiar with the trade for many years, I received, upwards of a twelvemonth ago, the following statement. He is well known for his humour, and is a leading man in his fraternity. After some conversation about "cocks," the most popular of which, my informant said, was the murder at Chigwell-row, he continued:

"That's a trump to the present day. Why, I'd go out now, sir, with a dozen of Chigwell-rows, and earn my supper in half an hour off of'em. The murder of Sarah Holmes at Lincoln is good, too — that there has been worked for the last five year successively every winter. Poor Sarah Holmes! Bless her! she has saved me from walking the streets all night many a time. Some of the best of these have been in work twenty years — the Scarborough murder has full twenty years. It's called 'THE SCARBOROUCH TRAGEDY.' I've worked it myself. It's about a noble and rich young naval officer seducing a poor clergyman's daughter. She is confined in a ditch, and destroys the child. She is taken up for it, tried, and executed. This has a great run. It sells all round the country places, and would sell now if they had it out. Mostly all our customers is females. They are the chief dependence we have. The Scarborough Tragedy is very attractive. It draws tears to the women's eyes to think that a poor clergyman's daughter, who is remarkably beautiful, should murder her own child; it's very touching to every feeling heart. There's a copy of verses with it, too.

"Then there's the Liverpool Tragedy — that's very attractive. It's a mother murdering her own son, through gold. He had come from the East Indies, and married a rich planter's daughter. He came back to England to see his parents after an absence of thirty years. They kept a lodging-house in Liverpool for sailors; the son went there to lodge, and meant to tell his parents who he was in the morning. His mother saw the gold he had got in his boxes, and cut his throat—severed his head from his body; the old man, upwards of seventy years of age, holding the candle. They had put a washing-tub under the bed to catch his blood. The morning after the murder, the old man's daughter calls and enquires for a young man. The old man denies that they have had any such person in the house. She says he had a mole on his arm, in the shape of a strawberry. The old couple go up-stairs to examine the corpse, and find they have murdered their own son, and then they both put an end to their existence. This is a deeper tragedy than the Scarborough Murder. That suits young people better; they like to hear about the young woman being seduced by the naval officer; but the mothers take more to the Liverpool Tragedy—it suits them better. Some of the 'cocks' were in existence long before ever I was born or thought of. The 'Great and important battle between two young ladies of fortune,' is what we calls a 'ripper.' I should like to have that there put down correct," he added, "'cause I've taken a tidy lot of money out of it."

My informant, who had been upwards of 20 years in the running patter line, told me that he commenced his career with the "Last Dying Speech and Full Confession of William Corder." He was sixteen years of age, and had run away from his parents. "I worked that there," he said, "down in the very town (at Bury) where he was executed. I got a whole hatful of halfpence at that. Why, I wouldn't even give 'em seven for sixpence—no, that I wouldn't. A gentleman's servant come out and wanted half a dozen for his master and one for himself in, and I wouldn't let him have no such thing. We often sells more than that at once. Why, I sold six at one go to the railway clerks at Norwich about the Manning affair, only about a fortnight back. But Steinburgh's little job—you know he murdered his wife and family, and committed suicide after—that sold as well as any 'die'. Pegsworth was an out-and-out lot. I did tremendous with him, because it happened in London, down Ratcliff-highway—that's a splendid quarter for working—there's plenty of feelings—but, bless you, some places you go to you can't move no how, they've hearts like paving-stones. They wouldn't have the 'papers' if you'd give them to 'em—especially when they knows you. Greenacre didn't sell so well as might have been expected, for such a diabolical out-an-out crime as he committed; but you see he came close after Pegsworth, and that took the beauty off him. Two murders together is never no good to nobody.

"Why, there was Wilson Gleeson, as great a villain as ever lived — went and murdered a whole family at noon-day — but Rush coopered him — and likewise that girl at Bristol — made it no draw to any one. Daniel Good, though, was a first rater; and would have been better if hadn't been for that there Madam Toosow. You see, she went down to Roehampton, and guv £2, for the werry clogs as he used to wash his master's carriage in; so, in course, when the harristocracy could go and see the real things — the werry identical clogs — in the Chamber of 'Orrors, why the people wouldn't look at our authentic portraits of the fiend in human form. Hocker wasn't any particular great shakes. There was a deal expected from him, but he didn't turn out well. Courvoisier was much better; he sold very well, but nothing to Blakesley. Why, I worked him for six weeks. The wife of a murdered man kept the King's Head that he was landlord on open on the morning of the execution, and the place was like a fair. I even went and sold papers outside the door myself. I thought if she war'n't ashamed, why should I be? After that we had a fine 'fake' — that was the fire of the Tower of London — it sold rattling. Why we had forty apprehended for that — first we said two soldiers was taken up that couldn't obtain their discharge, and then we declared it was a well-known sporting nobleman who did it for a spree. The boy Jones in the Palace wasn't much of an affair for the running patterers; the ballad singers — or street screamers, as we calls 'em — had the pull out of that. The patter wouldn't take; they had read it all in the newspapers before. Oxford, and Francis, and Bean were a little better, but nothing to crack about. The people doesn't care about such things as them.

"There's nothing beats a stunning good murder, after all. Why, there was Rush — I lived on him for a month or more. When I commenced with Rush, I was 14s. in debt for rent, and in less than fourteen days I astonished the wise men in the east by paying my landlord all I owed him. Since Dan'el Good there had been little or nothing doing in the murder line — no one could cap him — till

Rush turned up a regular trump for us. Why, I went down to Norwich expressly to work the execution. I worked my way down there with '*a sorrowful lamentation*' of his own composing, which I'd got written by the blind man expressly for the occasion. On the morning of the execution we beat all the regular newspapers out of the field; for we had the full, true, and particular account down, you see, by our own express, and that can beat anything that ever they can publish; for we gets it printed several days afore it comes off, and goes and stands with it right under the drop; and many's the penny I've turned away when I've been asked for an account of the whole business *before* it happened.

"So you see, for herly and correct hinformation, we can beat the *Sun*—aye, or the moon either, for the matter of that. Irish Jem, the Ambassador, never goes to bed but he blesses Rush the farmer; and many's the time he's told me we should never have such another windfall as that. But I told him not to despair; there's a good time coming, boys, says I, and, sure enough, up comes the Bermondsey tragedy. We might have done very well, indeed, out of the Mannings, but there was too many examinations for it to be any great account to us. I've been away with the Mannings in the country ever since. I've been through Hertfordshire, Cambridgeshire, and Suffolk, along with George Frederick Manning and his wife—travelled from 800 to 1,000 miles with 'em, but I could have done much better if I had stopped in London. Every day I was anxiously looking for a confession from Mrs. Manning. All I wanted was for her to clear her conscience afore she left this here whale of tears (that's what I always calls it in the patter), and when I read in the papers (mind they was none of my own) that her last words on the brink of heternity was, 'I've nothing to say to you, Mr. Rowe, but to thank you for kindness,' I guv her up entirely—had completely done with her. In course the public looks to us for the last words of all monsters in human form, and as for Mrs. Manning's, they were not worth the printing."

From the same man I had the following account of his vocation up to the present time:

"Well, sir," he said. "I think, take them altogether, things hasn't been so good this last year as the year before. But the Pope, God bless him! he's been the best friend I've had since

Rush, but Rush licked his Holiness. You see, the Pope and Cardinal Wiseman is a one-sided affair; of course the Catholics won't buy anything against the Pope, but *all* religions could go for Rush. Our mob once thought of starting a Cardinal's dress, and I thought of wearing a red hat myself. I did wear a shovel hat when the Bishop of London was our racket; but I thought the hat began to feel too hot, so I shovelled it off. There was plenty of paper that would have suited to work with a cardinal's hat. There was one, — 'Cardinal Wiseman's Lament,' — and it was giving his words like, and a red hat would have copped it. It used to make the people roar when it came to snivelling, and grumbling at little Jack Russell — by Wiseman, in course; and when it comes to this part — which alludes to that 'ere thundering letter to the Bishop of Durham — the people was stunned:

> '*He called me a buffalo, bull, and a monkey,*
> *And then with a soldier called Old Arthur conkey*
> *Declared they would buy me a ninepenny donkey,*
> *And send me to Rome to the Pope.*'

"They shod me, sir. *Who's* they? Why, the Pope and Cardinal Wiseman. I call my clothes after them I earn money by to buy them with. My shoes I call Pope Pius; my trowsers and braces, Calcraft; my waistcoat and shirt, Jael Denny; and my coat, Love Letters. A man must show a sense of gratitude in the best way he can. But I didn't start the cardinal's hat; I thought it might prove disagreeable to Sir Robert Peel's dress lodgers. There was very little doing for some time after I gave you an account before; hardly a slum worth a crust and a pipe of tobacco to us. A slum's a paper fake, — make a foot-note of that, sir. I think Adelaide was the first thing I worked after I told you of my tomfooleries. Yes, it was, — her helegy. She weren't of no account whatsomever, and Cambridge was no better nor Adelaide.

"But there was poor Sir Robert Peel, — he *was* some good; indeed, I think he was as good as 5*s*. a day to me for the four or five days when he was freshest. Browns were thrown out of the windows to us, and one copper cartridge was sent flying at us with 13$^1/_2$*d*. in it, all copper, as if it had been collected.

I worked Sir Robert at the West End, and in the quiet streets and squares. Certainly we had a most beautiful helegy. Well, poor gentleman, what we earned on him was some set-off to us for his starting his new regiment of Blues—the Cook's Own. Not that they've troubled me much. I was once before Alderman Kelly, when he was Lord Mayor, charged with obstructing, or some humbug of that sort. 'What are you, my man?' says he quietly, and like a gentleman. 'In the same line as yourself, my lord,' says I. 'How's that?' says he. 'I'm a paper-worker for my living, my lord,' says I. I was soon discharged; and there was such fun and laughing, that if I'd had a few slums in my pocket, I believe I could have sold them all in the justice-room.

"Haynau was a stunner, and the draymen came their caper just in the critical time for us, as things was growing very taper. But I did best with him in chaunting; and so, as you want to hear about chaunting, I'll tell you after. We're forced to change our patter—first running, then chaunting, and then standing—oftener than we used to.

"Then Calcraft was pretty tidy browns. He was up for starving his mother,—and what better can you expect of a hangman? Me and my mate worked him down at Hatfield, in Essex, where his mother lives. It's his native, I believe. We sold her one. She's a limping old body. I saw the people look at her, and they told me arterards who she was. 'How much?' says she. 'A penny, marm,' say I. 'Sarve him right,' says she. We worked it, too, in the street in Hoxton where he lives, and he sent out for two, which shows he's a sensible sort of character in some points, after all. Then we had a 'Woice from the Gaol! or the Horrors of the Condemned Cell! Being the Life of William Calcraft, the present Hangman.' It's written in the high style, and parts of it will have astonished the hangman's nerves before this. Here's a bit of the patter now:

'Let us look at William Calcraft,' says the eminent author, 'in his earliest days. He was born about the year 1801, of humble but industrious parents, at a little village in Essex. His infant ears often listened to the children belonging to the Sunday schools of his native place, singing the well-known words of Watt's beautiful hymn,

'When e'er I take my walks abroad
How many poor I see, &c.'

But alas for the poor farmer's boy, he never had the opportunity of going to that school to be taught how to "shun the broad way leading to destruction." To seek a chance fortune he travelled up to London where his ignorance and forlorn condition shortly enabled the fell demon which ever haunts the footsteps of the wretched, to mark him for her own.'

"Isn't that stunning, sir? Here it is in print for you. 'Mark him for her own!' Then, poor dear, he's so sorry to hang anybody. Here's another bit:

'But in vain he repents, he has no real friend in the world but his wife, to whom he can communicate his private thoughts, and in return receive consolation, can any lot be harder than this? Hence his nervous system is fast breaking down, every day rendering him less able to endure the excruciating and agonizing torments he is hourly suffering, he is haunted by remorse heaped upon remorse, every fresh victim he is required to strangle being so much additional fuel thrown upon that mental flame which is scorching him.'

"You may believe me, sir, an I can prove the fact — the author of that beautiful writing ain't in parliament! Think of the mental flame, sir! O, dear.

"Sirrell was no good either. Not salt to a herring. Though we worked him in his own neighbourhood, and pattered about gold and silver all in a row. 'Ah!' says one old woman, 'he was a 'spectable man.' 'Werry, marm,' says I.

"Hollest weren't no good either, 'cause the wictim was a parson. If it had happened a little later, *we'd* have had it to rights; the newspapers didn't make much of it. We'd have shown it was the 'Commencement of a Most a Horrid and Barbarious Plot got up by the Pope and Cardinal Wiseman *for-r* the Mas-ser-cree-ing of all good Protestant Ministers.' That would have been the dodge, sir! A beautiful idear, now, isn't it? But the murder came off badly, and you can't expect fellows like them murderers to have any regard for the interest of art and literature. Then there's so long to wait between the murder and the trial, that unless the fiend in human form keeps writing beautiful love-letters, the excitement can't be kept up. *We* can write love-letters for the fiend in human? That's quite true, and we once had a great pull that way over the newspapers. But Lord love you, there's plenty of 'em gets more and more into our line. They treads in our footsteps, sir; they follows our bright example. O! isn't there a nice rubbing and polishing up. This here copy won't do. This must be left out, and that put in; 'cause it suits the walk of the paper. Why, you must know, sir. *I* know. Don't tell me. You can't have been on the *Morning Chronicle* for nothing.

"Then there was the 'Horrid and Inhuman Murder, Committed by T. Drory, on the Body of Jael Denny, at Donninghurst, a Village in Essex.' We worked it in every way. Drory had every chance given to him. We had half-sheets, and copies of werses, and books. A werry tidy book it was, setting off with showing how 'The secluded village of Donninghurst has been the scene of a most determined and diabolical murder, the discovery of which early on Sunday, the 12th, in the morning, has thrown the whole of this part of the country into a painful state of excitement.' Well, sir, well—werry well; that bit was taken from a newspaper. Oh, we're not above acknowledging when we condescends to borrow from any of 'em. If you remember, when I saw you about the time, I told you I thought Jael Denny would turn out as good as Maria Martin. And without any joke or nonsense, sir, it really is a most shocking thing. But she didn't. The weather coopered her, poor lass! There was money in sight, and we couldn't touch it; it seemed washed away from us, for you may remember how wet it was. I made a little by her, though.

"For all that, I haven't done with Master Drory yet. If God spares my life, he shall make it up to me. Why, now sir, is it reasonable, that a poor man like me should take so much pains to make Drory's name known all over the country, and walk miles and miles in the rain to do it, and get only a few bob for my labour? It can't be thought on. When the Wile and Inhuman Seducer takes his trial, he must pay up my just claims. I'm not going to take all that trouble on his account, and let him off so easily.

"My last paying caper was the Sloanes. They beat Haynau. I declare to you, sir, the knowingest among us couldn't have invented a cock to equal the conduct of them Sloanes. Why, it's disgusting to come near the plain truth about them. I think, take it altogether, Sloane was as good as the Pope, but he had a stopper like Pius the Ninth, for that was a one-sided affair, and the Catholics wouldn't buy; and Sloane was too disgusting for the gentry, or better sort, to buy him. But I've been in little streets where some of the windows was without sashes, and some that had sashes had stockings thrust between the frames and I've taken half a bob in ha'pennies. Oh! you should have heard what poor women said about him, for it was women that bought him most. They was more savage against him than against her. Why, they had fifty deaths for him. Rolling in a barrel, with lots of sharp nails inside, down Primrose-hill, and turned out to the women on Kennington-common, and boiled alive in oil or stuff that can't be mentioned, or hung over a slow fire. 'O, the poor dear girl,' says they, 'what she's suffered.' We had accounts of Mistress Sloane's apprehension before the papers. We had it at Jersey, and they had it at Boulogne, but we were first. Then we discovered, because we *must* be in advance of the papers, that Miss Devaux was Sloane's daughter by a former wife, and Jane Wilbred was Mrs. Sloane's daughter by a former husband, and was entitled to £1,000 by rights. Haynau was a fool to Sloane.

"I don't know of anything fresh that's in hand, sir. One of our authors is coming out with something spicy, against Lord John, for doing nothing about Wiseman; 'cause he says as no one thing that he's written for Lord John ever sold well, something against him may."

OTHER PATTERERS

I PROCEED to abduce an account of the different grades of patterers generally, for patter has almost as many divisions as literature. There is patter pathetic, as from beggars; bouncing, to puff off anything of little or no value; comic, as by clowns; descriptive, as in the cases where the vendor describes, however ornately, what he really sells; religious, as occasionally by the vendors of tracts; *real patter* (as it is understood by the profession) to make a thing believed to be what it is not; classical, as in the case of the sale of stenographic cards, &c.; and sporting, as in race cards.

The pattering tribe is by no means confined to the traffic in paper, though it may be the principle calling as regards the acuteness of its professors. Among these street-folk are the running and standing patterers (or stationers as they are sometimes, but rarely, styled) — and in these are included, the Death and Fire Hunters; Chaunters; Second Edition-sellers; Reciters; Conundrum-sellers; Board-workers; Strawers; Sellers of (Sham) Indecent Publications; Street Auctioneers; Cheap Jacks; Mountebanks (quacks); Clowns; the various classes of Showmen; Jugglers; Conjurors; Ring-sellers for wagers; Sovereign-sellers; Corn-curers; Grease-removers; French-polishers; Blacking-sellers; Nostrum-vendors; Fortune-tellers; Oratorical-beggars; Turnpike-sailors; the classes of Lurkers; Stenographic Card-sellers, and the Vendors of Race-cards or lists.

The following accounts have been written for me by a gentleman who has for some years resided among the class, and has pursued a street calling for his existence. His remarks have of course all the weight due to personal experience, as well as to close observation.

"I wish," says the writer in question, "in the disclosures I am now about to make concerning the patterers generally, to *do more* than merely put the public on their guard. I take no cruel delight in dragging forth the follies of my fellow-men. Before I have done with my subject, I hope to draw forth and exhibit some of the

33

latent virtues of the class under notice, many of whom I know to sigh in secret over that one imprudent step (whatever its description), which has furnished the censorious with a weapon they have been but too ready to wield. The first thing for me to do is to give a glance at the *habitations* of these outcasts, and to set forth their usual conduct, opinions, conversations and amusements. As London (including the ten mile circle), is the headquarters of lodging-house life, and least known, because most crowded, I shall lift the veil which shrouds the vagrant hovel where the patterer usually resides.

"As there are many individuals in lodging-houses who are not regular patterers or professional vagrants, being rather, as they term themselves, 'travellers' (or tramps), so there are multitudes who do *not* inhabit such houses who really belong to the fraternity, pattering, or vagrant. Of these some take up their abode in what they call 'flatty-kens,' that is, houses the landlord of which is not 'awake' or 'fly' to the 'moves' and dodges of the trade; others resort to the regular 'padding-kens,' or houses of call for vagabonds; while others—and especially those who have families —live constantly in furnished rooms, and have little intercourse with the 'regular' travellers, tramps, or wanderers.

"The medium houses the London vagrant haunts, (for I have no wish to go to extremes either way,) are probably in Westminster, and perhaps the fairest 'model' of the '*monkry*' is the house in Orchard-street—once the residence of royalty—which has been kept and conducted for half a century by the veteran who some fifty years ago was the *only* man who amused the population with that well-known ditty,

> '*If I'd as much money as I could tell,*
> *I would not cry young lambs to sell.*'

Mister (for that is the old man's title) still manufactures lambs, but seldom goes out himself; his sons (obedient and exemplary young men) take the toys into the country, and dispose of them at fairs and markets. The wife of this man is a woman of some beauty and good sound sense, but far too credulous for the position of which she is the mistress.

34

"So much for the establishment. I have now to deal with the inmates.

"No one could be long an inmate of Mr.——s' without discerning in the motley group persons who had seen better days, and, seated on the same bench, persons who are 'seeing' the best days they *ever* saw. When I took up my abode in the house under consideration, I was struck by the appearance of a middle-aged, lady-like woman, a native of Worcester, bred to the glove trade, and brought up in the lap of plenty, and under the high sanction of religious principle. She had evidently some source of mental anguish. I believe it was the conduct of her husband, by whom she had been deserted, and who was living with a woman to whom, it is said, the wife had shown much kindness. By her sat a giant in size, and candour demands that I should say a 'giant in sin.' When Navy Jem, as he is called, used to *work* for his living (it was a long while ago) he drove a barrow at the formation of the Great Western Railway. At present the man lies in bed till midday, and when he makes his appearance in the kitchen,

> '*The very kittens on the hearth*
> *They dare not even play.*'

His breakfast embraces all the good things of the season. He divides his delicacies with a silver fork—where did he get it? The mode in which this man obtains a livelihood is at once a mixture and a mystery. His prevailing plan is to waylay gentlemen in the decline of life, and to extort money by threats of accusation and exposure, to which I can do no more than allude. His wife, a notorious shop-lifter, is now for the third time 'expiating her offences' in Coldbathfields.

"Next to Navy Jem may be perceived a little stunted woman, of pretended Scotch, but really Irish extraction, whose husband has died in the hospital for consumption at least as many times as the hero of Waterloo has seen engagements. At last the man *did* die, and his widow has been collecting money to bury him for eight years past, but has not yet secured the required sum. This woman, whose name I never knew, has a boy and a girl; to the former she is very kind, the latter she beats without mercy, always before breakfast, and with such (almost) unvaried punctuality that her brother will sometimes whisper (after saying grace), 'Mother, has our Poll had her licks yet?'

"Among the records of mortality lately before the public, is the account of a notorious woman, who was found suffocated in a stagnant pool, whether from suicide or accident it was impossible to determine. She had been in every hospital in town and country, suffering from a disease, entirely self-procured. She applied strong acids to wounds previously punctured with a pin, and so caused her body to present one mass of sores. She was deemed incurable by the hospital doctors, and liberal collections were made for her among the benevolent in various places. The trick, however, was ultimately discovered, and the failure of her plan (added to the bad state of health to which her bodily injuries had gradually led) preyed upon her mind and hastened her death.

"This woman had been the paramour of 'Peter the crossing-sweeper,' a man who for years went about showing similar wounds, which he pretended had been inflicted while fighting in the Spanish Legion — though, truth to say, he had never been nearer Spain than Liverpool is to New York. He had followed the 'monkry' from a child, and chiefly, since manhood, as a 'broken-down weaver from Leicester,' and after singing through every one of the provinces 'We've got no work to do,' he scraped acquaintance with a 'school of shallow coves;' that is, men who go about half-naked, telling frightful tales about ship-wrecks, hair-breadth escapes from houses on fire, and such like aqueous and ingenous calamities. By these Peter was initiated in the '*scaldrum dodge*,' or the art of burning the body with a mixture of acids and gunpowder, so as to suit the hues and complexions of the accident to be deplored. Such persons hold every morning a 'committee of ways and means,' according to whose decision the movements of the day are carried out. Sometimes when on their country rounds, they go singly up to the houses of the gentry and wealthy farmers, begging shirts, which they hide in hedges while they go to another house and beg a similar article. Sometimes they go in crowds, to the number of from twelve to twenty; they are most successful when the 'swell' is not at home; if they can meet with the 'Burerk' (Mistress), or the young ladies, they 'put it on them for dunnage' (beg a stock of general clothing), flattering their

victims first and frightening them afterwards. A friend of mine
was present in a lodging-house in Plymouth, when a school of
shallow coves returned from their day's work with *six suits of
clothes, and twenty-seven shirts, besides children's apparel and shoes,*
(all of which were sold to a broker in the same street), and, besides
these, the donations in money received amounted to 4*s.* 4*d.* a man.

"At this enterprise 'Peter' continued several years, but—to use
his own words—'everything has but a time,' the country got
'dead' to him, and people got 'fly' to the 'shallow brigade'; so
Peter came up to London to 'try his hand at something else.'
Housed in the domicile of 'Sayer the barber,' who has enriched
himself by beer-shops and lodging-house-keeping, to the tune it is
said of £20,000, Peter amused the 'travellers' of Wentworth-
street, Whitechapel, with recitals of what he had seen and done.
Here a profligate, but rather intelligent man, who had really been
in the service of the Queen of Spain, gave him an old red jacket,
and with it such instructions as equipped him for the imposition.
One sleeve of this jacket usually hung loosely by his side, while
the arm it should have covered was exposed naked, and to all
appearance withered. His rule was to keep silence till a crowd
assembled around him, when he began to '*patter*' to them to the
following effect: 'Ladies and gentlemen, it is with feelings of no
common reluctance that I stand before you at this time; but
although I am not without *feelings,* I am totally without friends,
and frequently without food. This wound (showing his disfigured
arm) I received in the service of the Queen of Spain, and I have
many more on different parts of my person. I received a little
praise for my brave conduct, but not a penny pension, and here
I am (there's no deception you see) ill in health—poor in pocket,
and exposed without proper nourishment to wind and weather—
the cold is blowing through me till I am almost perished.' His
'*Doky*' stood by and received the 'voluntary contributions' of the
audience in a soldier's cap, which our hero emptied into his pocket,
and after snivelling out his thanks, departed to renew the exhibition in the nearest available thoroughfare. Peter boasted that
he could make on an average fifteen of these pitches a day, and
as the proceeds were estimated as something considerable in each
pitch (he has been known to take as much as half-a-crown in

pence at one standing), he was able to sport his figure at Astley's in the evening – to eat 'spring lamb,' and when reeling home under the influence of whiskey, to entertain the peaceful inhabitants with the music of – 'We won't go home till morning ——'

"Whether the *game got stale*, or Peter became honest, is beyond the purport of my communication to settle. If any reader, however, should make his purchases at the puffing fish-monger's in Lombard-street, they may find Peter now pursuing the more honest occupation of sweeping the crossing, by the church of St. Gabriel, Fenchurch-street.

"Among the most famous of the 'lurking patterers' was 'Captain Moody,' the son of poor but honest parents in the county of Cornwall, who died during his boyhood, leaving him to the custody of a maiden aunt. This lady soon, and not without reason, got tired of her incorrigible charge. Young Moody was apprenticed successively to three trades, and wanted not ability to become expert in any of them, but having occasional interviews with some of the gipsy tribe, and hearing from themselves of their wonderful achievements, he left the sober walks of life and joined this vagrant fraternity.

"His new position, however, was attractive only while it was novel. Moody, who had received a fair education, soon became disgusted with the coarseness and vulgarity of his associates. At the solicitation of a neighbouring clergyman, he was restored to the friendship of his aunt, who had soon sad reason to regret that her compassion had got the better of her prudence; for one Sunday afternoon, while she was absent at church, young Moody who had pleaded indisposition and so obtained permission to stay at home, decamped (after dispatching the servant to the town, a mile distant, to fetch the doctor) in the meantime, emptying his aunt's 'safety cupboard' of a couple of gold watches and £72 in cash and country notes.

"His roving disposition then induced him to try the sea, and the knowledge he obtained during several voyages fitted him for those maritime frauds which got him the name of 'Captain Moody, the lurker.' The frauds of this person are well known, and often recounted with great admiration among the pattering fraternity. On one occasion the principal butcher in Gosport was summoned to meet a gentleman at an hotel. The *Louisa,* a brig, had just arrived at Portsmouth, the captain's name was Young, and this gentleman Moody personated for the time being. 'I have occasion,' said he to the butcher, 'for an additional supply of beef for the *Louisa;* I have heard you spoken of by Captain Harrison' (whom Moody knew to be an old friend of the butcher's), 'and I have thus given you the preference. I want a bullock, cut up in 12 lb. pieces; it must be on board by three tomorrow.' The price was agreed upon, and the captain threw down a few sovereigns in payment, but, of course, discovered that he had not gold enough to cover the whole amount, so he proposed to give him a cheque he had just received from Captain Harrison for £100, and the butcher could give him the difference. The tradesman was nothing loth, for a cheque upon 'Vallance, Mills, and West,' with Captain Harrison's signature, was reckoned equal to money any day, and so the butcher considered the one he had received, until the next morning, when the draft and the order proved to be forgeries. The culprit was, of course, nowhere to be found, nor, indeed, heard of till two years after, when he had removed the scene of his depredations to Liverpool.

"In that port he had a colleague, a man whose manners and appearance were equally prepossessing. Moody sent his pal into a jeweller's shop, near the corner of Lord-street, who there purchased a small gold seal, paid for it, and took his leave. Immediately afterwards, Moody entered the shop under evident excitement, declaring that he had seen the person, who had just left the shop, secrete two, if not three, seals up his coat-sleeve; adding, that the fellow had just gone through the Exchange, and that if the jeweller were quick he would be sure to catch him. The jeweller ran out without his hat, leaving his kind friend in charge of the shop, and soon returned with the supposed criminal in his custody. The 'captain,' however, in the meantime, had decamped, taking with him a tray from the window, containing precious materials to the value of £300.

"At another time, the 'captain' prepared a document, setting forth 'losses in the Baltic trade,' and a dismal variety of disasters; and concluding with a melancholy shipwreck, which had really taken place just about that time in the German Ocean. With this he travelled over great part of Scotland, and with almost unprecedented success. Journeying near the Firth of Forth, he paid a visit to Lord Dalmeny—a nobleman of great benevolence—who had read the account of the shipwreck in the local journals, and wondered that the petition was not signed by influential persons *on the spot;* and, somewhat suspicious of the reality of the 'captain's' identity, placed a terrestrial globe before him, and begged to be shown 'in what latitude he was cast away.' The awkwardness with which Moody handled the globe showed that *he* was 'out of *his* latitude' altogether. His lordship thereupon committed the document to the flames, but generously gave the 'captain' a sovereign and some good advice; the former he appropriated at the nearest public-house, of the latter he never made the least use.

"Old, and worn out by excesses and imprisonment, he subsists now by 'sitting pad' about the suburban pavements; and when, on a recent evening, he was recognised in a low public-house in Deptford, he was heard to say, with a sigh: 'Ah! once I could "screeve a fakement" (write a petition) or "cooper a monekur" (forge a signature) with any man alive, and my heart's game now; but I'm old and asthmatic, and got the rheumatics, so that I ain't worth a d—n.'

" 'The Lady Lurker.'—Of this person very little is known, and *that* little, it is said, makes her an object of pity. Her father was a dissenting minister in Bedfordshire. She has been twice married; her first husband was a schoolmaster at Hackney, and nephew of a famous divine who wrote a Commentary on the Bible, and was chaplain to George III. She afterwards married a physician in Cambridgeshier (a Dr. S——), who is alleged to have treated her ill, and even to have attempted to poison her. She has no children; and, since the death of her husband, has passed through various grades, till she is now a cadger. She dresses becomingly in black, and sends in her card (Mrs. Dr. S——) to the houses whose occupants are known, or supposed, to be charitable. She talks with them for a certain time, and then draws forth a few boxes of lucifers, which, she says, she is compelled to sell for a living. These lucifers are merely excuses, of course, for begging; still, nothing is known to have ever transpired in her behaviour wholly unworthy of a distressed gentlewoman. She lives in private lodgings."

I continue the account of these habitations, and of the wretched occupants, from the pen of the same gentleman whose vicissitudes (partly self-procured) led him to several years' acquaintance with the subject.

"Padding-kens" (lodging-houses) in the country are certainly preferable abodes to those of St. Giles's, Westminster, or Whitechapel; but in country as in town, their condition is extremely filthy and disgusting; many of them are scarcely ever washed, and as to sweeping, once a week is miraculous. In most cases they swarm with vermin, and, except where their position is very airy, the ventilation is imperfect, and frequent sickness the necessary result. It is a matter of surprise that the nobility, clergy, and gentry of the realm should permit the existence of such horrid dwellings.

"I think," continues my informant, "that the majority of these poor wretches are without even the idea of respectability or 'home comforts,' — many of them must be ranked among the worst of our population. Some, who could live elsewhere, prefer these wretched abodes, because they answer various evil purposes. With beggars, patterers, hawkers, tramps, and vendors of their own manufacture, are mingled thieves, women of easy virtue, and men of no virtue at all; a few, and by far the smallest portion, are persons who once filled posts of credit and affluence, but whom bankruptcy, want of employment, or sickness has driven to these dismal retreats. The vast majority of London vagrants take their summer vacation in the country, and the 'dodges' of both are interchanged, and every new 'move' circulates in almost no time.

"I will endeavour to sketch a few of the most renowned 'performers' on this theatre of action. By far the most illustrious is 'Nicholas A———,' a name known to the whole cadging fraternity as a *real* descendant from Bamfylde Moore Carew, and the 'prince of lurkers' and patterers for thirty years past. This man owes much of his success to his confessedly imposing appearance, and many of his escapes to the known respectability of his connections. His father — yet alive — is a retired captain in the Royal Navy, a gentleman of good private property, and one of her Majesty's justices of peace for the county of Devon – the southern extremity of which was the birth-place of Nicholas. But little is known of his early days. He went to school at Tavistock, where he received a good education, and began life by cheating his school-fellows.

"The foolish fondness of an indulgent mother, and some want of firmness in paternal discipline, accelerated the growth of every weed of infamy in Nicholas, and baffled every experiment, by sea and land, to set him up in life.

"Scarcely was he out of his teens, when he honoured the sister country with his visits and his depredations. About the centre of Sackville-street, Dublin, there lived a wealthy silversmith of the name of Wise. Into his shop (accompanied by one of his pals in livery) went Nicholas, whose gentlemanly exterior, as I have already hinted, would disarm suspicion in a stranger.

" 'Good morning, sir, is your name Wise? – Yes, sir. – Well, that is *my* name. – Indeed, of the English family, I suppose? – Yes, sir, East Kent. – Oh, indeed! related to the ladies of Leeds Castle, I presume? – I have the honour to be their brother. – James, is your name James or John? – Neither, sir, it is Jacob. – Oh, indeed! a very ancient name. – Well, I have occasion to give a party at the Corn Exchange Tavern, and I want a little plate on hire, can you supply me?' – A very polite affirmative settled this part of the business. Plate to the amount of £150 was selected and arranged, when Nicholas discovered that his pocket-book was at home (to complete the deception, his right arm was in a sling). 'Will you, Mr. Wise (you see my infirmity), write me a few lines?' – 'With the greatest pleasure,' was the silversmith's reply. – 'Well, let me see.

"My dear, do not be surprised at this; I want £150, or all the money you can send, per bearer; I will explain at dinner-time.

J. WISE."

" 'Now, John, take this to your mistress, and be quick.' As John was not very hasty in his return, Nicholas went to look for him, leaving a strict injunction that the plate should be sent to the Corn Exchange Tavern, as soon as the deposit was received. This happened at eleven in the forenoon — the clock struck five and no return of either the master or the man.

"The jeweller left a message with his apprentice, and went home to his dinner. He was met at the door of his suburban villa by his 'better-half,' who wondered what made him so late, and wished to know the nature of the exigency which had caused him to send home for so much money? The good man's perplexity was at an end when he saw his own handwriting on the note; and every means within the range of constabulary vigilance was taken to capture the offender, but Nicholas and his servant got clear off.

"This man's ingenuity was then taxed as to the next move, so he thought it expedient to *tax* somebody else. He went with his 'pal' to a miscellaneous repository, where they bought a couple of old ledgers — useful only as waste paper, a bag to hold money, two ink-bottles, &c. Thus equipped, they waited on the farmers of the district, and exhibited a 'fakement,' setting forth parliamentary authority for imposing a tax upon the geese! They succeeded to admiration, and weeks elapsed before the hoax was discovered. The coolness of thus assuming legislatorial functions, and being, at the same time, the executive power, has rarely been equalled.

"There is an old proverb, that 'It is an ill wind that blows *nobody* good.' The gallant 'captain' was domiciled at a lodging-house in Gainsborough, Lincolnshire, where he found all the lodgers complaining of the badness of the times — most of them were makers of nets. He sallied forth to all the general shops, and left his (fictitious) 'captain' card at each, with an order for an unusual number of nets. This 'dodge' gave a week's work to at least twenty poor people; but whether the shopkeepers were 'caught in a net,' or the articles were paid for and removed by the 'captain,' or whether it was a piece of pastime on his part, I did not stay long enough to ascertain.

"Nicholas A——is now in his sixty-second year, a perfect hypochondriac. On his own authority — and it is, no doubt, too true — he has been 'lurking' on every conceivable system, from forging a bill of exchange down to '*maundering on the fly*,' for the greater part of his life; and, excepting the 'hundred and thirteen times' he has been in provincial jails, society has endured the scourge of his deceptions for a quarter of a century at least. He now lives with

43

a young prostitute in Portsmouth, and contributes to her wretched earnings an allowance of 5*s*. a week, paid to him by the attorney of a distant and disgusted relative."

The writer of this account was himself two whole years on the "monkry," before he saw a lodging-house for tramps; and the first he *ever* saw was one well-known to every patterer in Christendom, and whose fame he says is "gone out into all lands," for its wayfaring inmates are very proud of its popularity.

"It may be as well," writes the informant in question, "before submitting the following account, to state that there are other, and more elaborate marks – the hieroglyphics of tramping – than those already given. I will accordingly explain them.

"Two hawkers (pals) go together, but separate when they enter a village, one taking each side of the road, and selling different things; and, so as to inform each other as to the character of the people to whose houses they call, they chalk certain marks on their door-posts:

"⌒+ means 'Go on. *I* have called here; don't *you* call – it's no go.'

"⌒+ means 'Stop – you may call here; they want' (for instance) 'what *you* sell, though not what *I* sell; or else,' 'They had no change when I was there, but may have it now;' or, 'If they don't buy, at least they'll treat you civilly.'

" ꝺ+ on a corner-house, or a sign-post, means, 'I went this way;' or 'Go on in this direction.'

" ꝺ+ on a corner-house, or sign-post, means 'Stop – don't go any further in this direction.'

" ⊙ means 'danger.'

"Like many other young men, I had lived above my income, and, too proud to crave parental forgiveness, had thrown off the bonds of authority for a life of adventure. I was now homeless upon the world. With a body capable of either exertion or fatigue, and a heart not easily terrified by danger, I endured rather than enjoyed my itinerant position. I sold small articles of Tunbridge ware, perfumery, &c. &c., by 'munging' (begging) over them – sometimes in Latin – got a better living than I expected, or probably deserved. I was always of temperate and rather abstemious habits, but ignorant of the haunts of other wanderers, (whom I saw in dozens every day upon every road, and every conceivable pursuit) I took up my nightly quarters at a sort of third-rate public-house, and supposed that my contemporaries did the same. How long my ignorance might have continued (if left to myself) I can hardly determine; an adventure at a road-side inn, however, removed the veil from my eyes, and I became gradually and speedily 'awake' to 'every move on the board.' It was a lovely evening in July, the air was serene and the scenery romantic; my own feelings were in unison with both, and enhanced perhaps by the fact that I had beguiled the last two miles of my deliberate walk with a page out of my pocket-companion, 'Burke on the Sublime and Beautiful.' I was now smoking my pipe and quaffing a pint of real 'Yorkshire stingo' in the 'keeping room' (a term which combines parlour and kitchen in one word) of a *real* 'Yorkshire village,' Dranfield, near Sheffield. A young person of the other sex was my only and accidental companion; she had been driven into the house by the over officiousness of a vigilant village constable, who finding that she sold lace without a license, and — infinitely worse — refused to listen to his advances, had warned her to 'make herself scarce' at her 'earliest possible convenience.'

"Having elicited what I did for a living, she popped the startling question to me, 'Where do you "hang out" in Sheffield?' I told her that I had never been in Sheffield, and did not 'hang out' my little wares, but used my persuasive art to induce the purchase of them. The lady said, 'Well, you are "green." I mean, where do you *dos*?' This was no better, it seemed like Greek, — '*delta, omicron, sigma*.' [I retain the "patterer's" own words to show the education of the class] — but the etymology was no relief to the perplexity. 'Where do you mean to sleep?' she inquired. I referred to my usual practice of adjourning to an humble public-house. My companion at once threw off all manner of disguise, and said, 'Well, sir, you are a young man that I have taken a liking to, and if you think you should like my company, I will take you to a lodging where there is plenty of travellers, and you will see "all sorts of life."' I liked the girl's company, and our mutual acquiescence made us companions on the road. We had not got far before we met the aforesaid constable in company

45

with an unmistakable member of the Rural Police. They made some inquiries of me, which I thought exceeded their commission. I replied to them with a mutilated Ode of Horace, when they both determined that I was a Frenchman, and allowed us to 'go on our way rejoicing.'

"The smoky, though well-built, town of Sheffield was now near at hand. 'The daylight was past,' and the 'shades of the evening were stretching out;' we were therefore enabled to journey through the thoroughfares without impertinent remarks, or perhaps any observation, except from a toothless old woman, of John Wesley's school, who was 'sorry to see two such nice young people going about the country,' and wondered if we 'ever thought of eternity!'

"After a somewhat tedious ramble, we arrived at Water-lane; —at the 'Bug-trap,' which from time immemorial has been the name of the most renowned lodging-house in that or perhaps any locality. Water-lane is a dark narrow street, crowded with human beings of the most degraded sort—the chosen atmosphere of cholera, and the stronghold of theft and prostitution. In less than half an hour, my fair companion and myself were sipping our tea, and eating Yorkshire cake in this same lodging-house.

" 'God bless every happy couple!' was echoed from a rude stentorian voice, while a still ruder hand bumped down upon our tea-table a red earthen dish of no small dimensions, into which was poured, from the mouth of a capacious bag, fragments of fish, flesh, and fowl, viands and vegetables of every sort, intermingled with bits of cheese and dollops of Yorkshire pudding. The man to whom this heterogeneous mass belonged, appeared anything but satisfied with his lot. 'Well,' said he, 'I don't know what this 'ere monkry *will* come to, after a bit. Three bob and a tanner, and that there dish o' scran' (enough to feed two families for a fortnight) 'is all I got this blessed day since seven o'clock in the morning, and now it's nine at night.' I ventured to say something, but a remark, too base for repetition, 'put the stunners on me,' and I held my peace.

"I was here surprised, on conversing with my young female companion, to find that she went to church, said her prayers night and morning, and knew many of the collects, some of which she repeated, besides a pleasing variety of Dr. Watt's hymns. At the death of her mother, her father had given up housekeeping; and, being too fond of a wandering life, had led his only child into habits like his own.

"As the night advanced, the party at the 'Bug-trap' more than doubled. High-flyers, shallow-coves, turnpike-sailors, and swells out of luck, made up an assembly of fourscore human beings, more than half of whom were doomed to sleep on a 'make-shift' —in other words, on a platform, raised just ten inches above the floor of the garret, which it nearly equalled in dimensions. Here were to be huddled together, with very little covering, old men and women, young men and children, with no regard to age, sex, or propensities.

"The 'mot' of the 'ken' (nickname for 'matron of the *establishment*') had discovered that I was a 'more bettermost' sort of person, and hinted that, if I would 'come down' with twopence more (threepence was the regular nightly charge), I, and the young gal as I was with, might have a little 'crib' to ourselves in a little room, along with another woman wot was married and had a 'kid,' and whose husband had got a month for 'griddling in the main drag' (singing in the high street), and being 'cheekish' (saucy) to the beadle.

"Next morning I bade adieu to the 'Bug-trap,' and I hope for ever."

The same informant further stated that he was some time upon "tramp" before he even knew of the existence of a common lodging-house: "After I had 'matriculated' at Sheffield," he says, "I continued some time going to public-houses to sleep, until my apparel having got shabby and my acquaintance with misfortune more general, I submitted to be the associate of persons whom I never spoke to out of doors, and whose even slight aquaintance I have long renounced. My first introduction to a London paddin' ken was in Whitechapel, the place was then called Cat and Wheel-alley (now Commercial-street). On the spot where St. Jude's church now stands was a double lodging-house, kept by a man named Shirley—one side of it was for single men and women, the other married couples; as these 'couples' made frequent exchanges, it is scarcely probable that Mr. Shirley ever 'asked to see their marriage lines.' These changes were, indeed, as common as they were disgusting. I knew two brothers (Birmingham nailers) who each brought a young woman out of service from the country. After a while each became dissatisfied with his partner. The mistress of the house (an old procuress from Portsmouth) proposed that they should change their wives. They did so, to the amusement of nine other couples sleeping on the same floor, and some of whom followed the example, and more than once during the night.

"When Cat and Wheel-alley was pulled down, the crew removed to George-yard; the proprietor died, and his wife sold the concern to a wooden-legged Welshman named Hughes (commonly called 'Taff'). I was there some time. 'Taff' was a notorious receiver of stolen goods. I knew two little boys, who brought home six pairs of new Wellington boots, which this miscreant bought at 1s. per pair; and, when they had no luck, he would take the strap off his wooden-leg, and beat them through the nakedness of their rags. He boarded and lodged about a dozen Chelsea and Greenwich pensioners. These he used to follow and watch closely till they got paid; then (after they had settled with him) he would make them drunk, and rob them of the few shillings they had left.

"One of these dens of infamy may be taken as a specimen of the whole class. They have generally a spacious, though often ill-ventilated, kitchen, the dirty dilapidated walls of which are hung with prints, while a shelf or two are generally, though barely, furnished with crockery and kitchen utensils. In some places knives and forks are not provided, unless a penny is left with the 'deputy,' or manager, till they are returned. A brush of any kind is a stranger, and a looking-glass would be a miracle. The average number of nightly lodgers is in winter 70, and in summer (when many visit the provinces) from 40 to 45. The general charge is, if two sleep together, 3d. per night, or 4d. for a single bed. In either case, it is by no means unusual to find 18 or 20 in one small room, the heat and horrid smell from which are insufferable; and, where there are young children, the staircases are the lodgement of every kind of filth and abomination. In some houses there are rooms for families, where, on a rickety machine, which they dignify by the name of a bedstead, may be found the man, his wife, and a son or daughter, perhaps 18 years of age; while the younger children, aged from 7 to 14, sleep on the floor. If they have linen, they take it off to escape vermin, and rise naked, one by one, or sometimes brother and sister together. This is no ideal picture; the subject is too capable of being authenticated to need that meaningless or dishonest assistance called 'allowable exaggeration.' The amiable and deservedly popular minister of a district church, built among lodging-houses, has stated that he has found 29 human beings in one apartment; and that having with difficulty knelt down between two beds to pray with a dying woman, his legs became so jammed that he could hardly get up again.

"Out of some fourscore such habitations," continues my informant, "I have only found *two* which had any sort of a garden; and, I am happy to add, that in neither of these two was there a single case of cholera. In the others, however, the pestilence raged with terrible fury.

"Of all the houses of this sort, the best I know is the one, (previously referred to) in Orchard-street, Westminster and another in Seven Dials, kept by a Mr. Mann (formerly a wealthy butcher). Cleanliness is inscribed on every wall of the house; utensils of every kind are in abundance, with a plentiful supply of water and gas. The beds do not exceed five in a room, and they are changed every week. There is not one disorderly lodger; and although the master has sustained heavy losses, ill health, and much domestic affliction, himself and his house may be regarded as patterns of what is wanted for the London poor.

"As there is a sad similarity between these abodes, so there is a sort of *caste* belonging in general, to the inmates. Of them it may be averred that whatever their pursuits, they are more or less alike in their views of men and manners. They hate the aristocracy. Whenever there is a rumour or an announcement of an addition to the Royal Family, and the news reaches the paddingken, the kitchen, for half-an-hour, becomes the scene of uproar — 'another expense coming on the b—y country!' The 'patterers' are very fond of the Earl of Carlisle, whom, in their attachment, they still call Lord Morpeth; they have read many of his lordship's speeches at *soirées* &c., and they think he wishes well to a poor man. Sir James Graham had better not show face among them; they have an idea (whence derived we know not) that this nobleman invented fourpenny-pieces, and now, they say, the swells give a 'joey' where they used to give a 'tanner'. The hero of Waterloo is not much amiss 'if he lets politics alone.' The name of a bishop is but another name for a Beelzebub; but they are very fond of the inferior clergy. Lay-agents and tract-distributors they cannot bear; they think they are spies come to see how much 'scran' (food) they have got, and then go and 'pyson' the minds of the public against the poor people.

"I was once (says our informant) in a house of this kind, in George-street, St. Giles's—the missionary who visited them on that occasion (Sunday afternoon) had the misfortune to be suspected as the author of some recent exposure in the newspapers. —They accused him, and he rebutted the accusation; they replied, and he rejoined; at last one of the men said, 'What do you want poking your nose in here for?' 'The City Mission,' was the answer 'had authorised——.' 'Authorised be d—d! are you ordained? 'No, not yet, friend.' The women then tore the poor gentleman's nether garments in a way I must not describe. The men carried him into the yard, filled his mouth with flour and mustard and then put him in a water-butt.

"It is, I am satisfied, quite a mistake to suppose that there is much real infidelity among these outcast beings. They almost all believe in a hereafter; most of them think that the wicked will be punished for a few years, and then the whole universe of people be embraced in the arms of one Great Forgiving Father. Some of them think that the wicked will not rise at *all;* the punishment of 'losing Heaven' being as they say 'Hell enough for anybody.' Points of doctrine they seldom meddle with.

"There are comparatively few Dissenters to be found in padding-kens, though many whose parents were Dissenters. My own opinion (writes my informant) is, that dissent seldom lasts long in one family. In eight years' experience I have found two hundred apparently pious men and women, and at least two thousand who call themselves Protestants, but never go to any church or chapel.

"The politics of these classes are, perhaps, for the most part, 'liberal Tory.' In most lodging-houses they take one or two papers:

the *Weekly Dispatch,* and *Bell's Weekly Messenger,* are the two usually taken. I know of no exception to this rule. The beggars hate a Whig Ministry, and I know that many a tear was shed in the hovels and cellars of London when Sir Robert Peel died. I know a publican, in Westminster, whose daily receipts are enormous, and whose only customers are soldiers, thieves, and prostitutes, who closed his house the day of the funeral, and put himself, his family, and even his beer-machines and gas-pipes, into mourning for the departed statesman.

"The pattering fraternity, that I write of, are generally much given to intemperance. Their amusements are the theatre, the free-and-easy, the skittle-ground, and sometimes cards and dominoes. They read some light works, and some of them subscribe to libraries, and a few, very few, attend lectures. Eliza Cook is a favourite writer with them, and Capt. Marryat, the 'top-sawyer,' as a novelist. Ainsworth is the idol of another class, when they can read. Mr. Dickens *was* a favourite, but he has gone down sadly in the scale since his *Household World* 'came it so strong' against the begging letter department. These poor creatures seldom rise in society. They make no effort to extricate themselves, while by others they are unpitied because unknown. To this rule, however, there are some happy and honourable exceptions.

"Taken as a body, patterers, lukers &c. are by no means quick-sighted as to the sanctions of moral obligations. They would join the hue and cry against the persecutors of Jane Wilbred, but a promiscuous robbery, even accompanied by murder—if it was 'got up clever' and 'done clean', so long as the parties escaped detection—might call forth a remark that 'there was no great harm done,' and perhaps some would applaud the perpetrators."

Before quitting this part of my subject (viz. the character, habits, and opinions of *all* classes of patterers) I will give an account of the pretended missionary proceedings of a man, well-known to the vagrant fraternity as "Chelsea George." I received the following narrative from the gentleman whose statements I have given previously. The scheme was concocted in a low lodging house:

"After a career of incessant 'lurking' and deceit, Chelsea George left England, and remained abroad," writes my informant, "four or five years. Exposure to the sun, and allowing his beard to grow a prodigious length, gave him the appearance of a foreigner. He had picked up enough French and Italian, with a little Dutch and German, and a smattering of Spanish, to enable him to 'hail for any part of the globe,' and from the designed inarticulateness with which he spoke (sometimes four languages in one sentence) added to his sun-burnt and grotesque appearance, it was difficult to *pall* him upon any *racket* (detect him in any pretence), so that the most incredulous — though often previously imposed upon — gave credence to his story, relief to his supposed necessities, and sometimes letters of introduction to their friends and neighbours.

"Some time after his return to England, and while pursuing the course of a 'high-flyer' (genteel beggar), he met with an interruption to his pursuits which induced him to alter his plan without altering his behaviour. The newspapers of the district, where he was then located, had raised before the eye and mind of the public, what the 'patterers' of his class proverbially call a 'stink' — that is, had opened the eyes of the unwary to the movements of 'Chelsea George;' and although he ceased to renew his appeals from the moment he heard of the notice of him, his appearance was so accurately described that he was captured and committed to Winchester jail as a rogue and vagabond. The term of his imprisonment has escaped my recollection. As there was no definite charge against him, probably he was treated as an ordinary vagrant and suffered a calendar month in durance. The silent system was not then in vogue, consequently there existed no barrier to mutual intercourse between prisoners, with all its train of conscience-hardening tendencies. I do not say this to intimate unqualified approval of the solitary system, I merely state a fact which has an influence on my subject.

"George had by this time scraped acquaintance with two fellow-prisoners — Jew Jem and Russia Bob. The former in 'quod' for 'pattering' as a 'converted Jew', the latter for obtaining money under equally false, though less theological, pretences.

"Liberated about one time, this trio laid their heads together — and the results was a plan to evangelize, or rather victimize, the inhabitants of the collier villages in Staffordshire and the adjoining counties. To accomplish this purpose, some novel and imposing representation must be made, both to lull supicion and give the air of piety to the plan, and disinterestedness to the agents by whom it was carried out.

"George and his two fellow-labourers were 'square-rigged' — that is, well dressed. Something, however, must be done to colour up the scene, and make the appeal for money touching, unsuspected, and successful. Just before the time to which I allude, a missionary from Sierra Leone had visited the larger towns of the district in question, while the inhabitants of the surrounding hamlets had been left in ignorance of the 'progress of missions in Africa and the East.' George and his comrades thought it would be no great harm at once to enlighten and fleece this scattered and anxious population. The plan was laid in a town of some size and facility. They 'raised the wind' to an extent adequate to some alteration of their appearances, and got bills printed to set forth the merits of the cause. The principal actor was Jew Jem, a converted Israelite, with 'reverend' before his name, and half the letters of the alphabet behind it. He had been in all the islands in the South Sea, on the coast of Africa, all over Hindostan, and half over the universe; and after assuring the villagers of Torryburn that he had carried the Gospel to various dark and *uninhabited* parts of the earth, he introduced Russia Bob (an Irishman who had, however, been in Russia) as his worthy and self-denying colleague, and Chelsea George as the first-fruits of their ministry — as one who had left houses and land, wife and children, and taken a long and hazardous voyage to show Christians in England that their sable brethren, children of one common Parent, were beginning to cast their idols to the moles and to the bats. Earnest was the gaze and breathless the expectation with which the poor deluded colliers of Torryburn listened to this harangue; and as argument always gains by illustration, the orator pulled out a tremendous black doll, bought for a 'flag' (fourpence) of a retired rag-merchant, and dressed up in Oriental style. This, Jew Jem assured the audience, was an idol brought from Murat in Hindostan. He presented it to Chelsea George for his worship and embraces. The convert indignantly repelled the insinuation, pushed the idol from him, spat in its face, and cut as many capers as a dancing-bear. The trio at this stage of the performances began 'puckering' (talking privately) to each other in murdered French, dashed with a little Irish; after which, the missionaries said that their convert (who had only a few words of English) would now profess his faith. All was attention as Chelsea George came forward. He stroked his beard, put his hand in his breast to keep down his dickey, and turning his eyes upwards, said: 'I believe in Desus Tist—dlory to 'is 'oly name!'

"This elicited some loud 'amens' from an assemblage of nearly 1,000 persons, and catching the favourable opportunity, a 'school of pals,' appointed for the purpose, went round and made the collection. Out of the abundance of their credulity and piety the populace contributed sixteen pounds! The whole scene was enacted out of doors, and presented to a stranger very pleasing impressions. I was present on the occasion, but was not then aware of the dodge. One verse of a hymn, and the blessing pronounced, was the signal for separation. A little shaking of hands concluded the exhibition, and 'every man went into his own house.'

"The missionary party and their 'pals' took the train to Manchester, and as none of them were teetotallers, the proceeds of their imposition did not last long. They were just putting on their considering caps, for the contrivance of another dodge, when a gentleman in blue clothes came into the tap-room, and informed Jew Jem that he was 'wanted.' It appears that 'Jem' had come out of prison a day or two before his comrades, and being 'hard up,' had ill-used a lady, taken her purse, and appropriated its contents. Inquiries, at first useless, had now proved successful— the 'missionary' stood his trial, and got an 'appointment' on Norfolk Island. Russia Bob took the cholera and died, and 'George the convert' was once more left alone to try his hand at something else.''

THE SELLER OF THE PENNY
SHORT-HAND CARDS

ALL LADIES and gentlemen who "take their walks abroad", must have seen, and of course heard, a little man in humble attire engaged in selling at one penny each a small card, containing a few sentences of letter-press, and fifteen stenographic characters, with an example, by which, it is asserted, anybody and everybody may "learn to write short-hand in a few hours." With the merits of the production, self-considered, this is not the place to meddle; suffice it that it is one of the many ways of getting a crust common to the great metropolis, and perhaps the most innocent of all the street performances. A kind of a street lecture is given by the vendor, in which the article is sufficiently puffed off. Of course this lecture is, so to speak, stereotyped, embracing the same ideas in nearly the same words over and over and over again. The exhibitor, however, pleads that constant exchange and interchange of passengers, and his desire to give each and all a fair amount of information, makes the repetition admissible, and even necessary. It is here given as a specimen of the style of the educated "patterer."

The Lecture

"Here is an opportunity which has seldom if ever been offered to the public before, whereby any person of common intellect may learn to write short-hand in a few hours, without any aid from a teacher. The system is entirely my own. It contains no vowels, no arbitrary characters, no double consonants, and no terminations; it may therefore properly be called 'stenography', an expression which conveyes its own meaning; it is derived from two Greek words; *stenos*, short, and *grapho*, I write, or *graphi*, the verb *to write*, and embraces all that is necessary in fifteen characters. I know that a prejudice obtains to a great extent against any thing and everything said or done in the street, but I have nothing to do with either the majority or minority of street pretenders. I am an educated man, and not a mere pretender, and if the justice or genuineness of a man's pretensions would always lead him to success I had not been here to-day. But against the tide of human disappointment, the worthy and the undeserving are so equally compelled to struggle, and so equally liable to be overturned by competition, that till you can prove that wealth is the gauge of character, it may be difficult to determine the ability or morality of a man from his position.

"I was lately reading an account of the closing life of that leviathan in literature, Dr. Johnson, and an anecdote occurred, which I relate, conceiving that it applies to one of the points at issue — I mean the ridicule with which my little publication has sometimes been treated by passers-by, who have found it easier to speculate on the texture of my coat, than on the character of my language. The Doctor had a niece who had embraced the peculiarities of Quakerism; after he had scolded her some time, and in rather unmeasured terms, her mother interfered and said, 'Doctor, don't scold the girl — you'll meet her in heaven, I hope.' — 'I hope not,' said the Doctor, 'for I hate to meet *fools* anywhere.' I apply the same observation to persons who bandy about the expressions 'gift of the gab,' 'catch-penny,' &c., &c., which in my case it is somewhat easier to circulate that to support. At any rate they ought to be addressed to *me* and not to the atmosphere. The man who meets a foe to the face, gives him an equal chance of defence, and the sword openly suspended from the belt is a less dangerous, because a less cowardly weapon than the one which, like that of Harmodius, is concealed under the wreaths of a myrtle.

"If you imagine that professional disappointment is confined to people out of doors, you are very much mistaken. Look into some of the middle-class streets around where we are standing; you will find here and there, painted or engraved on a door, the words 'Mr. So-and so, surgeon.' The man I am pre-supposing shall be qualified — qualified in the technical sense of the expression, a Member of the College of Surgeons, a Licentiate of Apothecaries' Hall, and a Graduate of some University. He may possess the talent of Galen or Hippocrates; or, to come to more recent date, of Sir Astley Cooper himself, but he never becomes popular, and dies unrewarded because unknown: before he dies, he may crawl out of his concealed starvation into such a thoroughfare as this, and see Professor Morrison, or Professor Holloway, or the Proprietor of Parr's Life Pills, or some other quack, ride by in their carriage; wealth being brought them by the same waves that have wafted misfortune to himself; though that wealth has been procured by one undeviating system of Hypocrisy and Humbug, of Jesuitism and Pantomime, such as affords no parallel since the disgusting period of Oliverian ascendancy. Believe me, my friends, a man may form his plans for success with profound sagacity, and guard with caution against every approach to extravagance, but neither the boldness of enterprise not the dexterity of stratagem will always secure the distinction they deserve. Else that policemen would have been an inspector!

"I have sometimes been told, that if I possessed the facilities I professedly exhibit, I might turn them to greater personal advantage: in coarse, unfettered, Saxon English, 'That's a LIE;' for on the authority of a distinguished writer, there are 2,000 educated men in London and its suburbs, who rise every morning totally ignorant where to find a breakfast. Now I am not *quite* so bad as that, so that it appears I am an exception to the rule, and not the rule open to exception. However, it is beyond all controversy, that the best way to keep the fleas from biting you in bed is to 'get out of bed;' and by parity of reasoning, the best way for you to sympathize with me for being on the street is to take me off, as an evidence of your sympathy.

"I remember that, some twenty years ago, a poor man of foreign name, but a native of this metropolis, made his appearance in Edinburgh, and advertised that he would lecture on mnemonics or the art of memory. As he was poor, he had recourse to an humble lecture-room, situated up a dirty court. Its eligibility may be determined by the fact that sweeps' concerts were held in it, at $1/_2 d$. per head, and the handbill mostly ended with the memorable words: 'N.B.—No gentleman admitted without shoes and stockings.' At the close of his first lecture (the admission to which was 2*d*.), he was addressed by a scientific man, who gave him 5*s*.—(it will relieve the monotony of the present address if some of you follow his example)—and advised him to print and issue some cards about his design, which he did. I saw one of them—the ink on it scarcely dry—as he had got it back at the house of a physician, and on it was inscribed: 'Old birds are not caught with chaff. From Dr. M——, an old bird.' The suspicious doctor, however, was advised to hear the poor man's twopenny lecture, and was able, at the end of it, to display a great feat of memory himself. What was the result? The poor man no longer lectured for 2*d*. But it is tedious to follow him through a series of years. He was gradually patronised throughout the kingdom, and a few months ago he was lecturing in the Hanover-square Rooms, with the Earl of Harrowby in the chair. Was he not as clever a man when he lectured in the sweeps' concert-room? Yes; but he had not been brought *under the shadow of a great name.* Sometimes that 'great name' comes too late. You are familiar with the case of Chatterton. He had existed, rather than lived, three days on a penny loaf; then he committed suicide, and was charitably buried by strangers. Fifty years or more had elapsed, when people found out how clever he had been, and collected money for the erection of that monument which now stands to his memory by St. Mary Redcliff Church, in Bristol. Now, if you have any idea of doing that for me, please to collect some of it while I am *alive!*"

On occasions when the audience is not very liberal, the lecturer treats them to the following hint:

"When in my golden days—or at least they were silver ones compared to these—I was in the habit of lecturing on scientific subjects, I always gave the introductory lecture *free*. I suppose this is an 'introductory lecture,' for it yields very little money at present. I have often thought, that if everybody a little richer than myself was half as conscientious, I should either make a rapid fortune, or have nobody to listen to me at all; for I never sanction long with my company anything I don't believe. Now if what I say is untrue or grossly improbable, it does not deserve the sanction of an audience; if otherwise, it must be meritorious, and deserve more efficient sanction. As to any insults I receive, Christianity has taught me to forgive, and philosophy to despise them."

These very curious, and perhaps unique, specimens of street elocution are of course interrupted by the occasional sale of a card,

and perhaps some conversation with the purchaser. The stenographic card-seller states that he has sometimes been advised to
use more commonplace language. His reply is germane to the
matter. He says that a street audience, like some other audiences,
is best pleased with what they least understand, and that the
way to appear sublime is to be incomprehensible. He can occasionally be a little sarcastic. A gentleman informed me that he
passed him at Bagnigge-wells on one occasion, when he was interrupted by a "gent," fearfully disfigured by the small-pox, who
exclaimed: "It's a complete humbug." "No, sir," retorted Mr.
Shorthand, "but if any of the ladies present were to call you
handsome, *that* would be a humbug." On another occasion a man
(half-drunk) had been annoying him some time, and getting tired
of the joke, said: "Well—I see you are a learned man, you must
pity my ignorance." "No," was the reply, "but I pity your
father." "Pity my father!—why?" was the response. "Because
Solomon says, 'He that begetteth a fool shall have sorrow of
him'." This little *jeu-d'esprit*, I was told, brought forth loud
acclamations from the crowd, and a crown-piece from a lady who
had been some minutes a listener. These statements are among
the most curious revelations of the history of the streets.

The short-hand card-seller makes no secret of having been
fined for obstructing a thoroughfare, having been bound down
to keep the peace, and several times imprisoned as a defaulter.
He tells me that he once "got a month" in one of the metropolitan
jails. It was the custom of the chaplain of the prison in which he
was confined, to question the prisoners every Wednesday, from
box to box (as they were arranged before him) on some portion
of Holy Writ, and they were expected, if able, to answer. On
one occasion, the subject being the Excellence of Prayer, the
chaplain remarked that, "even among the heathen, every author,
without exception, had commended prayer to a real or supposed
Deity." The card-seller, I am told, cried out "Question!" "Who
is that?" said the chaplain. The turnkey pointed out the question-
er. "Yes," said the card-seller, "you know what Seneca says:
—'Quid opus votis? Fac te ipsum felicem, vel bonum.' 'What need
of prayer? Make thou thyself happy and virtuous.' Does *that*
recommend prayer?" The prisoners laughed, and to prevent a

mutiny, the classical querist was locked up, and the chaplain closed the proceedings. It is but justice, however, to the worthy minister to state, his querist came out of durance vile better clothed than he went in.

The stenographic trade, of which the informant in question is the sole pursuer, was commenced eleven years ago. At that time 300 cards were sold in a day; but the average is now 24, and about 50 on a Saturday night. The card-seller tells me that he is more frequently than ever interrupted by the police, and his health being delicate, wet days are "nuisances" to him. He makes an annual visit to the country, he tells me, to see his children, who have been provided for by some kind friends. About two years ago he was returning to London and passed through Oxford. He was "hard up," he says, having left his coat for his previous night's lodging. He attended prayers (without a coat) at St. Mary's church, and when he came out, seated himself on the pavement beside the church, and wrote with chalk inside an oval border.

$$\text{"}Δελίμφαπολλυμαί.\text{" } - \text{Lucam xv. } 17.[1]$$
"I perish with hunger."

He was not long unnoticed, he tells me, by the scholars; some of whom "rigged him out," and he left Oxford with £6 10s. in his pocket.

"Let us indulge the hope," writes one who knows this man well, "that whatever indiscretions may have brought a scholar, whom few behold without pity, or converse with without respect for his acquirements, to be a street-seller, nevertheless his last days will be his best days, and that, as his talents are beyond dispute and his habits strictly temperate, he may yet arise out of his degradation."

Of this gentleman's history I give an account derived from the only authentic source. It is, indeed, given in the words of the writer from whom it was received. —

"The *Reverend* Mr. Shorthand" (his real name is of no consequence—indeed, it would be contrary to the rule of this work to print it) "was born at Hackney, in the county of Middlesex,

---

[1] This line is printed here precisely as in the original edition. [Publisher's Note.]

on Good Friday, the 15th of April, 1808; he is, therefore, now in his 43rd year. Of his parents very little is known; he was brought up by guardians, who were 'well to do,' and who gave him every indulgence and every good instruction and example. From the earliest dawn of reason he manifested a strong predilection for the church; and, before he was seven years old, he had preached to an infant audience, read prayers over a dead animal, and performed certain mimic ceremonies of the church among his schoolfellows.

"The directors of his youthful mind were strong Dissenters, of Antinomian sentiments. With half-a-dozen of the same denomination he went, before he was thirteen, to the anniversary meeting of the Countess of Huntingdon's College, at Cheshunt. Here, with a congregation of about forty persons, composed of the students and a few strangers, he adjourned, while the parsons were dining at the 'Green Dragon,' to the College Chapel, where, with closed doors, the future proprietor of the 'penny short-hand' delivered his first public sermon.

"Before he was quite fourteen the stenographic card-seller was apprenticed to a draper in or near Smithfield. In this position he remained only a few months, when the indentures were cancelled by mutual consent, and he resumed his studies, first at his native place, and afterwards as a day-scholar at the Charterhouse. He was now sixteen, and it was deemed high time for him to settle to some useful calling. He became a junior clerk in the office of a stock-broker and afterwards amanuensis to an 'M.D.,' who encouraged his thirst for learning, and gave him much leisure and many opportunities for improvement. While in this position he obtained two small prizes in the state lottery, gave up his situation, and went to Cambridge with a private tutor. As economy was never any part of his character, he there 'overrun the constable,' and to prevent," he says, "any constable running after him, he decamped in the middle of the night, and came to London by a waggon — all his property consisting of a Greek prayer-book, Dodd's Beauties of Shakespeare, two shirts, and two half-crowns.

"At this crisis a famous and worthy clergyman, forty years resident in Hackney (the Rev. H. H. N——, lately deceased), had issued from the press certain strictures against the Society for

Promoting Christianity among the Jews. The short-hand seller wrote an appendix to this work, under the title of the 'Church in Danger.' He took it to Mr. N——, who praised the performance and submitted to the publication. The impression cast off was limited, and the result unprofitable. It had, however, one favourable issue; it led to the engagement of its author as private and travelling tutor to the children of the celebrated Lady S——, who, though (for adultery) separated from her husband, retained the exclusive custody of her offspring. While in this employment, my informant resided chiefly at Clifton, sometimes in Bath, and sometimes on her ladyship's family property in Derbyshire. While here, he took deacon's orders, and became a popular preacher. In whatever virtues he might be deficient, his charities, at least, were unbounded. This profusion ill suited a limited income, and *a forgery* was the first step to suspension, disgrace, and poverty. In 1832 he married; the union was not felicitous.

"About this date my informant relates, that under disguise and change of name he supplied the pulpits of several episcopal chapels in Scotland with that which was most acceptable to them. Unable to maintain a *locus standi* in connexion with the Protestant church, he made a virtue of necessity, and avowed himself a seceder. In this new disguise he travelled and lectured, proving to a demonstration (always pecuniary) that 'the Church of England was the hospital of Incurables.'

"Always in delicate health, he found continued journeys inconvenient. The oversight of a home missionary station, comprising five or six villages, was advertised; the card-seller was the successful candidate, and for several years performed Divine service four times every Sunday, and opened and taught *gratuitously* a school for the children of the poor. Here report says he was much beloved, and here he ought to have remained; but with that restlessness of spirit which is so marked a characteristic of the class to which he now belongs, he thought otherwise, and removed to a similar sphere of labour near Edinburgh. The town, containing a population of 14,000, was visited to a dreadful extent with the pestilence of cholera. The future street-seller (to his honour be it spoken) was the only one among eight or ten ministers who was not afraid of the contagion. He visited many hundreds of cases, and, it is credibly asserted, added medicine, food, and nursing to his spiritual consolations. The people of his charge here embraced the Irving heresy; and unable, as he says, to determine the sense of 'the unknown tongues', he resigned his charge, and returned to London in 1837. After living some time upon his money, books, and clothes, till all was expended, he tried his hand at the 'begging-letter trade.' About this time, the card-seller declares that a man, also from Scotland, and of similar history and personal appearance, lodged with him at a house in the Mint, and stole his coat, and with it his official and other papers. This person had been either a city missionary or scripture-reader, having been dismissed for intemperance. The street card-seller states that he has 'suffered much persecution from the officers of the Mendicity Society, and in the opinion of the public, by the blending of his own history with that of the man who robbed him.' Be the truth as it may, or let his past faults have been ever so glaring, still it furnishes no present reason why he should be maltreated in the streets, where he is *now* striving for an honest living. Since the card-seller's return to London, he has been *five* times elected and re-elected to a temporary engagement in the Hebrew School, Goodman's-fields; so that at the worst, his habits of life cannot be *very* outrageous."

"The pomps and vanities of this wicked world," have, according to his own account, had very little share in the experience of the short-hand parson. He states, and there is no reason for doubting him, that he *never witnessed any sort of public amusement in his life;* that he was a hard student when he was young, and now keeps no company, living much in retirement. He "attends the ministry," he says, "of the Rev. Robert Montgomery—reads the daily lessons at home, and receives the communion twice every month at the early service in Westminster Abbey."

Of course these are matters that appear utterly inconsistent with his present mode of life. One well-known peculiarity of this extraordinary character is his almost idolatrous love of children, to whom, if he "makes a good Saturday night," he is very liberal in his way home. This, is perhaps, his "ruling passion" (an acquaintance of his, without knowing why I inquired, fully confirmed this account); and it displays itself sometimes in strong emotion, of which the following anecdote may be cited as an instance: — One of his favourite spots for stenographic demonstration is the corner of Playhouse-yard, close to *The Times* office. Directly opposite lives a tobacconist, who has a young family. One of his little girls used to stand and listen to him; to her he was so strongly attached, that when he heard of her death (he had missed her several weeks,) he went home much affected, and did not return to the spot for many months. At the death of the notorious Dr. Dillon, the card-seller offered himself to the congregation as a successor; they, however, declined the overture.

A STREET STATIONER

A MIDDLE-AGED man gave me the following account. He had pursued the trade for upwards of twelve years. He was a stout, cosy-looking man, wearing a loose great coat. The back of his tray rested against his double-breasted waiscoat; the pattern of which had become rather indistinct, but which was buttoned tightly up to his chin, as if to atone for the looseness of his coat. The corner of his mouth, towards his left ear, was slightly drawn down, for he seemed in "crying" to pitch his voice (so that it could be heard a street off) out of the corner of his only partially opened mouth.

"Middlin', sir," he said, "times is middlin' with me; they might be better, but then they might be worse. I can manage to live. The times is changed since I was first in business. There wasn't no 'velops (envelopes) then, and no note-paper—least I had none; but I made as good or a better living than I do now; a better indeed. When the penny-postage came in—I don't mind the year, but I hadn't been long in the trade (it was in 1840)—I cried some of the postage 'velops. They was big, figured things at first, with elephants and such like on them, and I called them at prime cost, if anything was bought wih'mem. The very first time, a p'liceman says, 'You mustn't sell the covers. What authority have you to do it?' 'Why, the authority to earn a dinner,' says I; but it was no go. Another peeler came up and said I wasn't to cry them again, or he'd have me up; and so that spec. came to nothing. I sell to ladies and gentlemen, and to servant-maids, and mechanics, and their wives; and indeed all sorts of people. Some fine ladies, that call me to the door on the sly, do behave very shabby. Why, there was one who wanted five half-quire of note for 4*d*., and I told her I couldn't afford it, and so she said 'that she knew the world, and never gave nobody the price they first asked.' 'If that's it, ma'am,' says I, 'people that knows your plan can 'commodate you.' That knowing card of a lady, sir, as she reckons herself, had as much velvet to her body—such a gown!—as would

pay *my* tailor's bills for twenty year. But I don't employ a fashion-
able tailor, and can patch a bit myself, as I was two years with
a saddler, and was set to work to make girths and horse-clothes.
My master died, and all went wrong, and I had to turn out,
without nobody to help me, — for I had no parents living; but I
was a strong young fellow of sixteen. I first tried to sell a few
pairs of girths, and a roller or two, to livery-stable keepers, and
horse-dealers, and jobmasters. But I was next to starving. They
wouldn't look at anything but what was good, and stuff was
too high, and the profit too little — for I couldn't get regular
prices, in course — and so I dropped it. There's no men in the
world so particular about good things as them as is about vally-
able horses. I've often thought if rich people cared half as much
about poor man's togs, that was working for them for next to
nothing, as they cared for their horse-clothes, it would be a better
world. I was dead beat at last; but I went down to Epsom and
sold a few race-cards. I'd borrowed 1*s*. of a groom to start with,
and he wouldn't take it back when I offered it; and that wax is
bought at general warehouses, known as 'swag shops' (of which I
may speak hereafter), at 8*d*. the pound, there being 48 round
sticks in, was my beginning in the paper trade. I felt queer at
first, and queerer when I wasn't among horses, as at the races
like — but one gets reconciled to anything, 'cept, to a man like
me, a low lodging-house. A stable's a palace to it. I got into
stationery at last, and it's respectable.

"I've heard people say how well they could read and write, and
it was no good to them. It has been, and is still, a few pence to me;
though I can only read and write middlin'. I write notes and
letters for some as buys paper of me. Never anything in the
beggin' way — never. It wouldn't do to have my name mixed up
that way. I've often got extra pennies for directing and doing up
valentines in nice 'velops. Why, I spoke to a servant girl the other
day; she was at the door, and says I, 'Any nice paper today, to
answer your young man's last love-letter, or to write home and
ask your mother's consent to your being wed next Monday week?'
That's the way to get them to listen, sir. Well. I finds that she
can't write, and so I offers to do it for a pint of beer, and she to
pay for paper of course. And then there was so many orders what

to say. Her love to no end of aunts, and all sorts of messages and inquiries about all sorts of things; and when I'd heard enough to fill a long 'letter' sheet, she calls me back and says, 'I'm afraid I've forgot uncle Thomas.' I makes it all short enought in the letter, sir. 'My kind love to all inquiring friends,' takes in all uncle Thomases. I writes them when I gets a bite of dinner. Sometimes I posts them if I'm paid beforehand; at other times I leaves them next time I pass the door. There's no mystery made about it. If a missus says, 'What's that?' I've heard a girl answer, 'It's a letter I've got written home, ma'am. I haven't time myself', or 'I'm no scholar, ma'am.' But that's only where I'm known. I don't write one a week the year round — perhaps forty in a year. I charge 1d. or 2d., or if it's a very poor body, and no gammon about it, nothing. Well, then, I think I never wrote a love-letter. Women does that one for another, I think, when the young housemaid can't write as well as she can talk. I jokes some as I knows, and says I writes all sorts of letters but love-letters, and for them, you see, says I, there's wanted the best gilt edge, and a fancy 'velop, and a diction-ary. I take more for note and 'velops than anything else, but far the most for note. Some has a sheet folded and fitted into a 'velop when they buys, as they can't fit it so well themselves, they say. Perhaps I make 2s. a day, take it all round. Some days I may make as much as 3s. 6d.; at others, 'specially wet days, not 1s. But I call mine a tidy round, and better than average. I've only myself, and pays 1s. 9d. a week for a tidy room, with a few of my own sticks in it. I buy sometimes in Budge-row, and sometimes in Drury-lane. Very seldom at a swag-shop, for I don't like them.

"Well, now, I've heard, sir, that poor men like me ain't to be allowed to sell anything in the Park at the Great Exhibition. How's that, sir?" I told him I could give no information on the subject.

"It's likely enough to be true," he resumed; "the nobs'll want to keep it all to theirselves. I read *Lloyd's Weekly Newspaper* on a Sunday, and what murders and robberies there is now! What will there be when the Great Exhibition opens! for rogues is worst in a crowd, and they say they'll be plenty come to London from all arts and parts? Never mind; if I can see anything better to do in a fair way at the Exhibition, I'll cut the streets.

"Perhaps my earnings is half from working people, and half from private houses; that's about it. But working people's easiest satisfied."

I have given this man's statement more fully than I should have thought necessary, that I might include his account of letter-writing. The letter-writer was at one period a regular street-labourer in London, as he is now in some continental cities — Naples, for instance. The vocation in London seems in some respects to have fallen into the hands of the street-stationer, but the majority of letters written for the uneducated—and their letter-receiving or answering is seldom arduous—is done, I believe, by those who are rather vaguely but emphatically described as— "friends."

I am told that there are 120 street-stationers in London, a small majority of whom may be itinerant, but chiefly on regular rounds. On a Sunday morning, in such places as the Brill, are two or three men, but not regularly, who sell stationery only on Sunday mornings. Taking the number, however, at 120, I am assured that their average profits may be taken at 8s. weekly, each stationer. On note-paper of the best sort the profit is sometimes only 50 per cent.; but, take the trade altogether, we may calculate it at cent. per cent. (on some things it is higher); and we find £4,992 yearly expended in street-stationery.

A STREET AUTHOR, OR POET

I CALLED upon one on the recommendation of a neighbouring tradesman, of whom I made some inquiries. He could not tell me the number of the house in the court where the man lived, but said I had only to inquire for the Tinker, or the Poet, and anyone would tell me.

I found the poor poet, who bears a good character, on a sick bed; he was suffering, and had long been suffering, from abscesses. He was apparently about forty-five, with the sunken eyes, hollow cheeks, and, not pale but thick and rather sallow complexion, which indicate ill-health and scant food. He spoke quietly, and expressed resignation. His room was not very small, and was furnished in the way usual among the very poor, but there were a few old pictures over the mantelpiece. His eldest boy, a lad of thirteen or fourteen, was making dog-chains; at which he earned a shilling or two, sometimes 2s. 6d., by sale in the streets.

"I was born at Newcastle-under-Lyne," the man said, "but was brought to London when, I believe, I was only three months old. I was very fond of reading poems, in my youth, as soon as I could read and understand almost. Yes, very likely, sir; perhaps it was that put it into my head to write them afterwards. I was taught wire-working, and jobbing, and was brought up to hawking wire-work in the streets, and all over England and Wales. It was never a very good trade—just a living. Many and many a weary mile we've travelled together,—I mean, my wife and I have: and we've sometimes been benighted, and had to wander or rest about until morning. It wasn't that we hadn't money to pay for a lodging, but we couldn't get one. We lost count of the days sometimes in wild parts; but if we did lose count, or thought we had, I could always tell when it was Sunday morning by the look of nature; there was a mystery and a beauty about it as told me. I was very fond of Goldsmith's poetry always. I can repeat 'Edwin and Emma' now. No, sir; I never read the 'Vicar of Wakefield.' I found 'Edwin and Emma' in a book called the

'Speaker.' I often thought of it in travelling through some parts of the country.

"Above fourteen years ago I tried to make a shilling or two by selling my verses. I'd written plenty before, but made nothing by them. Indeed I never tried. The first song I ever sold was to a concert-room manager. The next I sold had great success. It was called the 'Demon of the Sea,' and was to the tune of 'The Brave Old Oak.' Do I remember how it began? Yes, sir, I remember every word of it. It began:

> *'Unfurl the sails*
> *We've easy gales;*
> *And helmsman steer aright,*
> *Hoist the grim death's head—*
> *The Pirate's head—*
> *For a vessel heaves in sight!'*

That song was written for a concert-room, but it was soon in the streets, and ran a whole winter. I got only 1s. for it. Then I wrote the 'Pirate of the Isles', and other ballads of that sort. The concert-rooms pay no better than the printers for the streets.

"Perhaps the best thing I ever wrote was the 'Husband's Dream.' I'm very sorry indeed that I can't offer you copies of some of my ballads, but I haven't a single copy myself of any of them, not one, and I dare say I've written a thousand in my time, and most of them were printed. I believe 10,000 were sold of the 'Husband's Dream.' It begins:

> *'O Dermot, you look healthy now,*
> *Your dress is neat and clean;*
> *I never see you drunk about,*
> *Then tell me where you've been.*
>
> *Your wife and family — are they well?*
> *You once did use them strange:*
> *O, are you kinder to them grown,*
> *How came this happy change?'*

"Then Dermot tells how he dreamed of his wife's sudden death, and his children's misery as they cried about her dead body, while he was drunk in bed, and as he calls out in his misery, he wakes, and finds his wife by his side. The ballad ends:

> *'I pressed her to my throbbing heart,*
> *Whilst joyous tears did stream;*
> *And ever since, I've heaven blest,*
> *For sending me that dream.'*

"Dermot turned teetotaller. The teetotallers were very much pleased with that song. The printer once sent me 5s. on account of it.

"I have written all sorts of things—ballads on a subject, and copies of verses, and anything ordered of me, or on anything I thought would be accepted, but now I can't get about. I've been asked to write indecent songs, but I refused. One man offered me 5s. for six such songs. — 'Why, that's less than the common price,' said I, 'instead of something over to pay for the wickedness.' — All those sort of songs come now to the streets, I believe all do, from the concert-rooms. I can imitate any poetry. I don't recollect any poet I've imitated. No, sir, not Scott or Moore, that I know of, but if they've written popular songs, then I dare say I have imitated them. Writing poetry is no comfort to me in my sickness. It might if I could write just what I please. The printers like hanging subjects best, and I don't. But when any of them sends to order a copy of verses for a 'Sorrowful Lamentation' of course I must supply them. I don't think much of what I've done that way. If I'd my own fancy, I'd keep writing acrostics, such as one I wrote on our rector." "God bless him", interrupted the wife, "he's a good man." "That he is," said the poet, "but he's never seen what I wrote about him, and perhaps never will." He then desired his wife to reach him his big Bible, and out of it he handed me a piece of paper, with the following lines written on it, in a small neat hand enough:

> *"Celestial blessings hover round his head,*
> *Hundreds of poor, by his kindness were fed,*
> *And precepts taught which he himself obeyed.*
> *Man, erring man, brought to the fold of God,*
> *Preaching pardon through a Saviour's blood.*

No lukewarm priest, but firm to Heaven's cause;
Examples showed how much he loved its laws.
Youth and age, he to their wants attends,
Steward of Christ — the poor man's sterling friend."

"There would be some comfort, sir," he continued, "if one could go on writing at will like that. As it is, I sometimes write verses all over a slate, and rub them out again. Live hard! yes, indeed, we do live hard. I hardly know the taste of meat. We live on bread and butter, and tea; no, not any fish. As you see, sir, I work at tinning. I put new bottoms into old tin tea-pots, and such like. Here's my sort of bench, by my poor bit of a bed. In the best weeks I earn 4s. by tinning, never higher. In bad weeks I earn only 1s. by it, and sometimes not that — and there are more shilling than four shilling weeks by three to one. As to my poetry, a good week is 3s., and a poor week is 1s. — and sometimes I make nothing at all that way. So I leave you to judge, sir, whether we live hard; for the comings in, and what we have from the parish, must keep six of us — myself, my wife and four children. It's a long, hard struggle." "Yes, indeed," said the wife, "it's just as you've heard my husband tell, sir. We've 2s. a week and four loaves of bread from the parish, and the rent's 2s. 6d., and the landlord every week has 2s., — and 6d. he has done for him in tinning work. Oh, we do live hard, indeed."

As I was taking my leave, the poor man expressed a desire that I would take a copy of an epitaph which he had written for himself. "If ever," he said, "I am rich enough to provide for a tombstone, or my family is rich enough to give me one, this shall be my epitaph" (I copied it from a blank page in his Bible):

"Stranger, pause, a moment stay,
Tread lightly o'er this mound of clay.
Here lies J—— H——, in hopes to rise,
And meet his Saviour in the skies.
Christ his refuge, Heaven his home,
Where pain and sorrow never come.
His journey's done, his trouble's past,
With God he sleeps in peace at last."

A CHEAP-JOHN

THE FOLLOWING narrative, relative to this curious class, who, in many respects, partake of the characteristics proper to the mountebank of old, was taken from one of the fraternity. It may be cited as an example of those who are bred to the streets:—

"My father and mother," said he, "both followed a travelling occupation, and were engaged in vending different things, from the old brimstone matches up to clothes lines, clothes props, and clothes pegs. They never got beyond these—the other articles were thread, tapes, nutmeg graters, shoe-ties, stay-laces, and needles. My father, my mother used to tell me, was a great scholar, and had not always been a travelling vagrant. My mother had never known any other life. I, however, did not reap any benefit from my father's scholarship. At a very early age, five or six perhaps, I recollect myself a poor little neglected wretch, sent out each day with a roll of matches, with strict injunctions not to come home without selling them, and to bring home a certain sum of money, upon pain of receiving a sound thrashing, which threat was mostly put into execution whenever I failed to perform the task imposed upon me.

"My father seldom worked, that is, seldom hawked, but my mother, poor thing, had to travel and work very hard to support four of us—my father, myself, and a sister, who is since dead. I was but little assistance, and sometimes when I did not bring home the sum required, she would make it up, and tell my father I had been a good boy. My father was an inveterate drinker, and had a very violent temper. My mother, I am sorry to say, used to drink too, but I believe that ill-usage drove her to it. They led a dreadful life; I scarcely felt any attachment for them; home we had none, one place was as good as another to us. I left my parents when scarcely eight years old. I had received a thrashing the day before for being a defaulter in my sale, and I determined the following morning to decamp; and, accordingly, with my nine-pennyworth of matches (the quantity generally allotted me), I set out to begin the world upon my own account. Although this occurred 25 years ago, I have never met my parents since. My father, I heard, died a few years after my leaving, but my mother I know not whether she be living or dead. I left my parents at Dover, and journeyed on to London.

"I knew there were lodging-houses for travellers in every town, some of them I had stopped at with my father and mother. I told the people of these houses that my parents would arrive the following day, and paid my 2d. for the share of a third, fourth, fifth, or even sixth part of a bed, according to the number of children who inhabited the lodging-house upon that particular night. My matches I could always sell if I tried, but I used to play my time away, and many times night had arrived before I thought of effecting sales sufficient to pay my expenses at the beggar's hotel. Broken victuals I got in abundance, indeed more than sufficient for my own consumption. The money I received for the matches, after paying my lodging, and purchasing a pennyworth of brimstone to make more (the wood I begged at the carpenters), I gambled away at cards. Yes, young as I was, I understood blind hookey. I invariably lost; of course I was cheated.

"I remained in a lodging house in Mill-lane, Deptford, for two years, discontinued the match-selling, and, having a tidy voice, took to hawking songs through the public-houses. The sailors used to ask me to sing, and there were few days that I did not accumulate 2s. 6d., and from that to 4s., especially when I chose to be industrious; but my love of pitch and toss and blind hookey always kept me poor. I often got into debt with my landlady, and had no difficulty in doing so, for I always felt a pride in paying. From selling the printed songs, I imbibed a wish to learn to read, and, with the assistance of an old soldier, I soon acquired sufficient knowledge to make out the names of each song, and shortly afterwards I could study a song and learn the words without anyone helping me. I stopped in Deptford until I was something more than twelve years old. I had then laid the songs aside, and taken to hawking small wares, tapes, thread, &c.; and in the winter season I was a buyer of rabbit and hare skins. I kept at this for about three years, sometimes entirely without a stock. I had run it out perhaps gambled it away; and at such times I suffered great privations. I never could beg. I have often tried, but never could. I have approached a house with a begging intention, knocked at the door, and when it has been opened I have requested a drink of water.

When I was about 16 I joined in partnership with a man who used to make phosphorus boxes. I sold them for him. A piece of phosphorus was stuck in a tube, the match was dipped into the phosphorus, and it would ignite by friction. I was hawking these boxes in Norwich, when the constable considered they were dreadful affairs, and calculated to encourage and assist thieves and burglars. He took me before the magistrate, at the beak's own private house, and he being equally horrified, I was sent to prison for a month. I have often thought since that the proceeding was illegal. What would be said now if a man was to be sent to jail for selling lucifer matches? In Norwich prison I associated with the rest, and if I had been inclined to turn thief I had plenty of opportunities and offers of gratuitous instruction. The separate or silent system was not in vogue then. I worked on the treadmill. Dinner was allowed to be sent in on the Sunday by the prisoner's friends. My dinner was sent in on the first Sunday by the man I sold the boxes for, as it was on the second, third, and fourth; but I had lost it before I received it. I had always gambled it away, for there were plenty of opportunities of doing so in the prisons then.

"On leaving the jail I received 1s., with this I purchased some songs and travelled to Yarmouth. I could do best among sailors. After a few weeks I had accumulated about 8s., and with that sum I purchased some hardware at the swag-shop, commenced hawking, and cut the vocal department altogether: still I gambled and kept myself in poverty. In the course of time, however, I had amassed a basket of goods, worth, perhaps, £3. I gambled and lost them all in one night. I was so downcast and unhappy from this circumstance, that it caused me to reflect seriously, and I made an oath that I never would gamble again. I have kept it, and have reason to bless the day that I made so good a resolution. After losing my basket of goods, the winner gave me articles amounting to a few shillings, and I began the world once more. Shortly afterwards I commenced rag gatherer, and changed my goods for old rags, of course not refusing cash in payment. My next step was to have some bills printed, whereon I requested all thrifty wives to look out their old rags or old metal, or old bones, &c.; stating at the bottom that the bill would be called for, and that a good price in ready money would be given for all useless lumber, &c. Some months at this business realized me a pretty sum of money. I was in possession of nearly £5. Then I discontinued the rag-gathering; not that the trade was declining, but I did not like it — I was ambitious.

"I purchased a neat box, and started to sell a little Birmingham jewellery. I was now respectably dressed, was getting a living, and had entirely left off stopping at common lodging-houses; but I confined my visits to small villages — I was afraid of the law; and as I was pursuing my calling near Wakefield, a constable inquired for my hawker's licence. I had none to produce. He took me into custody, and introduced me to a magistrate, who committed me to prison for a month, and took away my box of goods. I endured the month's imprisonment upon the silent system; they cut my hair short; and at the expiration of the term I was thrust out upon the world heart-broken, without a shilling, to beg, to steal, or to starve.

"I proceeded to Leeds, the fair was on at this time. I got engaged to assist a person, from whom I had been accustomed occasionally to purchase goods. He was a 'Cheap-John.' In the course of the day he suggested that I should have a try at the hand-selling. I mounted the platform, and succeeded beyond my own expectations or that of my master. He offered me a regular engagement, which I accepted. At times I would help him sell, and at other times I hawked with his licence. I had regular wages, besides all I could get above a certain price that he placed upon each of the goods. I remained with this person some fifteen months, at the end of which period I commenced for myself, having saved nearly £25. I began at once the hand-selling, and purchased a hawker's licence, which enabled me to sell without danger. Then I always called at the constable's house, and gave a louder knock at his door than any other person's, proud of my authority, and assured of my safety. At first I borrowed an empty cart, in which I stood and sold my wares. I could chaff as well as the best, and was as good a salesman as most of them. After that I purchased a second-hand cart from a person who had lately started a waggon. I progressed and improved in circumstances, and at last bought a very handsome waggon for myself. I have now a nice caravan, and a good stock of goods, worth at least £50. Money I have but little. I always invest it in goods. I am married, and have got a family. I always travel in the summer, but remain at home during the winter. My wife never travels. She remains behind, and manages a little swag-shop, which always turns in at least the family expenses.''

THE STREET-SELLERS OF RINGS
AND SOVEREIGNS FOR WAGERS

THIS CLASS is hardly known in the streets of London at present. Country fairs and races are a more fitting ground for the ring-seller's operations. One man of this class told me that he had been selling rings, and occasionally medals, for wagers for this last fifteen years. "It's only a so-so game just now," he said; "the people get so fly to it. A many hold out their penny for a ring, and just as I suppose I'm a going to receive it, they put the penny into their pockets, and their thumb upon their nose. I wish I had some other game, for this is a very dickey one. I gives 3d. a dozen for the rings at the swag shop, and sometimes sells a couple of dozen in a day, but seldom more. Saturday is no better day than any other. Country people are my best customers. I know them by their appearance. Sometimes a person in the crowd whispers to the others that he bought one the other day and went and pawned it for 5s., and he'd buy another but he's got no money. I don't ask for such assistance; I suppose it's done for a lark, and to laugh at others if they buy. Several times since I have been on this dodge, women have come back and abused me because the ring they bought for a penny was not gold. Some had been to the pawn shop, and were quite astonished that the pawn-broker wouldn't take the ring in. I do best in the summer at the races: people think it more likely that two sporting gents would lay an out of the way wager (as you know I always make out) then than at any other time. I have been interfered with at races before now for being an impostor, and yet at the same time the gamblers was allowed to keep their tables; but of course theirs was all fair — no imposition about them — oh no! I am considered about one of the best patterers among our lot.

"I dare say there may be twenty on us all together, in town and country, on rings and sovereigns. Sometimes, when travelling on foot to a race or fair, I do a little in the *Fawney dropping* line;" (fawneys are rings) "but that is a dangerous game. I never did it but two or three times. There were some got lagged for it, and that frightened me. In ring-dropping we pretend to have found a ring, and ask some simple-looking fellow if it's good gold, as it's only just picked up. Sometimes it is immediately pronounced *gold:* 'Well it's no use to me,' we'll say, 'will you buy it?' Often they are foolish enough to buy, and it's some satisfaction to one's conscience to know that they think they are a taking you in, for they give you only a shilling or two for an article which if really gold would be worth eight or ten. Some ring-droppers write out an account and make a little parcel of jewellery, and when they pick out their man, they say, 'If you please, sir, will you read this for me, and tell me what I should do with these things, as I've just found them?' Some people advise they should be taken to the police office—but very few say that; some, that they should be taken to the address; others, that they should be sold, and the money shared; others offer a price for them, stating that they're not gold, they're only trumpery they say, but they'll give half-a-crown for them. It's pleasant to take such people in. Sometimes the finder says he's in haste, and will sell them for anything to attend to other business, and he then transfers his interest at perhaps 200 per cent profit. This game won't friz now, sir, it's very dangerous. I've left it off long since. I don't like the idea of quod. I've been there once."

Another plan of dropping rings is to write a letter. This is the style:—

"My dear Anne,

"I have sent you the ring, and hope it will fit.—Excuse me not bringing it. John will leave it with you.—You know I have so much to attend to.—I shall think every minute a year until the happy day arrives.

"Yours devotedly,

"James Brown."

This love epistle containing the wedding-ring was most successful when it first came up, but the public now are too wide awake. According to another informant, the ring-dropping "lurk" is now carried on this way, for the old style is "coopered". "A woman," he says, "is made up so as to appear in the family-way — pretty far gone — and generally with a face as long as a boy's kite. Up she goes to any likely ken, where she knows there are women that are married or expect to get married, and commences begging. Then comes the tale of woe, if she can get them to listen — 'I'm in the family-way,' she says, 'as you can plainly see *young ladies* (this she says to the *servants,* and that prides them, you know). My husband has left me after serving me in this way. I don't know where he is, and am forced to solicit the ladies' charity.' Well, the servants will bring broken victuals and make a little collection among themselves for the 'unprotected female;' for which in return, with many thanks for their kindness, she offers her gold wedding-ring for sale, as she wants to get back to her suffering kids to give them something to eat, poor things, and they shall have the gold ring, she says, for half what it's worth; or if they won't buy it, will they lend 2*s.* or 3*s.* on it till she can redeem it, as she hasn't been in the habit of pledging! The girls are taken off their guard (she not being in the habit of pledging is a choker for them) by the woman's seeming simplicity, and there's a consultation. One says to the other — 'Oh, you'll want it, Mary, for John;' and another, 'No, you'll want it first, Sally, for William.' But the woman has her eye on the one as says least, as the likeliest of all to want it, and so she says to the John and William girls, 'Oh, you don't want it; but *here* (touching the silent one), here's a *young lady* as does' (that sweetens the servant girl up directly). She says, 'I don't want it, bless you,' with a giggle, 'but I'll lend you a trifle, as you are in this state, and have a family, and are left like this by your husband — ain't he cruel, Sally?' (she adds to her fellow-servant). The money the ring-woman gets, sir, depends upon the servant's funds; if it is just after quarter-day, she generally gets a tidy tip — if not, 4 or 5 bob. I've known one woman get 10*s.* and even 12*s.* this way. The ring is made out of brass gilt buttons, and stunning well: it's faked up to rights, and takes a good judge even at this day to detect it without a test.

"The best sort of rings for *fawney dropping* is the Belchers. They are a good thick looking ring, and have the crown and V.R. stamped upon them. They are 7*d.* a dozen. I takes my stand now, in my ring-selling, as if I was in a great hurry, and pulls out my watch. I used to have a real one, but now it's a dummy. 'Now, ladies and gentlemen,' says I, 'I am not permitted to remain more than ten minutes in one spot. I have rings to sell to decide a wager recently made between two sporting noblemen, to the effect that I do not sell a certain quantity of these rings in a given time, at a penny a piece. I can recommend the article as being well worth the money I ask for it, perhaps something more. I do not say they are gold; in fact, I must not say too much, as there is a person in this company watching my proceedings, and seeing that I do not remain more than ten minutes in this spot,' — here I always looks very hard at the most respectable and gentlemanly looking person among my hearers and sometimes gives him a wink, and sometimes a nod, — 'but if you should hear anything more about these rings, and you want to purchase, don't be vexed if I am gone when you want me. The ten minutes has nearly expired; three minutes more; any more buyers? It makes no difference to me whether I sell or not — I get my pay all the same; but if you take my advice, buy; and perhaps if you was to call at the sign of the Three Balls, as you go home, you may be agreeably surprised, and hear something to your advantage. Perhaps I have said too much. I have one minute more, before I close the establishment. After shutting the box, I dare not sell another in this spot, if you were to offer me £5 for it; therefore, if you wish to purchase, now is your time.' I make many a pitch, and do not sell a single ring; and the insults I receive used to aggravate me very much, but I do not mind them now, I'm used to it.

"The flyest cove among all us ring-sellers is little Ikey, the Jew. There were two used to work the game. They had a real gold ring, just like the ones they were selling, and they always used to pitch near a pawnbroker's shop. Ikey's pal would buy a ring for a penny, of the street-seller, and would then say, loud enough to be heard by the bystanders, 'There's a pawn shop — I'll go and ask them to take it in.' A crowd would follow him. He would enter the pawnbroker's — present a real gold ring — obtain a loan of 5s., and would present the ticket to the bystanders, who would then buy very fast. When the pitch was over, Ikey's pal would take the ring out of pawn, and away the two would go to work near some other pawnbroker's. I have heard Ikey say they have pawned the ring thirty-five times in a day. I tried the same caper; but my pal cut with the gold ring the first day, and I've never had another go at that *fake* since.

"Before I commenced the jewellery line," continued my candid informant, "a good many years ago, I used to hold horses about Bond-street. Afterwards I was taken as an errand boy at a druggist's, was out of an errand one day and got 6*d*. for holding a gentleman's horse, which kept me nearly an hour; when I went back to my master's I was told I wasn't wanted any more. I had been cautioned about stopping of errands two or three times before; however I didn't like the situation, it was too confining. I next got a place as pot-boy, in Brick Lane. Here I was out one day gathering in the pots. I hung the strap of pots to a railing to have a game at chances (pitch and toss), somebody prigged my strap of pots, and I cut. A few weeks after I was grabbed for this, and got a month at the mill; but I was quite innocent of prigging —I was only careless. When I came out of prison, I went to Epsom races, thinking to get a job there at something, or other. A man engaged me to assist him in 'pitching the hunters.' Pitching the hunters is the three sticks a penny, with the snuffboxes stuck upon sticks; if you throw your stick, and they fall out of the hole, you are entitled to what you knock off.

"I came to London with my master the pitcher-hunter, he went to a swag shop in Kent-street, in the Borough, to purchase a new stock. I saw a man there purchasing rings, this was little Ikey, the Jew; some days afterwards I saw him making a pitch, and selling very fast. I had fourpence in my pocket; went to Kent-street, to the swag shops, bought a dozen rings, and commenced selling them. I sold that day three dozen; that wasn't bad considering that my toggery was very queer, and I looked anything but like one who would be trusted with ten pounds' worth of gold rings. This wager between the two sporting noblemen has been a long time settling. I've been at it more than fifteen years. The origin of it was this here: when sovereigns were first coined, the Jew boys and others used to sell medals and card-counters upon particular occasions, the same as they do now, and shove them in a saucepan lid, with silver paper under them. Captain

Barclay, and another of the same sort, bet a wager, that one of these Jew-boys could not dispose of a certain number of real sovereigns in a given time, supposing the Jew-boy cried out nothing more than 'here's sovereigns, only a penny a piece.' The number he was to sell was 50 within the hour, and to take his station at London Bridge. The wager was made, the Jew-boy procured, and the sovereigns put into the pot lid. 'Here are real sovereigns a penny a piece, who'll buy?' he cried; but he sold only a few. The number disposed of, within the hour, I have heard was seventeen. Those who purchased, when they found that they had really bought sovereigns at a penny a piece, returned for more, but the salesman was gone. A good harvest was afterwards reaped among the Jews, who got up a medal something like a sovereign, and sold them in every quarter of London, for the Captain's wager soon spread about everywhere. It's a stale game now; it was so before my time, but I've heard the Jews talk about it.

"The second day I tried the ring dodge, I was a little more successful; indeed every day for some time exceeded the day before, for, as I improved in patter, my sales increased. My appearance, too, was improving. At one time I was a regular swell, sported white kid gloves, white choker, white waistcoat, black ribbon, and a quizzing glass. Some people used to chaff me, and cry out 'there's a swell.' I never was saving, always spent my money as fast as I got it. I might have saved a goodish bit, and I wish I had now. I never had a wife, but I have had two or three broomstick matches, though they never turned out happy. I never got hold of one but what was fond of lush.

"I live in Westminster, at a padding-ken. I'd rather not tell you where, not that I've anything to fear, but people might think I was a *nose*, if anybody came after me, and they would crab me. I'd rather get something else to do if I could, but I think this is the best street game I could follow. I don't believe any of the ring-sellers dispose of any more than myself, except little Ikey; he now adds other articles, a silver thimble (he calls it), some conundrums, a song-book and a seal, and all for a penny. I tried the same thing, but found I could do just as well with the rings alone. We expects to do great things during the Exhibition. I think all of us ought to be allowed to sell in the parks. Foreigners are invited to witness specimens of British Industry, and it's my opinion they should see all, from the highest to the lowest. We *did* intend petitioning the Prince on the subject, but I don't suppose it would be any go, seeing as how the slang coves" (the showmen), "have done so, and been refused."

TWO ORPHAN FLOWER GIRLS

OF THESE girls the elder was fifteen and the younger eleven. Both were clad in old, but not torn, dark print frocks, hanging so closely, and yet so loosely, about them as to show the deficiency of under-clothing; they wore old broken black chip bonnets. The older sister (or rather half-sister) had a pair of old worn-out shoes on her feet, the younger was barefoot, but trotted along, in a gait at once quick and feeble—as if the soles of her little feet were impervious, like horn, to the roughness of the road. The elder girl had a modest expression of countenance, with no pretensions to prettiness except in having tolerably good eyes. Her complexion was somewhat muddy, and her features somewhat pinched. The younger child had a round, chubby, and even rosy face, and quite a healthful look. Her portrait is here given.

They lived in one of the streets near Drury-lane. They were inmates of a house, not let out as a lodging-house, in separate beds, but in rooms, and inhabited by street-sellers and street-labourers. The room they occupied was large, and one dim candle lighted it so insufficiently that it seemed to exaggerate the dimensions. The walls were bare and discoloured with damp. The furniture consisted of a crazy table and a few chairs, and in the centre of the room was an old four-post bedstead of the larger size. This bed was occupied nightly by the two sisters and their brother, a lad just turned thirteen. In a sort of recess in a corner of the room was the decency of an old curtain—or something equivalent, for I could hardly see in the dimness—and behind this was, I presume, the bed of the married couple. The three children paid 2s. a week for the room, the tenant, an Irishman out of work, paying 2s. 9d., but the furniture was his, and his wife aided the children in their trifle of washing, mended their clothes, where such a thing was possible, and such like. The husband was absent at the time of my visit, but the wife seemed of a better stamp, judging by her appearance, and by her refraining from any direct, or even indirect, way of begging, as well as from the "Glory be to Gods!" "the heavens be your honour's bed!" or "it's the truth I'm telling of you, sir," that I so frequently met with on similar visits.

The elder girl said, in an English accent, not at all garrulously, but merely in answer to my questions: "I sell flowers, sir; we live almost on flowers when they are to be got. I sell, and so does my sister, all kinds, but it's very little use offering any that's not sweet. I think it's the sweetness as sells them. I sell primroses, when they're in, and violets, and wall-flowers, and stocks, and roses of different sorts, and pinks, and carnations, and mixed flowers, and lilies of the valley, and green lavender, and mignonette (but that I do very seldom), and violets again at this time of the year, for we get them both in spring and winter." (They are forced in hot-houses for winter sale, I may remark.) "The best sale of all is, I think, moss-roses, young moss roses. We do best of all on them. Primroses are good, for people say: 'Well, here's spring again to a certainty.' Gentlemen are our best customers. I've heard that they buy flowers to give to the ladies. Ladies have sometimes said: 'A penny, my poor girl, here's three-half-pence for the bunch.' Or they've given me the price of two bunches for one; so have gentlemen. I never had a rude word said to me by a gentleman in my life. No, sir, neither lady nor gentleman ever gave me 6*d.* for a bunch of flowers. I never had a sixpence given to me in my life—never. I never go among boys, I know nobody but my brother. My father was a tradesman in Mitchelstown, in the County Cork. I don't know what sort of a tradesman he was. I never saw him. He was a tradesman I've been told. I was born in London. Mother was a chairwoman, and lived very well. None of us ever saw a father." [It was evident that they were illegitimate children, but the landlady had never seen the mother, and could give me no information.] "We don't know anything about our fathers. We were all 'mother's children.' Mother died seven years ago last Guy Faux day. I've got myself, and my brother and sister a bit of bread ever since, and never had any help but from the neighbours. I never troubled the parish. O, yes, sir, the neighbours is all poor people, very poor, some of them. We've lived with her" (indicating her landlady by a gesture) "these two years, and off and on before that. I can't say how long."

The Orphan Flower Girl

"Well, I don't know exactly," said the landlady, "but I've had them with me almost all the time, for four years, as near as I can recollect; perhaps more. I've moved three times, and they always followed me." In answer to my inquiries the landlady assured me that these two poor girls were never out of doors all the time she had known them after six at night. "We've always good health. We can all read." [Here the three somewhat insisted upon proving to me their proficiency in reading, and having produced a Roman Catholic book, the "Garden of Heaven," they read very well.] "I put myself," continued the girl, "and I put my brother and sister to a Roman Catholic school — and to Ragged schools — but *I* could read before mother died. My brother can write, and I pray to God that he'll do well with it. I buy my flowers at Covent Garden; sometimes, but very seldom, at Farringdon. I pay 1*s.* for a dozen bunches, whatever flowers are in. Out of every two bunches I can make three, at 1*D.* a piece. Sometimes one or two over in the dozen, but not so often as I would like. We make the bunches up ourselves. We get the rush to tie them with for nothing. We put their own leaves round these violets [she produced a bunch]. The paper for a dozen costs a penny; sometimes only a halfpenny. The two of us doesn't make less than 6*d.* a day, unless it's very ill luck. But religion teaches us that God will support us, and if we make less we say nothing. We do better on oranges in March or April, I think, it is, than of flowers. Oranges keep better than flowers, you see, sir. We make 1*s.* a day, and 9*d.* a day, on oranges, the two of us. I wish they was in all the year. I generally go St. John's-wood way, and Hampstead and Highgate way with my flowers. I can get them nearly all the year, but oranges is better liked than flowers, I think. I always keep 1*s.* stock-money, if I can. If it's bad weather, so bad that we can't sell flowers at all, and so if we've had to spend our stock-money for a bit of bread, *she* [the landlady] lends us 1*s.*, if she has one, or she borrows one of a neighbour, if she hasn't, or if the neighbours hasn't it, she borrows it at a dolly-shop" [the illegal pawnshop]. "There's 2*d.* a week to pay for 1*s.* at a dolly, and perhaps an old rug left for it; if it's very hard weather, the rug must be taken at night time, or we are starved with the cold. It sometimes has to be put into the dolly again next morning, and then there's 2d. to pay for it for the day. We've had a frock in for 6d., and that's a penny a week, and the same for a day. We never pawned anything; we have nothing they would take in at the pawnshop. We live on bread and tea, and sometimes a fresh herring of a night. Sometimes we don't eat a bit all day when we're out; sometimes we take a bit of bread with us, or buy a bit. My sister can't eat taturs; they sicken her. I don't know what emigrating means." [I informed her and she continued]: "No, sir, I wouldn't like to emigrate and leave brother and sister. If they went with me I don't think I should like it, not among strangers. I think our living costs us 2s. a week for the two of us; the rest goes in rent. That's all we make."

The brother earned from 1s. 6d. to 2s. a week, with an occasional meal, as a costermonger's boy. Neither of them ever missed mass on a Sunday.

A FLOWER GIRL

SOME OF these girls are, as I have stated, of an immoral character, and some of them are sent out by their parents to make out a livelihood by prostitution. One of this class, whom I saw, had come out of prison a short time previously. She was not nineteen, and had been sentenced about a twelvemonth before to three months' imprisonment with hard labour, "for heaving her shoe," as she said, "at the Lord Mayor, to get a comfortable lodging, for she was tired of being about the streets." After this she was locked up for breaking the lamps in the street. She alleged that her motive for this was a belief that by committing some such act she might be able to get into an asylum for females. She was sent out into the streets by her father and mother, at the age of nine, to sell flowers. Her father used to supply her with the money to buy the flowers, and she used to take the proceeds of the day's work home to her parents. She used to be out frequently till past midnight, and seldom or never got home before nine. She associated only with flower girls of loose character. The result may be imagined.

She could not state positively that her parents were aware of the manner in which she got the money she took home to them. She supposes that they must have imagined what her practices were. He used to give her no supper if she "didn't bring home a good bit of money." Her father and mother did little or no work all this while. They lived on what she brought home. At thirteen years old she was sent to prison (she stated) "for selling combs in the street" (it was winter, and there were no flowers to be had). She was incarcerated fourteen days, and when liberated she returned to her former practices. The very night that she came home from gaol her father sent her out into the streets again. She continued in this state, her father and mother living upon her, until about twelve months before I received this account from her, when her father turned her out of his house, because she didn't bring home money enough.

She then went into Kent, hop-picking, and there fell in with a beggar, who accosted her while she was sitting under a tree. He said, "You have got a very bad pair of shoes on; come with me, and you shall have some better ones." She consented, and walked with him into the village close by, where they stood out in the middle of the streets, and the man began addressing the people, "My kind good Christians, me and my poor wife here is ashamed to appear before you in the state we are in." She remained with this person all the winter, and travelled with him through the country, begging. He was a beggar by trade. In the spring she returned to the flower-selling, but scarcely got any money either by that or other means. At last she grew desperate, and wanted to get back to prison. She broke the lamps outside the Mansion-house, and was sentenced to fourteen days' imprisonment. She had been out of prison nearly three weeks when I saw her, and was in training to go into an asylum. She was sick and tired, she said, of her life.

A WATERCRESS GIRL

THE LITTLE watercress girl who gave me the following statement, although only eight years of age, had entirely lost all childish ways, and was, indeed, in thoughts and manner, a woman. There was something cruelly pathetic in hearing this infant, so young that her features had scarcely formed themselves, talking of the bitterest struggles of life, with the calm earnestness of one who had endured them all. I did not know how to talk with her. At first I treated her as a child, speaking on childish subjects; so that I might, by being familiar with her, remove all shyness, and get her to narrate her life freely. I asked her about her toys and her games with her companions; but the look of amazement that answered me soon put an end to any attempt at fun on my part. I then talked to her about the parks, and whether she ever went to them. "The parks!" she replied in wonder, "where are they?" I explained to her, telling her that they were large open places with green grass and tall trees, where beautiful carriages drove about, and people walked for pleasure, and children played. Her eyes brightened up a little as I spoke; and she asked, half doubtingly, "Would they let such as me go there—just to look?" All her knowledge seemed to begin and end with watercresses, and what they fetched. She knew no more of London than that part she had seen on her rounds, and believed that no quarter of the town was handsomer or pleasanter than it was at Farringdon-market or at Clerkenwell, where she lived. Her little face, pale and thin with privation, was wrinkled where the dimples ought to have been, and she would sigh frequently. When some hot dinner was offered to her, she would not touch it, because, if she ate too much, "it made her sick," she said; " and she wasn't used to meat, only on a Sunday."

The poor child, although the weather was severe, was dressed in a thin cotton gown, with a threadbare shawl wrapped round her shoulders. She wore no covering to her head, and the long rusty hair stood out in all directions. When she walked she shuffled along, for fear that the large carpet slippers that served her for shoes should slip off her feet.

"I go about the streets with water-creases, crying, 'Four bunches a penny, water-creases.' I am just eight years old — that's all, and I've a big sister, and a brother and a sister younger than I am. On and off, I've been very near a twelvemonth in the streets. Before that, I had to take care of a baby for my aunt. No, it wasn't heavy — it was only two months old; but I minded it for ever such a time — till it could walk. It was a very nice little baby, not a very pretty one; but, if I touched it under the chin, it would laugh. Before I had the baby, I used to help mother, who was in the fur trade; and, if there was any slits in the fur, I'd sew them up. My mother learned me to needle-work and to knit when I was about five. I used to go to school, too; but I wasn't there long. I've forgot all about it now, it's such a time ago; and mother took me away because the master whacked me, though the missus use'n't to never touch me. I didn't like him at all. What do you think? he hit me three times, ever so hard, across the face with his cane, and made me go dancing down stairs; and when mother saw the marks on my cheek, she went to blow him up, but she couldn't see him — he was afraid. That's why I left school.

"The creases is so bad now, that I haven't been out with 'em for three days. They're so cold, people won't buy 'em; for when I goes up to them, they say, 'They'll freeze our bellies.' Besides, in the market, they won't sell a ha'penny handful now — they're ris to a penny and tuppence. In summer there's lots, and 'most as cheap as dirt; but I have to be down at Farringdon-market between four and five, or else I can't get any creases, because everyone almost — especially the Irish — is selling them, and they're picked up so quick. Some of the saleswomen — we never calls 'em ladies — is very kind to us children, and some of them altogether spiteful. The good one will give you a bunch for nothing, when they're cheap; but the others, cruel ones, if you try to bate them a farden less than they ask you, will say, 'Go along with you, you're no good.' I used to go down to market along with another girl, as must be about fourteen, 'cos she does her back hair up. When we've bought a lot, we sits down on a door-step, and ties up the bunches. We never goes home to breakfast till we've sold out; but, if it's very late, then I buys a penn'orth of pudden, which is very nice with gravy. I don't know hardly one of the people, as goes to Farringdon, to talk to; they never speaks to me, so I don't speak to them. We children never play down there, 'cos we're thinking of our living. No; people never pities me in the street — excepting one gentleman, and he says, says he, 'What do you do out so soon in the morning?' but he gave me nothink — he only walked away.

"It's very cold before winter comes on reg'lar — specially getting up of a morning. I gets up in the dark by the light of the lamp in the court. When the snow is on the ground, there's creases. I bears the cold — you must; so I puts my hands under my shawl, though it hurts 'em to take hold of the creases, especially when we takes 'em to the pump to wash 'em. No; I never see any children crying — it's no use.

"Sometimes I make a great deal of money. One day I took 1s. 6d., and the creases cost 6d.; but it isn't often I get such luck as that. I oftener makes 3d. or 4d. than 1s.; and then I'm at work, crying, 'Creases, four bunches a penny, creases!' from six in the morning to about ten. What do you mean by mechanics? — I don't know what they are. The shops buys most of me. Some of 'em says, 'Oh! I ain't a-goin' to give a penny for these;' and they want 'em at the same price as I buys 'em at.

"I always give mother my money, she's so very good to me. She don't often beat me; but, when she do, she don't play with me. She's very poor, and goes out cleaning rooms sometimes, now she don't work at the fur. I ain't got no father, he's a father-in-law. No; mother ain't married again — he's a father-in-law. He grinds scissors, and he's very good to me. No; I don't mean by that that he says kind things to me, for he never hardly speaks. When I gets home, after selling creases, I stops at home. I puts the room to rights; mother don't make me do it, I does it myself. I cleans the chairs, though there's only two to clean. I takes a tub and scrubbing-brush and flannel, and scrubs the floor — that's what I do three or four times a week.

"I don't have no dinner. Mother gives me two slices of bread and butter and a cup of tea for breakfast, and then I go to till tea, and has the same. We has meat of a Sunday, and, of course, I should like to have it every day. Mother has just the same to eat as we has, but she takes more tea — three cups, sometimes. No; I never has no sweet-stuff; I never buy none — I don't like it. Sometimes we has a game of 'honeypots' with the girls in the court, but not often. Me and Carry H—— carries the little 'uns. We plays, too, at 'kiss-in-the-ring.' I knows a good many games, but I don't play at 'em, 'cos going out with creases tires me. On a Friday night, too, I goes to a Jew's house till eleven o'clock on a Saturday night. All I has to do is to snuff the candles and poke the fire. You see they keep their Sabbath then, and they won't touch anything; so they gives me my vittals and $1\frac{1}{2}d.$, and I does it for 'em. I have a reg'lar good lot to eat. Supper of Friday night, and tea after that, and fried fish of a Saturday morning, and meat for dinner, and tea, and supper, and I like it very well.

"Oh, yes; I've got some toys at home. I've a fire-place, and a box of toys, and a knife and fork, and two little chairs. The Jews gave 'em to me where I go to on a Friday; and that's why I said they was very kind to me. I never had no doll; but I misses little sister — she's only two years old. We don't sleep in the same room; for father and mother sleeps with little sister in the one pair, and me and brother and other sister sleeps in the top room. I always goes to bed at seven, 'cos I has to be up so early.

"I am a capital hand at bargaining — but only at buying water-creases. They can't take me in. If the woman tries to give me a small handful of creases, I says, 'I ain't agoin' to have that for a ha'porth,' and I go to the next basket, and so on, all round. I know the quantities very well. For a penny I ought to have a full market hand, or as much as I could carry in my arms at one time, without spilling. For $3d.$ I has a lap full, enough to earn about a shilling; and for $6d.$ I gets as many as crams my basket. I can't read or write, but I knows how many pennies goes to a shilling, why, twelve, of course, but I don't know how many ha'pence there is, though there's two to a penny. When I've bought $3d.$ of creases, I ties 'em up into as many little bundles as I can. They must look biggish, or the people won't buy them, some puffs them out as much as they'll go. All my money I earns I puts in a club and draws out to buy clothes with. It's better than spending it in sweet-stuff, for them as has a living to earn. Besides it's like a child to care for sugar-sticks, and not like one who's got a living and vittals to earn. I ain't a child, and I shan't be a woman till I'm twenty, but I'm past eight, I am. I don't know nothing about what I earns during the year. I only know how many pennies goes to a shilling, and two ha'pence goes to a penny, and four fardens goes to a penny. I knows, too, how many fardens goes to tuppence — eight. That's as much as I wants to know for the markets."

A TIN-WARE SELLER

THE FOLLOWING street-biography was communicated to me in writing. It is, I believe, a striking instance of the vicissitudes and privations to which a street-life is subject. It forms, moreover, a curious example of those moral contradictions which make the same individual at one time give way *hopelessly* to the force of circumstances, and at another resolutely control them.

"My object," says my correspondent, "for writing this, what some folks no doubt will call a nonsensical epistle, is merely to show how much human nature is capable of enduring in the shape of privations. People in easy circumstances will scarcely credit what I am about to relate; and many of the poor will smile at what I have termed hardships, and at my folly in endeavouring to paint the misery I have endured, which will appear slight when compared to what they themselves have suffered.

"I am the son of a mechanic who was accidentally drowned some weeks previous to my birth. My mother, through industry and perseverance, endeavoured to support me and my sister till we arrived at the ages of 15 and 18, I being the younger. I entered a gentleman's service as pantry-boy, where I continued until I considered myself competent to take a higher situation. Still a servant's life was not the bent of my inclinations; martial music and viewing soldiers on parade made me think that a rifle was a more graceful tool than a toasting-fork. I resolved to serve his Majesty, and for that purpose enlisted in the 60th Rifles on the route for India, but Providence ordained it otherwise. On the afternoon on which I 'listed I fell by accident and broke my leg, and as I was not sworn in I was entitled to no pension. I was six months confined to my bed, it was three years before I could go without my crutch. Grief for my misfortunes had borne my mother to an early grave, and I was left a cripple and destitute. Whether by design or accident I do not recollect, but I met with the lady (Lady M——) in whose service I first entered as pantry-boy; she took pity on my forlorn condition, and kindly

invited me to her Mansion, where I remained until completely
restored to health, but still crippled. After this I was employed
painting and glazing, &c., and, considering myself competent to
get my living in that line, I resolved to go to London — the theatre
of all my misery to come, for I was disappointed.

"On reaching the metropolis my paint-brush was turned into
a shovel, my paint-pot into a dust sieve, for I could only get
employed by a man to work in a dust-yard at 10s. a week. From
thence I went to a firm belonging to a friend at Beckenham, near
Croydon, as working time-keeper, or foreman; but during a fair
in that village I neglected to back the time, and being discharged
was cast upon the world again with only 3s, in my pocket, which
I eat and drank up, having no idea of street trading, Then came
my trials; but having had sufficient food during the day I did
not feel much the effects of my first night in the streets. The next
day I had no food, and towards dusk began bitterly to feel my
situation; that night I slept, or rather lay, in an empty house.
Towards noon of the next day I felt weak, and drank large
quantities of water, for I had no particular desire for food. Passing
by a shop where old clothes were offered for sale, I saw a man
disposing of an old vest for a few pence. I caught the malady
and was instantly spoiled of my coat, having received in exchange
for it 2s. and an old frock — such as are generally worn by
waggoners or countrymen. I more than once smiled at my novel
appearance. A penny loaf, a drink of water, and a threepenny
lodging was the first assault upon my 2s. I regretted, however,
the 3d. paid for my lodging, and determined not to risk another,
for my bedfellows were so numerous, and of such teazing propensities, that they would not allow me to sleep; truly indeed is
it said that 'poverty makes us aquainted with strange bedfellows.'

"At this time I formed an acquaintance with a man whose
condition was similar to my own; he engaged to put me 'fly to
a dodge' or two; an explanation from him was necessary to make
me acquainted with the sense of his words, which I soon found
simply meant artful manoeuvres. One of these dodges was to
snooze (a term for sleeping) in the Adelphi-arches; I felt grateful
for such a mark of disinterested friendship, and next day my
friend and me fared sumptuously on the produce of my coat,

and at night we repaired to the Arches in question, and there found a comfortable lodging in a hay-loft. I lay for some time, but did not sleep. I was several times addressed by my companion in an undertone, 'Are you asleep,' he whispered, 'ain't it a stunning dos?' (which means a good bed). I was not in a mood for conversation, and made no reply; to silence him completely I affected to snore, and this had the desired effect. For a few minutes he was quite quiet, and then he commenced with great caution to unlace my boots, with a view to stealing them. I perceived his object, and immediately left my lodging and companion.

"I felt grieved and disappointed at the loss of one in whom I placed all confidence; but this time wisdom was purchased cheaply, inasmuch as I suffered no loss except that my money might have lasted me a little longer. The remainder of that night I strayed about the Strand and Charing-cross, after a drink of water; I took a seat on a kerb surrounding the pump; many wretched beings came and seated themselves beside me, and a conversation ensued respecting their several destinations during the day. One proposed going to Hungerford-market to do a feed on decayed shrimps or other offal laying about the market; another proposed going to Covent Garden to do a 'tightener' of rotten oranges, to which I was humorously invited; I accepted the invitation, and proceeded with my new companion. I fared well; I filled my hat, took a seat, and made a most delicious breakfast. I remained strolling about the Garden all day, and towards evening was invited by my companions to a 'dos' in an open shed in Islington; this I declined, alleging that I had a lodging, but that night I slept amongst a heap of stones near the pillar at Charing-cross.

"I continued to attend the Garden for several weeks, subsisting entirely on the offal of that market.

"One day I took notice of a man there selling chestnut leaves; I enquired how he obtained them: he told me he plucked them from the trees without hindrance, and directed me to where I could obtain some. I went to a grove in the vicinity of Kilburn, and lay there all night. Next morning I found no leaves, so I returned disappointed to town, and on going though the market a woman employed me to carry a bushel of pears some little distance for her for a penny. I felt quite elevated in anticipation of such a treat as a penny loaf, but alas! I fell down under the weight of the fruit and poverty; my employer, however, kindly gave me the penny, though some of her pears were injured, and I had not taken them half the required distance. With the money I purchased a loaf, and sat on a stone near the pump in Covent Garden and began my meal. Here I soon had a companion, who after rinsing a lettuce at the pump, began to devour it. I shared my loaf with him. 'O God!' said he, 'what are we destined to suffer. I have escaped the bullets of the Carlists in Spain to die in the streets of London with hunger.'

"I felt an interest in the poor fellow, who I ̄discovered in the course of conversation had been a gentleman's servant in his time; he assured me he had been living in the same way for several weeks as I myself had been. Towards night my companion asked me where I slept. I told him my different haunts, he told me I'd better go to the straw-yard with him; this was a place I had not yet heard of; it was the nightly refuge for the houseless poor. I accompanied him without hesitation; my confidence was not misplaced; I slept there several nights. Bread was distributed to us night and morning, and this was fortunate, for the Garden began to fail. In the course of conversation with some of the inmates of the Refuge, we found that we could obtain employment at stone-breaking; this we tried the next morning, and succeeded. We worked all day, and received 6d. each on leaving work. We then made up our minds to go to lodgings that we might have an opportunity of washing what were once shirts.

"Misery had not had that wasting influence on my companion as it had on me. I was at this time a complete skeleton; a puff of wind would cause me to stagger. I continued stone-breaking, but about noon of the third day I sunk exhausted on the heap of stones before me. Poverty had done its work, and I anticipated with pleasure approaching dissolution. I was assisted to my lodging by my companion, and went to bed. When the woman at the lodging-house discovered that I was ill, she ordered some of her domestics to dress me and put me in the street, alleging that she was under a penalty of £20 were it discovered that she lodged a sick stranger. I was, therefore, cast into the street at 12 o'clock at night. My companion then gave me the 3*d*. he had earned that day to procure me a lodging if possible, and he slept in the streets the remainder of the night. I went to another lodging, concealing as much as possible my illness; my money was taken, and I was conducted to bed. I spent a wretched night, and next morning I was very bad. The landlady led me to the workhouse; I was admitted directly; had they detained me asking questions I should have sunk on the floor. My disorder was pronounced English cholera. I lay three weeks in a precarious state, but at the end of seven weeks was recovered sufficiently to walk about. I was then discharged; but on going towards the Abbey in Westminster I fainted, and on recovery found myself surrounded by a number of persons. I was advised to return to the house; I did so, and was admitted for a short time, after which I was again discharged, but I received out-door relief twice a week; and for some time a small portion of bread and cheese as well. *I had now lost not only all hope, but even desire of bettering my condition;* during these trials I made none acquainted with my privations, save those situated as I was.

"I now altered my condition as regards sleeping; I walked about during the night, and slept a portion of the day on a heap of sand near Westminster-bridge. I then remembered to have a poor relative in Kensington; I did not plead distress, but merely asked whether she knew where I might procure employment. I had a cup of tea, the first I had tasted since I was in the workhouse, a period of five weeks. Being asked some question by my relative, I could not help making reference to some of my sufferings. At this place I found a young man of whom I had had a previous acquaintance; I told him of my inability to procure a lodging, and he allowed me without the knowledge of his parents to sleep in the stable-loft; the bed was hard, but the coal sacks kept me warm. Here I had many opportunities of earning a few pence, and I began to regain my spirits.

"On one occasion, seeing a lad ill-treated by a young man who was much his superior in size and strength, I interposed, and it may be conjectured in what manner. This circumstance procured me a friend, for, with the assistance of the lad I had protected,

I was enabled to live tolerably well, and after a short while I got a situation at a coal-shed at 10s. a week. I continued in this place eighteen months, but, my master giving up the business, I was again cast on the world. I then began to think seriously of some way of living, and for the first time asked for the loan of 15s. With this I purchased a few articles of furniture, laid out 7s. 6d for two hundred of oranges, with which I walked and hawked about two days, taking but 4d. during the time. I disposed of the remainder of my stock, wholesale, for 6s.; with this I purchased a small tin saucepan, a piece of marble slab, and commenced sugar-boiling. I retailed my manufacture in the streets.

"By dint of perseverance and economy I managed to live this way through the winter and a portion of the spring; but summer being now come, people needed none of my compounds to warm their mouths, so it was necessary for me to change my hand. What should I do? Thoughts came and vanished at their births. I recollected having seen a person selling rings at a penny each; I made up my mind to try the same. I laid out 5s. in a tray and stock; after arranging the goods to the best advantage I sallied into the streets. The glittering baubles took for a while, but when discoloured were useless. Having once a considerable stock of these soiled rings, I was prompted to begin "lot selling." After calculating the profits, I commenced selling in that line. As this continued for seven weeks I managed to get a living. The system then became general; every street in the metropolis contained a lot seller, so I was determined to change my hand. One day in the street I saw a girl with a bundle of old umbrellas going towards a marine store shop; I asked if the umbrellas were for sale; she replied in the affirmative; the price she asked was 4d.; I became a purchaser.

"With these old umbrellas I commenced a new life. I bought some trifling tools necessary for repairing umbrellas, and, after viewing well the construction of the articles I commenced operations. I succeeded, and in a little time could not only mend an old umbrella, but make a new one. This way of living I followed three years. In one of my walks through the streets crying old umbrellas to sell, I saw a street tinker repairing a saucepan; he seemed so very comfortable with his fire-pan before him, that I resolved from that moment to become a tinker, and for that purpose I bought a few tools, prepared a budget, and sallied into the streets with as much indifference as if I had been at the business since my birth. After a little practice I fancied I was fit for better things than mending old saucepans, and flattered myself that I was able to make a new one. This I resolved to attempt, and succeeded so well, that I at once abandoned the rainy-day system, and commenced manufacturing articles in tin-ware, such as are now sold in the streets, namely funnels, nutmeg-graters, penny mugs, extinguishers, slices, save-alls, &c. I soon became known to the street-sellers and swag-shop proprietors. The prices I get are low, and I am deficient in some of the tools necessary to forward the work, with the required speed to procure returns adequate to my expenses; but thanks to the Lord I am better off than ever I expected to be, with the difference only of a somewhat shattered constitution. There are many at the present day suffering as I have done, and they may be found in and about the different markets of the metropolis."

THE STREET-SELLERS OF "SMALL-WARE", OR TAPE, COTTON, ETC.

THE STREET-SELLERS of tape and cotton are usually elderly females; and during my former inquiry I was directed to one who had been getting her living in the street by such means for nine years. I was given to understand that the poor woman was in deep distress, and that she had long been supporting a sick husband by her little trade, but I was wholly unprepared for a scene of such startling misery, sublimed by untiring affection and pious resignation, as I there discovered.

I wish the reader to understand that I do not cite this case as a type of the sufferings of this particular class, but rather as an illustration of the afflictions which frequently befall those who are soley dependent on their labour, or their little trade, for their subsistence, and who, from the smallness of their earnings, are unable to lay by even the least trifle as a fund against any physical calamity.

The poor creatures lived in one of the close alleys at the east end of London. On inquiring at the house to which I was directed, I was told I should find them in "the two-pair back." I mounted the stairs, and on opening the door of the apartment I was terrified with the misery before me. There, on a wretched bed, lay an aged man in almost the last extremity of life. At first I thought the poor old creature was really dead, but a tremble of the eyelids as I closed the door, as noiselessly as I could, told me that he breathed. His face was as yellow as clay, and it had more the cold damp look of a corpse than that of a living man. His cheeks were hollowed in with evident want, his temples sunk, and his nostrils pinched close. On the edge of the bed sat his heroic wife, giving him drink with a spoon from a tea-cup. In one corner of the room stood the basket of tapes, cottons, combs, braces, nutmeg-graters, and shaving-glasses, with which she strove to keep her old dying husband from the workhouse. I asked her how long her good man had been ill, and she told me he had been confined to his bed five weeks last Wednesday, and that it was ten weeks since he had eaten the size of a nut in solid food. Nothing but a little beef-tea had passed his lips for months. "We have lived like children together," said the old woman, as her eyes flooded with tears, "and never had no dispute. He hated drink, and there was no cause for us to quarrel. One of my legs, you see, is shorter than the other," said she, rising from the bed-side, and showing me that her right foot was several inches from the ground as she stood. "My hip is out. I used to go out washing, and walking in my pattens I fell down. My hip is out of the socket three-quarters of an inch, and the sinews is drawn up. I am obliged to walk with a stick." Here the man groaned and coughed so that I feared the exertion must end his life. "Ah, the heart of stone would pity that poor fellow," said the good wife.

"After I put my hip out, I couldn't get my living as I'd been used to do. I couldn't stand a day if I had five hundred pounds for it. I must sit down. So I got a little stall, and sat at the end of the alley here with a few laces and tapes and things. I've done so for this nine year past, and seen many a landlord come in and go out of the house that I sat at. My husband used to sell small articles in the streets—black lead and furniture paste, and blacking. We got a sort of a living by this, the two of us together. It's very seldom though we had a bit of meat. We had 1s. 9d. rent to pay— Come, my poor fellow, will you have another little drop to wet your mouth?" said the woman, breaking off. "Come, my dearest, let me give you this," she added, as the man let his jaw fall, and she poured some warm sugar and water flavoured with cinnamon —all she had to give him—into his mouth.

"He's been an ailing man this many a year. He used to go of errands and buy my little things for me, on account of my being lame. We assisted one another, you see. He wasn't able to work for his living, and I wasn't able to go about, so he used to go about and buy for me what I sold. I am sure he never earned above 1s. 6d. in a week. He used to attend me, and many a time I've sat for ten and fourteen hours in the cold and wet and didn't take a sixpence. Some days I'd make a shilling, and some days less; but whatever I got I used to have to put a good part into the basket to keep my little stock." [A knock here came to the door; it was for a half-penny-worth of darning cotton.]

"You know a shilling goes further with a poor couple that's sober than two shillings does with a drunkard. We lived poor, you see, never had nothing but tea, or we couldn't have done anyhow. If I'd take 18*d*. in the day I'd think I was grandly off, and then if there was 6*d*. profit got out of that it would be almost as much as it would. You see these cotton braces here" (said the old woman, going to her tray). "Well, I gives 2*s*. 9*d*. a dozen for them here, and I sells 'em for 4^1/$_2$*d*., and oftentimes 4*d*. a pair. Now, this piece of tape would cost me seven farthings in the shop, and I sells it at six yards a penny. It has the *name* of being eighteen yards. The profit out of it is five farthings. It's beyond the power of man to wonder how there's a bit of bread got out of such a small way. And the times is so bad, too! I think I could say I get 8*d*. a day profit if I have any sort of custom, but I don't exceed that at the best of times. I've often sat at the end of the alley and taken only 6*d*., and that's not much more than 2*d*. clear —it ain't 3*d*. I'm sure.

"I think I could safely state that for the last nine years me and my husband has earned together 5*s*. a week, and out of that the two of us had to live and pay rent—1*s*. 9*d*. a week. Clothes I could buy none, for the best garment is on me; but I thank the Lord still. I've paid my rent all but three weeks, and that isn't due till tomorrow. We have often reckoned it up here at the fire. Some weeks we have got 5*s*. 3*d*., and some weeks less, so that I judge we have about 3*s*. to 3*s*. 6*d*. a week to live upon the two of us, for this nine years past. Half-a-hundred of coals would fit me the week in the depths of winter. My husband had the kettle always boiling for me against I came in. He used to sit here reading his book— he never was fit for work at the best—while I used to be out minding the basket. He was so sober and quiet too. His neighbours will tell that of him.

"Within the last ten weeks he's been very ill indeed, but still I could be out with the basket. Since then he's never earn't me a penny—poor old soul, he wasn't able! All that time I still attended to my basket. He wasn't so ill then but what he could do a little here in the room for hisself; but he wanted little, God knows, for he couldn't eat. After he fell ill, I had to go all my errands myself. I had no one to help me, for I had nothing to pay them, and I'd have to walk from here down to Sun-street with my stick, till my bad leg pained me so that I could hardly stand. You see the hip being put out has drawn all the sinews up into my groin, and it leaves me uncapable of walking or standing constantly; but I thank God that I've got the use of it anyhow. Our lot's hard enough, goodness knows, but we are content. We never complain, but bless the Lord for the little he pleases to give us. When I was on my errands, in course I couldn't be minding my basket; so I lost a good bit of money that way. Well, five weeks on Wednesday he has been totally confined to his bed, excepting when I lifted him up to make it some nights; but he can't bear *that* now. Still the first fortnight he was bad, I did manage to leave him, and earn a few pence; but, latterly for this last three weeks, I haven't been able to go out at all, to do anything."

"She's been stopping by me, minding me here night and day all that time," mumbled the old man, who now for the first time opened his grey glassy eyes and turned towards me, to bear, as it were, a last tribute to his wife's incessant affection. "She has been most kind to me. Her tenderness and care has been such that man never knew from woman before, ever since I lay upon this sick bed. We've been married five-and-twenty years. We have always lived happily — very happily indeed — together; until sickness and weakness overcome me I always strove to help myself a bit, as well as I could; but since then she has done all in her power for me — worked for me — ay, she has worked for me, surely — and watched over me. My creed through life has been repentance towards God, faith in Jesus Christ, and love to all my brethren. I've made up my mind that I must soon change this tabernacle, and my last wish is that the good people of this world will increase her little stock for her. She cannot get her living out of the little stock she has, and since I lay here it's so lessened, that neither she nor no one else can live upon it. If the kind hearts would give her but a little stock more, it would keep her old age from want, as she has kept mine. Indeed, indeed, she does deserve it. But the Lord, I know, will reward her for all she has done to me." Here the old man's eyelids dropped exhausted.

"I've had a shilling and a loaf twice from the parish," continued the woman. "The overseer came to see if my old man was fit to be removed to the workhouse. The doctor gave me a certificate that he was not, and then the relieving officer gave me a shilling and a loaf of bread, and out of that shilling I bought the poor old fellow a sup of port wine. I bought a quartern of wine, which was 4_d._, and I gave 5_d._ for a bit of tea and sugar, and I gave 2_d._ for coals; a halfpenny rushlight I bought, and a short candle, that made a penny — and that's the way I laid out the shilling. If God takes him, I know he'll sleep in heaven. I know the life he's spent, and am not afraid; but no one else shall take him from me — nothing shall part us but death in this world. Poor old soul, he can't be long with me. He's a perfect skeleton. His bones are starting through his skin."

I asked what could be done for her, and the old man thrust forth his skinny arm, and laying hold of the bed-post, he raised himself slightly in his bed, as he murmured "If she could be got into a little parlour, and away from sitting in the streets, it would be the saving of her." And, so saying, he fell back overcome with the exertion, and breathed heavily.

The woman sat down beside me, and went on. "What shocked him most was that I was obliged in his old age to go and ask for relief at the parish. You see, he was always a spiritful man, and it hurted him sorely that he should come to this at last, and for the first time in his lifetime. The only parish money that ever we had was this, and it _does_ hurt him every day to think that he must be buried by the parish after all. He was always proud, you see."

I told the kind-hearted old dame that some benevolent people had placed certain funds at my disposal for the relief of such distress as hers; and I assured her that neither she nor her husband should want for anything that might ease their sufferings.

The day after the above was written, the poor old man died. He was buried out of the funds sent to the "Morning Chronicle," and his wife received some few pounds to increase her stock; but in a few months the poor old woman went mad, and is now, I believe, the inmate of one of the pauper lunatic asylums.

THE BLIND BOOT-LACE SELLER

THE BLIND boot-lace seller who gave me the following history of his life was the original of the portrait. He was a tall strongly built man. In face he was ghastly, his cheek bones were sharp and high, his nose flat to his face, and his eyes were so deeply sunk in that he had more the appearance of a death's head than of a living man. His shirt was scrupulously clean. He wore a bright red cotton neckerchief and a plaid waistcoat of many colours. His dog accompanied him and never left his master's side one moment.

"It's very sorrowful — very sorrowful indeed to hear that," said the boot-lace seller to me, on my reading to him an account of a blind needle-seller; "it touches me much to hear that. But you see I don't grieve for the loss of my sight as he do, poor man. I don't remember ever seeing any object. If there was a thing with many colours in it, I could discern the highest colour. I couldn't tell one from another, but only the highest.

"I was born in Northumberland," he said, "about five-and-fifty years ago. My father was a grocer and had £1,000 worth of freehold property besides his business, which was very large for a small town; his was the principal shop, and in the general line. He had a cart of his own, in which he attended market. I was very comfortably brought up, never wanted for nothing, and had my mother lived I should have had an independent fortune. At five years old, while mother was still alive, I caught the smallpox. I had four sisters and one brother, and we all six had it at once; that was before the vaccination was properly established. I've heerd said that father did not want to have us inoculated, because of the people coming backwards and forwards to the shop. I only wish vaccination had been in vogue then as it is now, and I shouldn't have lost my eyes. God bless the man who brought it up, I say; people doesn't know what they've got to thank him for. Well, all my sisters and brothers had not a mark upon them. It laid hold of only me. They couldn't lay a finger upon me, they was obligated to lift me up in one of my father's shirts, by holding the corners of it like a sheet. As soon as ever the pock began to decay it took away my eyes altogether. I didn't lose both my eyeballs till about twenty years after that, though my sight was gone for all but the shadow of daylight and any high colours.

"At sixteen years of age my left eye bursted; I suffered terribly then — oh terribly! yes, that I did. The black-and-white like all mixed together, the pock came right through the star of the eye the doctor said; and when I was five-and twenty my other eyeball bursted, and then my eyes was quite out of my head. Till that time I could see a little bit; I could tell the daylight, and I could see the moon, but not the shape of it. I never could see a star, and do you know I grieved about the loss of that little bit of sight as much as if I was losing the whole of it. As my eye-ball sloughed day by day, I could see the light going away by little, every day till the week's end. When I looked at the daylight just before it all went, I could see the light look as red as fire — as red as blood; and when it all left me, oh, I was dreadful sorrowful, I thought I was lost altogether. But, I shouldn't have been so bad off, as I said, if mother had lived, but she died when I was about six year old. I didn't care much about her, indeed I took a dreadful dislike to her. I heerd her say one day to a person in the shop, that she would sooner see me dead and buried than be as I was, but now I know that it was her fondness for me.

"Mother catched a cold, and died after six days' illness. When she was gone, father got to neglect the business. He had no one then to attend to it, and he took and shut up the shop. He lost heart, you see. He took and turned all the tenants out of his property, and furnished all the rooms of a large house suitable for the quality that used to come to the town to bathe. He mortgaged the place for £250 to buy the furniture, and that was the ruin of him. Eighteen years afterwards the lawyers got the better of him, and all the family was turned out of the door without a penny. My father they'd put in jail before. He died a few years afterwards in the workhouse. When the family was turned out, there was only my eldest brother away at sea, and my eldest sister in service; so me and my three sisters was sent in the wide world without the means of getting a crust or a place to put our heads in. All my sisters after that got into service, and I went to drive some coal carts at North Shields. The coal carts was father's, and they was all he had left out of his property; so I used to go to Wall's End and fill the carts, then take them down to North Shields and sell them at the people's doors. We never used to sell less than the load. I did all this, blind as I was, without a person to guide, and continued at it night and day for about fifteen year. It was well known to the whole countryside. I was the talk for miles round. They couldn't believe I was blind; though they see my eyes was gone, still they couldn't hardly believe. Then, after the fifteen year, me and my father had a complete fall out. He took an advantage of my sister. He had borrowed £20 of her, and when he could, he wouldn't pay her. He behaved as bad as father could, and then I broke with him." (He then went over the whole story, and was affected, even to speechlessness, at the remembrance of his family troubles. Into these there is no necessity to enter here; suffice it, the blind man appears to have behaved very nobly.)

"I came away and went to my brother, who was well off at Hull; when I got there, I found he had gone to Russia and died there that very spring. While I was on my way to Hull, I used to go to sleep at the lodging-houses for travellers. I had never been in one before, and there I got to think, from what I heerd, that a roving life was a fine pleasant one. The very first lodging-house I went into was one in Durham, and there persons as was coming the same road persuaded me to go and beg with them, but I couldn't cheek it; it was too near hand at home. We came on to Darlington, that was 18 miles further, that day. They still kept company with me, and wanted me to beg, but I wouldn't; I couldn't face it. I thought people would know me. The next day we started on our way to Northallerton, and then my few shillings was all gone; so that night we went to seek relief, and got a pennyworth of milk, and a penny loaf each and our bed. The parish gave us a ticket to a lodging-house. The next morning we started from Northallerton, and then I was very hungry; all I had the day before was the pennyworth of bread I got from the parish.

"Then as we got about a mile out of the town, there was a row of houses, and the Scotchman who was with me says, 'If ye'll gang up wi' me, I'll speak for ye.' Well, we went up and got 3*d.*,

and plenty of bread and butter; almost every house we got something at; then I was highly delighted; thinks I, this is a business
—and so I did. We shared with the other man who had come on
the road with us, and after that we started once more, and then I
was all eager to go on with the same business. You see I'd never
had no pleasure, and it seemed to me like a new world—to be
able to get victuals without doing anything—instead of slaving as
I'd been with a couple of carts and horses at the coal-pits all the
time. I didn't think the country was half so big, and you couldn't
credit the pleasure I felt in going about it. I felt as if I didn't care
for nothing; it was so beautiful to be away there quite free, without any care in the world, for I could see plainly I could always
get the best of victuals, and the price of my lodgings. There's no
part in all England like Yorkshire for living. We used to go to
all the farm-houses, we wouldn't miss one if it was half a mile off
the road; if the Scotsman who was with me could only see a road
he'd take me up it, and we got nice bits of pie and meat, and
bread and cake, indeed as much as would serve four people, when
we got to the lodging-house at night and a few shillings beside.
I soon got not to care about the loss of my brother.

"At last we got to make so much money that I thought it was
made to chuck about the streets. We got it so easy, you see. It
was only 4s. or 5s. but then I was only a flatty or I could have
made 14s. or 15s. at least. This was in Boroughbridge, and there at
a place called, I think, Bridely-hill, there was a lodging-house
without never a bed in it at all; but only straw littered on the
ground, and here I found upwards of sixty or seventy, all tramps,
and living in different ways, pattering, and thieving, and singing,
and all sorts; and that night I got to think it was the finest scene
I had ever known. I grew pleaseder, and pleaseder, with the life,
and wondered how any one could follow any other. There was no
drunkenness, but it was so new and strange, and I'd never known
nothing of life before, that I was bewildered, like, with over-joy
at it. Then I soon got to think I'd have the summer's pleasure out
and wouldn't go near Hull till the back end of the year, for it
was the month of May, that what I'm talking about took place;
and so things went on. I never thought of home, or sisters, or anything, indeed. I was so over-joyed that I could think of nothing

THE BLIND BOOT-LACE SELLER

else. Whenever I got to a new county it seemed like getting into a new nation, and when I heard we were close upon a new place I used to long and long to get into it.

"At last I left the Scotchman and took up with an old sailor, a man-of-warsman, who was coming up to London to get his pension, and he was a regular 'cadger' like the other who had put me 'fly to the dodge,' though none of us weren't 'fly' to nothing then. I can't tell you, I wanted to, how I longed to be in town, and, as I came through the streets with him, I didn't know whether I carried the streets or they carried me. You see I had heard people talk about London in North Shields, and I thought there was no poor people there at all—none but ladies and gentlemen and sailors. In London the sailor drew his pension, and he and me got robbed and then the sailor left me, and then I started off without a penny into the country; and at Stratford-le-Bow I began for, the first time, to say, 'Pity the poor blind.' Up to this time I had never axed no one—never spoke, indeed—the cadgers who had been with me had done this for me, and glad to have the chance of sharing with me. A blind man can get a guide at any place, because they know he's sure to get something. I took only 5*d.* at Stratford-le Bow, and then started on my way to Romford; and there, in the lodging-house, I met a blind man, who took me in partnership with him, and larnt me my business complete—that he just did, and since then I've been following it, and that's about two or three and twenty year ago.

"Since I've been in London, and that's fourteen year, I've lived very regular, always had a place, and attended my church. If it hadn't been for the lodging-houses I should never, may be, have been as I am; though, I must confess, I always had a desire to find out travelling, but couldn't get hold of any one to put me in the way of it. I longed for a roving life and to shake a loose leg, still I couldn't have done much else after my quarrel with my father. My sister had offered to lend me money enough to buy a horse and cart for myself, but I didn't like that, and thought I'd get it of my brother at Hull; and that and the padding-kens is solely the cause of my being as I am; and since I first travelled there's more now than ever—double and treble as many."

A YOUNG PICKPOCKET

To SHOW the class of characters usually frequenting these lodging-houses, I will now give the statement of a boy — a young pick-pocket — without shoes or stockings. He wore a ragged, dirty, and very thin great coat, of some dark jean or linen, under which was another thin coat, so arranged that what appeared rents — and, indeed, were rents, but designedly made — in the outer garment, were slits through which the hand readily reached the pockets of the inner garment, and could there deposit any booty. He was a slim, agile lad, with a sharp but not vulgar expression, and small features. His hands were of singular delicacy and beauty. His fingers were very long, and no lady's could have been more taper. A burglar told me that with such a hand he ought to have made his fortune. He was worth £20 a week, he said, as a *"wire,"* that is a picker of ladies' pockets. When engaged "for a turn," as he told me he once was by an old pickpocket, the man looked minute-ly at his fingers, and approved of them highly. His hands, the boy said, were hardly serviceable to him when very cold. His feet were formed in the same symmetrical and beautiful mould as his hands.

"I am 15," he said. "My father was a potter, and I can't recol-lect my mother" (many of the thieves are orphans or motherless). "My father has been dead about five years. I was then working at the pottery in High-street, Lambeth, earning about 4s. a week; in good weeks, 4s. 6d. I was in work eight months after my father died; but one day I broke three bottles by accident, and the fore-man said 'I shan't want you any more;' and I took that as meant for a discharge; but I found afterwards that he didn't so mean it. I had 2s. and a suit of clothes then, and tried for work at all the potteries; but I couldn't get any. It was about the time Smithfield fair was on. I went, but it was a very poor concern. I fell asleep in a pen in the afternoon, and had my shoes stolen off my feet. When I woke up, I began crying. A fellow named Gyp then came along (I knew his name afterwards), and he said, 'What are you crying for?' and I told him, and he said, 'Pull off your stockings, and come with me, and I'll show you where to sleep.' So I did, and he took me to St. Olave's workhouse, having first sold my stockings. I had never stolen anything until then.

"There I slept in the casual ward, and Gyp slept there too. In the morning we started together for Smithfield, where he said he had a job to sweep the pens, but he couldn't sweep them without pulling off his coat, and it would look so queer if he hadn't a shirt — and he hadn't one. He promised to teach me how to make a living in the country if I would lend him mine, and I was persuaded — for I was an innocent lad then — and went up a gateway and stripped off my shirt and gave it to him, and soon after he went into a public-house to get half a pint of beer; he went in at one door and out at another, and I didn't see him for six months afterwards. That afternoon I went into Billingsgate market and met some boys, and one said. 'Mate, how long have you been knocking about; where did you doss?' I didn't know that they meant, and when they'd told me they meant where did I sleep? I told them how I'd been served. And they said, 'Oh! you must expect that, until you learn something,' and they laughed. They all know'd Gyp; he was like the head of a Billingsgate gang once.

"I became a pal with these boys at Billingsgate, and we went about stealing fish and meat. Some boys have made 2s. in a morning when fish is dear — those that had pluck and luck; they sold it at half-price. Billingsgate market is a good place to sell it; plenty of costermongers are there who will buy it, rather than off the salesmen. I soon grew as bad as the rest at this work. At first I sold it to other boys, who would get 3d. for what they bought at 1d. Now they can't do me. If I can get a thing cheap where I lodge, and have the money, and can sell it dear, that's the chance. I carried on this fish rig for about two years, and went begging a little, too. I used to try a little thieving sometimes in Petticoat-lane. They say the 'fliest' is easy to take in sometimes — that's the artfullest; but I could do no good there. At these two years' end, I was often as happy as could be; that is, when I had made money.

"Then I met B——, whom I had often heard of as an uncommon clever pickpocket; he could do it about as well as I can now, so as people won't feel it. Three of his mates were transported for stealing silver plate. He and I became pals, and started for the country with

1*d*. We went through Foot's Cray, and passed a farm where a man's buried at the top of a house; there's something about money while a man's above ground; I don't understand it, but it's something like that. A baker, about thirty miles from London, offended us about some bread; and B—— said 'I'll serve him out.' We watched him out, and B—— tried at his pocket, saying, 'I'll show you how to do a handkerchief;' but the baker looked round, and B—— stopped; and just after that I flared it [whisked, the handkerchief out]; and that's the first I did. It brought 1*s*. 3*d*. We travelled across country, and got to Maidstone, and did two handkerchiefs. One I wore round my neck, and the other the lodging-house-keeper pawned for us for 1*s*. 6*d*. In Maidstone, next morning, I was nailed, and had three months of it. I didn't mind it so much then, but Maidstone's far worse now, I've heard. I have been in prison three times in Brixton, three times in the Old Horse [Bridewell], three times in the Compter, once in the Steel, and once in Maidstone — thirteen times in all, including twice I was remanded, and got off; but I don't reckon that prison.

"Every time I came out harder than I went in. I've had four floggings; it was bad enough — a flogging was — while it lasted; but when I got out I soon forgot it. At a week's end I never thought again about it. If I had been better treated I should have been a better lad. I could leave off thieving now as if I had never thieved, if I could live without." [I am inclined to doubt this part of the statement.] "I have carried on this sort of life until now. I didn't often make a very good thing of it. I saw Manning and his wife hung. Mrs. Manning was dressed beautiful when she came up. She screeched when Jack Ketch pulled the bolt away. She was harder than Manning, they all said; without her there would have been no murder. It was a great deal talked about, and Manning was pitied. It was a punishment to her to come on the scaffold and see Manning with the rope about his neck, if people takes it in the right light. I did 4*s*. 6*d*. at the hanging — two handkerchiefs, and a purse with 2*s*. in it — the best purse I ever had; but I've only done three or four purses. The reason is, because I've never been well dressed. If I went near a lady, she would say, 'Tush, tush, you ragged fellow!' and would shrink away. But I would rather rob the rich than the poor; they miss it less. But 1*s*. honest goes

further than 5s. stolen. Some call that only a saying, but it's
true.

"All the money I got soon went — most of it a-gambling. Picking
pockets, when any one comes to think on it, is the daringest thing
that a boy can do. It didn't in the least frighten me to see Manning
and Mrs. Manning hanged. I never thought I should come to the
gallows, and I never shall — I'm not high-tempered enough for that.
The only thing that frightens me when I'm in prison is sleeping in
a cell by myself — you do in the Old Horse and the Steel — because I
think things may appear. You can't imagine how one dreams when
in trouble. I've often started up in a fright from a dream. I don't
know what might appear. I've heard people talk about ghosts and
that. Once, in the County, a tin had been left under a tap that went
drip — drip — drip. And all in the ward were shocking frightened;
and weren't we glad when we found out what it was! Boys tell
stories about haunted castles, and cats that are devils; and that
frightens one. At the fire in Monument-yard I did 5s. 7d. — 3s. in
silver and 2s. 3d. in handkerchiefs, and 4d. for three pairs of gloves.
I sell my handkerchiefs in the Lane (Petticoat-lane). I carry on
this trade still. Most times I've got in prison is when I've been
desperate from hunger, and have said to B—— 'Now I'll have
money, nailed or not nailed.'

"I can pick a woman's pocket as easy as a man's, though you
wouldn't think it. If one's in prison for begging, one's laughed at.
The others say, 'Begging! Oh, you cadger!' So a boy is partly
forced to steal for his character. I've lived a good deal in lodging-
houses, and know the ways of them. They are very bad places for a
boy to be in. Where I am now, when the place is full, there's upwards of 100 can be accommodated. I won't be there long, I'll do
something to get out of it. There's people there will rob their own
brother. There's people there talk backward — for one they say
eno, for two *owt*, for three *eerht*, for four *rouf*, for five *evif*, for six
exis. I don't know any higher. I can neither read nor write. In this
lodging-house there are no women. They talk there chiefly about
what they've done, or are going to do, or have set their minds
upon, just as you and any other gentlemen might do.

"I have been in lodging-houses in Mint-street and Kent-street,
where men and women and children all slept in one room. I think

the men and women who slept together were generally married, or lived together; but it's not right for a big boy to sleep in the same room. Young men have had beds to themselves, and so have young women there; but there's a deputy comes into the room, every now and then, to see there's nothing wrong. There's little said in these places, the people are generally so tired. Where I am there's horrid language—swearing, and everything that's bad. They are to be pitied, because there's not work for honest people, let alone thieves. In the lodging-houses the air is very bad, enough to stifle one in bed—so many breaths together. Without such places my trade couldn't be carried on; I couldn't live. Some though would find another way out. Three or four would take a room among them. Anybody's money's good—you can always get a room.

"I would be glad to leave this life, and work at a pottery. As to sea, a bad captain would make me run away—sure. He can do what he likes with you when you're out at sea. I don't get more than 2s. a week, one week with the other, by thieving; some days you do nothing until hunger makes your spirits rise. I can't thieve on a full belly. I live on 2s. a week from thieving, because I understand fiddling—that means, buying a think for a mere trifle, and selling it for double, or for more, if you're not taken in yourself. I've been put up to a few tricks in lodging-houses and now I can put others up to it. Everybody must look after themselves, and I can't say I was very sorry when I stole that 2s. from a poor woman, but I'd rather have had 1s. 6d. from a rich one. I never drink—eatin's my part.

"I spend chief part of my money in pudding. I don't like living in lodging-houses, but I must like it as I'm placed now—that sort of living, and those lodging-houses, or starving. They bring tracts to the lodging-houses—pipes are lighted with them; tracts won't fill your belly. Tracts is no good, except to a person that has a home; at the lodging-houses they're laughed at. They seldom are mentioned. I've heard some of them read by missionaries, but can't catch anything from them. If it had been anything bad, I should have caught it readily. If an innocent boy gets into a lodging-house, he'll not be innocent long—he can't. I know three boys who have run away, and are in the lodging-houses still, but I hope their father has caught them. Last night a little boy came to the lodging-house where I was. We all thought he had run away, by the way he spoke. He stayed all night, but was found out in two or three falsehoods. I wanted to get him back home, or he'll be as bad as I am in time, though he's nothing to me; but I couldn't find him this morning; but I'll get him home yet, perhaps.

"The Jews in Petticoat-lane are terrible rogues. They'll buy anything of you — they'll buy what you've stolen from their next-door neighbours — that they would, if they knew it. But they'll give you very little for it, and they threaten to give you up if you won't take a quarter of the value of it. 'Oh! I shee you do it', they say, 'and I like to shee him robbed, but you musht take vot I give.' I wouldn't mind what harm came to those Petticoat-laners. Many of them are worth thousands, though you wouldn't think it.

After this I asked him what he, as a sharp lad, thought was the cause of so many boys becoming vagrant pickpockets? He answered, "Why, sir, if boys runs away, and has to shelter in low lodging-houses — and many runs away from cruel treatment at home — they meet there with boys such as me, or as bad, and the devil soon lays his hand on them. If there wasn't so many lodging-houses there wouldn't be so many bad boys — there couldn't. Lately a boy came down to Billingsgate, and said he wouldn't stay at home to be knocked about any longer. He said it to some boys like me; and he was asked if he could get anything from his mother, and he said 'yes, he could.' So he went back, and brought a brooch and some other things with him to a place fixed on, and then he and some of the boys set off for the country; and that's the way boys is trapped. I think the fathers of such boys either ill-treat them, or neglect them; and so they run away. My father used to beat me shocking; so I hated home. I stood hard licking well, and was called 'the plucked one'." This boy first stole flowers, currants, and gooseberries out of the clergyman's garden, more by way of bravado, and to ensure the approbation of his comrades, then for anything else.

He answered readily to my inquiry, as to what he thought would become of him? — "Transportation. If a boy has great luck he may carry on for eight years. Three or four years is the common run, but transportation is what he's sure to come to in the end." This lad picked my pocket at my request, and so dexterously did he do his "work," that though I was alive to what he was trying to do, it was impossible for me to detect the least movement of my coat. To see him pick the pockets, as he did, of some of the gentlemen who were present on the occasion, was a curious sight. He crept behind much like a cat with his claws out, and while in the act held his breath with suspense; but immediately the handkerchief was safe in his hand, the change in the expression of his countenance was most marked. He then seemed almost to be convulsed with delight at the success of his perilous adventure, and, turning his back, held up the handkerchief to discover the value of his prize with intense glee evident in every feature.

A BEGGAR

A BEGGAR decently attired, and with a simple and what some would call even a respectable look, gave me the following account: —

"I am now twenty-eight, and have known all connected with the begging trade since I was fourteen. My grandfather (mother's father) was rich, owning three parts of the accommodation houses in St. Giles's; he allowed me 2s. a week pocket-money. My grandfather kept the great house, the old Rose and Crown, in Church-lane, opposite Carver-street, best known as the 'Beggar's Opera.' When a child of seven, I have seen the place crowded — crammed with nothing but beggars, first-rates — none else used the house. The money I saw in the hands of the beggars made a great impression upon me. My father took away my mother's money. I wish my mother had run away instead. He was kind, but she was always nagging. My father was a foreman in a foundry. I got a situation in the same foundry after my father cut. Once I was sent to a bank with a cheque for £38 to get cashed, in silver, for wages. In coming away, I met a companion of mine, and he persuaded me to bolt with the money, and go to Ashley's. The money was too much for my head to carry. I fooled all that money away. I wasn't in bed for more than a fortnight. I bought linnets in cages for the fancy of my persuader. In fact, I didn't know what use to put the money to. I was among plenty of girls. When the money was out I was destitute. I couldn't go back to my employers, and I couldn't face my mother's temper — that was worse; but for that nagging of hers I shouldn't have been as I am. She has thrashed me with a hand broom until I was silly; there's the bumps on my head still; and yet that woman would have given me her heart's blood to do me a good.

"As soon as I found myself quite destitute, I went wandering about the City, picking up the skins of gooseberries and orange peel to eat, to live on — things my stomach would turn at now. At last my mother came to hear that I tried to destroy myself. She

paid the £38, and my former employers got me a situation in Paddington. I was there a month, and then I met him as advised me
to steal the money before—he's called the ex-king of the costermongers now. Well, he was crying hareskins, and advised me again
to bolt, and I went with him. My mind was bent upon costermongering and a roving life. I couldn't settle to anything. I
wanted to be away when I was at work and when I was away
I wanted to be back again. It was difficult for me to stick to anything for five minutes together; it is so now. What I begin I can't
finish at the time—unless it's a pot of beer. Well, in four days my
adviser left me; he had no more use for me. I was a flat. He had
me for a 'go-along,' to cry his things for him. Then, for the first
time in my life, I went into a low lodging-house. There was forty
men and women sleeping in one room. I had to sleep with a black
man, and I slept on the floor to get away from the fellow. There
were plenty of girls there; some playing cards and dominoes. It
was very dirty—old Mother——, in Lawrence-lane—the Queen of
Hell she was called. There was one tub among the lot of us. I felt
altogether disgusted. Those who lived there were beggars, thieves,
smashers, coiners, purchasers of begged and stolen goods, and
prostitutes. The youngest prostitute was twelve, and so up to
fifty. The beastliest language went on. It's done to outrival one
another.

"There I met with a man called Tom Shallow [*shallow* is cant
for half-naked], and he took me out ballad-singing, and when we
couldn't get on at that (the songs got dead) he left me. I made him
10s. or 12s. a day in them days, but he only gave me my lodgings
and grub (but not half enough), and two pipes of tobacco a day to
keep the hunger down, that I mightn't be expensive. I then 'listed.
I was starving, and couldn't raise a lodging. I took the shilling,
but was rejected by the doctor. I 'listed again at Chatham afterwards, but was rejected again. I stayed jobbing among the soldiers
for some weeks, and then they gave me an old regimental suit,
and with that I came to London. One gave me a jacket, and
another a pair of military trousers, and another a pair of old
ammunition boots, and so on.

"About that time a batch of invalids came from Spain, where
they had been under General Evans. On my way up from

Chatham, I met at Gravesend with seven chaps out on '*the Spanish lurk*' as they called it—that is, passing themselves off as wounded men of the Spanish Legion. Two *had been* out in Spain, and managed the business if questions were asked; the others were regular English beggars, who had never been out of the country. I joined them as a serjeant, as I had a serjeant's jacket given me at Chatham. On our way to London—'the school' (as the lot is called) came all together—we picked up among us £4 and £5 a day—no matter where we went. 'The school' all slept in lodging-houses, and I at last began to feel comfortable in them. We spent our evenings in eating out-and-out suppers. Sometimes we had such things as sucking pigs, hams, mince pies—indeed we lived on the best. No nobleman could live better in them days. So much wine, too! I drank in such excess, my nose was as big as that there letter stamp; so that I got a sickening of it. We gave good victuals away that was given to us—it was a nuisance to carry them. It cost us from 6*d.* to 1*s.* a day to have our shoes cleaned by *poor* tramps, and for clean dickies.

"The clean dodge is always the best for begging upon. At Woolwich we were all on the fuddle at the Dust Hole, and our two spokesmen were drunk; and I went to beg of Major——, whose brother was then in Spain—he himself had been out previously. Meeting the major at his own house, I said, 'I was a serjeant in the 3rd Westminster Grenadiers, you know, and served under your brother.' 'Oh! yes, that's my brother's regiment', says he. 'Where was you, then, on the 16th of October?' 'Why, sir, I was at the taking of the city of Irun,' says I—(in fact, I was at that time with the costermonger in St. Giles's, calling cabbages, 'white heart cabbages, oh!') Then said the major, 'What day was Ernani taken on?' 'Why,' said I (I was a little tipsy, and bothered at the question), 'that was the 16th of October, too.' 'Very well, my man,' says he, tapping his boots with a riding whip he held, 'I'll see what I can do for you;' and the words were no sooner out of his mouth than he stepped up to me and gave me a regular pasting. He horse-whipped me up and down stairs, and all along the passages; my flesh was like sassages. I managed at last, however, to open the door myself, and get away. After that 'the school' came to London. In a day we used to make from £8 to £10 among us, by walking up Regent-street, Bond-street, Piccadilly, Pall-mall, Oxford-street, the parks—those places were the best beats. All the squares were good too. It was only like a walk out for air, and your 25s. a man for it. At night we used to go to plays, dressed like gentlemen. At first the beaks protected us, but we got found out, and the beaks grew rusty.

"The thing got so overdone, every beggar went out as a Spanish lurksman. Well, the beaks got up to the dodge, and all the Spanish lurksmen in their turns got to work the universal staircase, under the care of Lieutenant Tracy (Tothill-fields treadmill). The men that had really been out and got disabled were sent to that staircase at last, and I thought I would try a fresh lurk. So I went under the care and tuition of a sailor. He had been a sailor. I became a *turnpike sailor*, as it's called, and went out as one of the shallow brigade, wearing a Guernsey shirt and drawers, or tattered trousers. There was a school of four. We only got a tidy living—16s. or £1 a day among us. We used to call every one that came along—coalheavers and all—sea-fighting captains. 'Now, my noble sea-fighting captain, we used to say, 'fire an odd shot from your larboard locker to us, Nelson's bull-dogs;' but mind we never tried that dodge on at Greenwich, for fear of the old geese, the Collegemen. The Shallow got so grannied [known] in London, that the supplies got queer, and I quitted the land navy. Shipwrecks got so common in the streets, you see, that people didn't care for them, and I dropped getting cast away.

"I then took to *screeving* [writing on the stones]. I got my head shaved, and a cloth tied round my jaws, and wrote on the flags—

'*Illness and want,*'

though I was never better in my life, and always had a good bellyfull before I started of a morning. I did very well at first: 3s. or 4s. a day—sometimes more—till I got grannied. There is one man who draws Christ's heads with a crown of thorns and mackerel, on the pavement, in coloured chalks (there are four or five others at the same business); this one, however, often makes £1 a day now in three hours; indeed, I have known him come home with 21s., besides what he drank on the way. A gentleman who met him in Regent-street once gave him £5 and a suit of clothes to do Christ's heads with a crown of thorns and mackerel on the walls. His son does Napoleon's heads best, but makes nothing like so much as the father. The father draws cats' heads and salmon as well — but the others are far the best spec. He will often give thirteen-pence, and indeed fourteen-pence, for a silver shilling, to get rid of the coppers. This man's pitch is Lloyd-square, not far from Sadler's Wells. I have seen him commence his pitch there at half-past eleven, to catch the people come from the theatre. He is very clever. In wet weather, and when I couldn't chalk, as I couldn't afford to lose time, I used to dress tidy and very clean for the *'respectable broken-down tradesman or reduced gentleman'* caper. I wore a suit of black, generally, and a clean dickey, and sometimes old back kid gloves, and I used to stand with a paper before my face, as if ashamed —

> *'To a Humane Public.*
> *'I have seen better days.'*

"This is called standing pad with a fakement. It is a wet weather dodge, and isn't so good as screeving, but I did middling, and can't bear being idle. After this I mixed with the street patterers on *the destitute mechanic's lurk.* We went in a school of six at first, all in clean aprons, and spoke every man in his turn. It won't do unless you're clean. Each man wanted a particular article of dress. One had no shirt — another no shoes — another no hat — and so on. No two wanted the same. We said.: —

"Kind and benevolent Christians! — It is with feelings of deep regret, and sorrow and shame, that us unfortunate tradesmen are compelled to appear before you this day, to ask charity from the hands of strangers. We are brought to it from want — I may say, actual starvation.' (We always had a good breakfast before we started, and some of us, sir, was full up to the brim of liquor.) 'But what will not hunger and the cries of children compel men to do.' (We were all single men.) 'When we left our solitary and humble homes this morning, our children were crying for food, but if a farthing would have saved their lives, we hadn't it to give them. I assure you, kind friends, me, my wife, and three children, would have been houseless wanderers all last night, but I sold the shirt from off my back as you may see (opening my jacket) to pay for a lodging. We are, kind friends, *English* mechanics. It is hard that you won't give your own countrymen a penny, when you give so much to *foreign* hurdy-gurdies and organ-grinders. Owing to the introduction of steam and machinery and foreign manufactures we have been brought to this degraded state. Fellow countrymen, there are at this moment 4,000 men like ourselves, able and willing to work, but can't get it, and forced to wander the streets. I hope and trust some humane Christian within the sound of my voice will stretch out a hand with a small trifle for us, be it ever so small, or a bit of dry bread or cold potato, or anthing turned from your table, it would be of the greatest benefit to us and our poor children.' (Then we would whisper to one another. 'I hope they won't bring out any scran — only coppers.') 'We have none of us tasted food this blessed day. We have been told to go to our parishes, but that we cannot brook; to be torn from our wives and families is heart rending to think of — may God save us all from the Bastile!' (We always pattered hard at the overseers.)

"The next of the school that spoke would change the story some-how, and try to make it more heart-rending still. We did well at first, making about 5*s*. a day each, working four hours, two in the morning and two in the afternoon. We got a good deal of clothing too. The man who went without a shirt never went to a door to ask for one; he had to show himself in the middle of the road. The man that *did* go to the door would say, 'Do bestow a shirt on my poor shopmate, who hasn't had one for some days.' It's been said of me, when I had my shirt tied round my waist all the time out of sight. The man who goes without his shirt has his pick of those given; the rest are sold and shared. Whatever trade we represented we always had one or two really of the trade in the school. These were always to be met at the lodging-houses. They were out of work, and had to go to low lodging-houses to sleep. There they met with beggars who kiddied them on to the lurk. The lodging-houses is good schools for that sort of think, and when a mechanic once gets out on the lurk he never cares to go to work again. I never knew one return. I have been out oft and oft with weavers with a loom, and have woven a piece of ribbon in a gentleman's parlour — that was when we was Coventry ribbon weavers. I have been a stocking weaver from Leicester, and a lacemaker too from Nottingham. Distressed mechanics on their way to London get initiated into beggar's tricks in the low lodging-houses and the unions. This is the way, you see, sir. A school may be at work from the lodging-house where the mechanic goes to, and some of the school finds out what he is, and says, 'Come and work with us in a school: you'll do better than you can at your business, and you can answer any questions; we'll lurk on your trade.'

"I have been out with a woman and children. It's been said in the papers that children can be hired for that lurk at 4d. or 6d. a day — that's all fudge, all stuff, every bit of it — there's no children to be hired. There's many a labouring man out of work, who has a wife and three or more children, who is glad to let them go out with any patterer he knows. The woman is entitled to all the clothes and grub given, and her share of the tin — that's the way it's done; and she's treated to a drink after her day's work, into the bargain. I've been out on the *respectable family man lurk*. I was out with a woman and three kids the other day; her husband was on the pad in the country, as London was too hot to hold him. The kids draw, the younger the better, for if you vex them, and they're oldish, they'll blow you. Liverpool Joe's boy did so at Bury St. Edmund's to a patterer that he was out with, and who spoke cross to him. The lad shouted out so as the people about might hear, 'Don't you jaw me, you're not my father; my father's at home playing cards.' They had to crack the pitch [discontinue] through that.

"The respectable family dodge did pretty well. I've been on *the clean family* lurk too, with a woman and children. We dressed to give the notion that, however humble, at least we were clean in all our poverty. On this lurk we stand by the side of the pavement in silence, the wife in a perticler clean cap, and a milk-white apron. The kids have long clean pinafores, white as the driven snow; they're only used in clean lurk, and taken off directly they come home. The husband and father is in a white flannel jacket, an apron worn and clean, and polished shoes. To succeed in this caper there must be no rags, but plenty of darns. A pack of pawntickets is carried in the waistcoat pocket. (One man that I know stuck them in his hat like a carman's). That's to show that they've parted with their little all before they came to that. They are real pawn-tickets. I have known a man pay 2s. 6d. for the loan of a marriage certificate to go out on the clean lurk.

"If a question is asked, I say – 'We've parted with everything, and can get no employment; to be sure, we have had a loaf from the parish, but what's that among my family?' That takes the start out of the people, because they say, why not go to the parish? Some persons say, 'Oh, poor folks, they're brought to this, how clean they are – a darn is better than a patch any time.' The clean lurk is a bare living now – it was good – lots of togs came in, and often the whole family were taken into a house and supplied with flannel enough to make under clothing for them all; all this was pledged soon afterwards, and the tickets shown to prove what was parted with, through want.

"Those are some of the leading lurks. There's others. 'Fits', are now bad, and 'paralytics' are no better. *The lucifer lurk* seems getting up though. I don't mean the selling, but the dropping them in the street as if by accident. It's a great thing with the children; but no go with the old 'uns. I'll tell you another lurk: a woman I knows sends out her child with $1/4$ oz. of tea and half a quarter of sugar, and the child sits on a door step crying, and saying, if questioned, that she was sent out for tea and sugar, and a boy snatched the change from her, and threw the tea and sugar in the gutter. The mother is there, like a stranger, and says to the child: – 'And was that your poor mother's last shilling, and daren't you go home, poor thing?' Then there is a gathering – sometimes 18s. in a morning; but it's almost getting stale, that is. I've done *the shivering dodge* too – gone out in the cold weather half naked. One man has practised it so much that he can't get off shivering now. Shaking Jemmy went on with his shivering so long that he couldn't help it at last. He shivered like a jelly – like a calf's foot with the ague – on the hottest day in summer. It's a good dodge in tidy inclement seasons. It's not so good a lurk, by two bob a day, as it once was. This is a single-handed job; for if one man shivers less than another he shows that it isn't so cold as the good shiverer makes it out—then it's no go.

"Of the *maimed beggars,* some are really deserving objects, as without begging they must starve to death; that's a fact, sir. What's a labouring man to do if he's lost any of his limbs? But some of these even are impostors. I know several blind men who have pensions; and I know two who have not only pensions, but keep lodging-houses, and are worth money, and still go out a begging—though not near where they live. There's the man with the very big leg, who sits on the pavement, and tells a long yarn about the tram carriage having gone over him in the mine. He does very well—remarkable well. He goes tatting and billy-hunting in the country (gathering rags and buying old metal), and comes only to London when he has that sort of thing to dispose of. There's Paddy in the truck too; he makes a good thing, and sends money home to Ireland; he has a decrepit old mother, and it's to his credit. He never drinks. There's Jerry, the collier, he has lost both arms, and does a tidy living, and deserves it; it's a bad misfortune. There's Jack Tiptoe, he can't put one heel to the ground—no gammon; but Mr. Horsford and he can't agree, so Jack takes to the provinces now. He did very well indeed here.

"There used to be a society among us called *the Cadger's Club;* if one got into a prison there was a gathering for him when he came out, and 6s. a week for a sick member, and when he got out again two collections for him, the two amounting perhaps to £1. We paid 3d. a week each—no women were members—for thirteen weeks, and then shared what was in hand, and began for the next thirteen, receiving new members and transacting the usual business of a club. This has been discontinued these last five years; the landlord cut away with the funds. We get up raffles, and help one another in the best way we can now. At one time we had forty-five members, besides the secretary, the conductor, and under-conductor. The rules were read over on meeting nights— every Wednesday evening. They were very strict; no swearing, obscene or profane language was permitted. For the first offence a fine of 1d was inflicted, for the second 2d., and for the third the offender was ejected the room. There was very good order, and few fines had to be inflicted. Several respectable tradesmen used to pay a trifle to be admitted, out of curiosity, to see the proceedings, and used to be suprised at their regularity. Among the other rules were these: a fine of 1*d.* for any member refusing to sing when called on; visitors the same. All the fines went to the fund. If a member didn't pay for five meeting nights he was scratched. Very few were scratched.

"The secretary was a windmill cove (sold children's windmills in the streets), and was excused contributing to the funds. He had 1*d.* from each member every sharing night, once a quarter, for his labour; he was a very good scholar, and had been brought up well. The landlord generally gave a bob on a sharing night. The conductor managed the room, and the under-conductor kept the door, not admitting those who had no right to be there, and putting out those who behaved improperly. It was held in the Coachmakers' Arms, Rose-street, Longrave-street; tip-top swells used to come among us, and no mistake; real noblemen, sir. One was the nephew of the Duke of——, and was well-known to all of us by the nick-name Facer.

"I used to smoke a very short and very black pipe, and the honourable gent has often snatched it from my mouth, and has given me a dozen cigars for it. My face has been washed in the gin by a noble lord after he'd made me drunk, and I felt as if it was vitriol about my eyes. The beggars are now dispersed and broken up. They live together now only in twos and threes, and, in plain truth, have no money to spend; they can't get it. Upon an average, in former days a cadger could make his two or three guineas per week without working overtime; but now he can hardly get a meal, not even at the present winter, though it's been a slap up inclement season, to be sure. The Mendicity Society has ruined us—them men took me and gave me a month, and I can say from my concience, that I was no more guilty of begging at that time that an unborn baby. The beggars generally live in the low lodging-houses, and there of a night they tell their tales of the day, and inform each other of the good and bad places throughout London, and what 'lurks' do the best. They will also say what beats they intend to take the next day, so that those who are on the same lurk may not go over the same ground as to taunt me by offering to jump me" [invite him to a jumping].

"It is no use telling a lie, but the low lodging-houses throughout London and the country are nests for beggars and thieves. I know some houses that are wholly supported by beggars. In almost every one of the padding-kens, or low lodging-houses in the country, there is a list of walks, written on a piece of paper, and pasted up over the kitchen mantel-piece. Now at St. Alban's for instance, at the——, and at other places, there is a paper stuck up in each of the kitchens. This paper is headed 'WALKS OUT OF THIS TOWN,' and underneath it is set down the names of the villages in the neighbourhood at which a beggar may call when out on his walk, and they are so arranged as to allow the cadger to make a round of about six miles, each day, and return the same night. In many of those papers there are sometimes twenty walks set down. No villages that are in any way 'gammy' are ever mentioned in these papers, and the cadger, if he feels inclined to stop for a few days in the town, will be told by the lodging-house keeper, or the other cadgers that he may meet there, what gentleman's seats or private houses are of any account on the walk that he means to take. The names of the good houses are not set down in the paper, for fear of the police. Most of the lodging-house keepers buy the 'scran' [broken victuals] of the cadgers; the good food they either eat themselves or sell to the other travellers, and the bad they sell to parties to feed their dogs or pigs upon. The cadger's talk is quite different now to what it was in the days of Billy. You see the flats got awake to it, so in course we had to alter the patter.

"The new style of cadgers' cant is nothing like the thieves' cant, and is done all on the rhyming principle. This way's the caper. Suppose I want to ask a pal to come and have a *glass* of *rum* and smoke a *pipe* of *tobacco*, and have a game at *cards* with some *blokes* at *home* with me. I should say, if there were any flats present, 'Splodger, will you have a Jack-sur*pass* of finger-and-*thumb*, and below your yard of *tripe* of nosey me *knackert* and have a touch of the *broads* with me and the other heaps of *coke* at my *drum*. [In this it will be observed that every one of the 'cant' words rhymes with the words ordinarily used to express the same idea.] I can assure you what little we cadgers do get we earn uncommon hard. Why, from standing shaking – that is, being out nearly naked in the hardest-frosts — I lost the use of my left side for nearly three years, and wasn't able to stir outside the door. I got my living by card-playing in the low lodging-houses all that time. I worked the oracle — they were not up to it. I put the first and seconds on and the bridge also. I'd play at cards with any one. You see, sir, I was afeard to come to you at first because I had been 'a starving' on the pavement only a few days ago, not a hundred yards from your very door, and I thought you might know me."

THE STREET-SELLER OF RHUBARB AND SPICE

FROM A street-seller whose portrait has been given I received the following history. He appeared to be a very truthful and kindly-disposed old man: —

"I am one native of Mogadore in Morocco. I am an Arab. I left my countree when I was sixteen or eighteen year of age. I forget, sir. I don't know which, about eighteen, I tink it was. My fader was like market man, make de people pay de toll — he rent de whole market, you see, from de governemen, and make de people pay so much for deir stands. I can't tell you what dey call dem dere. I couldn't recollect what my fader pay for de market; but I know some of de people pay him a penny, some a ha'penny, for de stands. Dere everything sheap, not what dey are here in England. Dey may stop all day for de toll or go when de market is over. My fader was not very rish — not very poor — he keep a family. We have bread, meat, shicken, apples, grapes, all de good tings to eat, not like here — tis de sheapest countree in de world. My fader have two wifes, not at once you know, he bury de first and marry anoder. I was by second wife. He have seven shildren by her, four sons and tree daughters. By de first I tink dere was five, two sons and tree daughters. Bless you, by de time I was born dere was great many of'em married and away in de world. I don't know where dey are now. Only one broder I got live for what I know, wheder de oders are dead or where dey are I can't tell. De one broder I speak of is in Algiers now; he is dealer dere. What led me to come away, you say? Like good many I was young and foolish; like all de rest of young people, I like to see foreign countries, but you see in my countree de governemen don't like de people to come away, not widout you pay so mush, so Gibraltar was de only port I could go to, it was only one twenty miles across de water — close to us. You see you go to Gibraltar like smuggling — you smuggle yourself — you talk wid de Captain and he do it for you.

"My fader been dead years and years before I come away, I

suppose I was about ten year old when he die. I had been at school till time I was grown up, and after dat I was shoemaker. I make de slippers. Oh yes! my moder was alive den—she was dead when I was here in England. I get about one penny a pair for de slippers in my countree; penny dere as good as shilling here amost. I could make tree, four, five pair in one day. I could live on my gains den better dan what I could do here wid twelve times as mush—dat time I could. I don't know what it is now. Yes, my moder give me leave to go where I like. She never see me since" (sighing). "Oh yes, I love her very mush. I am old man now, but I never forgot her yet;" here the old man burst into tears and buried his face in his handkerchief for several minutes. "No, no! she don't know when I come away dat she never see me again, nor me neider. I tell I go Gibraltar, and den I tell her I go to Lisbon to see my broder, who was spirit merchant dere. I didn't say noting not at all about coming back to her, but I thought I should come back soon. If I had tought I never see no more, not all de gold in de world take me from her. She was good moder to me. I was de youngest but one. My broders kept my moder, you see. Where I came from it is not like here, if only one in de family well off, de oders never want for noting. In my country, you see, de law is you must maintain your fader and moder before you maintain your own family. You must keep dem in de house."

Here he repeated the law in Hebrew. "De people were Mahome-dans in Mogadore, but we were Jews, just like here, you see. De first ting de Jews teesh de schildren is deir duty to deir faders and deir moders. And dey love one anoder more than de gold; but dey love de gold more dan most people, for you see gold is more to dem. In my countree de governemen treat de Jews very badly, so de money all de Jews have to help dem. Often de governemen in my country take all deir money from de Jews, and kill dem after, so de Jews all keep deir money in secret places, put de gold in jars and dig dem in de ground, and de men worths hundreds go about wid no better clothes dan mine.

"Well, you see I leave my poor moder, we kissed one anoder, and cry for half an hour, and come away to Gibraltar. When I get dere, my broder come away from Lisbon to Gibraltar; dat time it was war time, and de French was coming to Lisbon, so everybody run. When I come away from Mogadore, I have about one hundred dollars—some my moder give me, and some I had save. When I got to Gibraltar, I begin to have a little stand in de street wid silk handkerschiefs, cotton handkerschiefs, shop goods you know. I do very well wid dat, so after I get licence to hawk de town, and after dat I keep shop. Altogeder, I stop in Gibraltar about six years. I had den about five or six hundred dollars. I live very well all de time I dere. I was wid my broder all de time. After I am six year in Gibraltar, I begin to tink I do better in England. I tink, like good many people, if I go to anoder part dat is risher —'t de rishest countree in de world—I do better still.

"So I start off, and get I here I tink in 1811, when de tree shilling-pieces first come out. I have about one hundred and tirty pound at dat time. I stop in London a good bit, and eat my money; it was most done before I start to look for my living. I try to look what I could do, but I was quite stranger you see. I am about fourteen or fifteen month before I begin to do anyting. I go to de play house; I see never such tings as I see here before I come. When I come here, I think I am in heaven altogether—God a'mighty forgive me—such sops [shops] and such beautiful tings. I live in Mary Axe Parish when I first come; same parish where I live now. Well, you see some of my countreemen den getting good living by selling de rhubard and spices in de street. I get to know dem all; and dat time you see was de good time, money was plenty, like de dirt here. Dat time dere was about six or seven Arabians in de street selling rhubard and spices, five of 'em was from Mogadore, and two from not far off; and dere is about five more going troo de country. Dey all sell de same tings, merely rhubard and spice, dat time; before den was good for tem tings— after dat dey get de silks and tings beside. I can't tell what first make dem sell de rhubarb and de spice; but I think it is because people like to buy de Turkey rhubarb of de men in de turbans. When I was little shild, I hear talk in Mogadore of de people of my countree sell de rhubarb in de streets of London, and make plenty money by it.

"Dere was one very old Arabian in de streets wen I first come; dey call him Sole; he been forty year at de same business. He wear de long beard and Turkish dress. He used to stand by

Bow Shursh, Sheapside. Everybody in de street know him. He was de old establish one. He been dead now, let me see — how long he been dead — oh, dis six or seven and twenty year. He die in Gibraltar very poor and very old — most ninety year of age. All de rhubarb-sellers was Jews. Dere was anoder called Ben Aforiat, and two broders; and anoder, his name was Azuli. One of Aforiat's broders use to stand in St. Paul's Shurshyard. He was very well know; all de oders hawk about de town like I do myself. Now dey all gone dead, and dere only four of us now in England; dey all in London, and none in de country.

"Two of us live in Mary Axe, anoder live in, what dey call dat — Spitalfield, and de oder in Petticoat-lane. De one wat live in Spitalfield is old man, I dare say going for 70. De one in Petticoat-lane not mush above 30. I am little better dan 73, and de oder wat live in Mary Axe about 40. I been de longest of all in de streets, about tirty-eight or tirty-nine year. All dat was here when I first come, die in London, except dat old man Sole wat I was telling of, dat die in Gibraltar. About tirteen or fourteen die since I come to England; some die in de Hospital of de Jews at Mile End; some die at home — not one of dem die worth no money. Six od dem was very old people, between 60 and 70; dere was some tirty, some forty. Some of dem die by inshes. Dere was one fine fellow, he was six foot two, and strong man, he take to his bed and fall away so; at last you see troo his hand; he was noting but de carcase; oders die of what you call de yellow jaundice; some have de fever, but deir time was come; de death we must be.

"When I first come to dis countree me make plenty of money by selling de rhubarb in de street. Five-and-twenty year ago I make a pound a day some time. Take one week wid another, I dare say I clear, after I pay all de cost of my living, tirty shillings; and now, God help me, I don't make not twelve shilling a week, and all my food to pay out of dat. One week wid anoder, when I go out I clear about twelve shilling. Everything is so sheep now, and dere is so many sops [shops], people has no money to buy tings with. I could do better when everyting was dear. I could live better, get more money, and have more for it. I have better food, better lodging, and better clothes. I don't know wat is de cause, as

The Street Rhubarb and Spice Seller

you say. I only know dat I am worse, and everybody is worse; dat is all I know. Bread is sheeper, but when it was one and ninepence de loaf I could get plenty to buy it wid, but now it is five pence, I can't get no five pence to have it. If de cow is de penny in de market what is de use of dat, if you can't get no penny to buy him?

"After I been selling my rhubarb for two years, when I fust come here, I save about a hundred and fifty pound, and den you see I agree wid tree oder my countrymen to take a sop [shop] in Exeter. De oder tree was rhubarb-sellers, like myself, and have save good bit of money as well. One have seven hundred pound; but he have brought tree or four hundred pound wid him to dis countree. Anoder of de tree have about two hundred, and de oder about one hundred; dey have all save deir money out of de rhubarb. We keep our sop, you see, about five year, and den we fall in pieces altogeder. We take and trust, and lose all our money. T'oders never keep a sop before, and not one uf us was English scholar; we was forced to keep a man, and dat way we lose all our money, so we was force to part, and every one go look for hisself. Den we all go selling rhubarb again about de country, and in London; and I never able to hold up my head since. When I come back to de rhubarb times is getting bad, and I not able to save no more money. All I am worth in de world is all I got in my box, and dat altogeder is not more dan ten shilling. Last week I haven't a pound of meat in de house, and I am obliged to pawn my waistcoat and handkerchief to get me some stock. It easy to put dem in but very hard to get dem out.

"I had two wives. After two or tree year when I come I marry my first. I had two shildren by my first, but both of dem die very young; one was about five year old an de oder about tree. When I travel the countree, my first wife she go wid me everywhere. I been to all parts — to Scotland, to Wales, but no to Ireland. I see enough of dem Irish in dis countree, I do not want no more of dem dere. Not one of my countree I tink ever been to Ireland, and only one beside myself been to Scotland; but dat no use, de Scotsh don't know wat spice is. All de time I am in Scotland I can't get no bread, only barley and pea meal, and dat as sour as de winegar — and I can't get no flour to make none too — so I begin to say, by God I come to wrong countree here. When I go across de countree of England I never live in no lodging-houses — always in de public — because you see I do business dere; de missus perhaps dere buy my spices of me. I lodge once in Taunton, at a house where a woman keep a lodging house for de Jewish people wat go about wid de gold tings — de jewellery. At oder towns I stop at de public, for dere is de company, and I sell my tings.

"I buy my rhubarb and my spice of de large warehouse for de drugs; sometimes I buy it of my countreemen. We all of us know de good spice from de bad. You look! I will show you how to tell de good nutmeg from de bad. Here is some in de shell: you see, I put de strong pin in one and de oil run out; dat is because dey has not been put in de spirit to take away de oil for to make de extract. Now, in de bad nutmeg all de oil been took out by de spirit, and den dere is no flavour, like dose you buy in de sheep sops [cheap shops]. I sell de Rhubarb, East Indy and Turkey, de Cloves, Cinnamons, Mace, Cayenne Pepper, White Pepper — a little of all sorts when I get de money to buy it wid. I take my solemn oat I never sheat in scales nor weight; because de law is, 'take weight and give weight,' dat is judge and justice. Dere is no luck in de sort weight — no luck at all. Never in my life I put no tings wid my goods. I tell you de troot, I grind my white pepper wid my own hands, but I buy me ginger ground, and *dat* is mixed I know. I tink it is pea flour dey put wid it, dere is no smell in dat, but it is de same colour — two ounces of ginger will give de smell to one pound of pea flour. De public-houses will have de sheep ginger and dat I buy. I tell you de troot.

"How am I tell what will become of me. Dat is de Almighty's work" (here he pointed to Heaven). "De Jews is very good to deir old people. If it was not for my old woman I be like a gentleman now in de hospital at Mile End; but you see, I marry de Christian woman and dat is against our people — and I would never leave her — no not for all de good in de world to come to myself. If I am poor, I not de only one. In de holiday times I send a petition, and perhaps dere is five shillings for me from de hospital. In de Jews' Hospital dere is only ten — what you call de Portuguese Jews. We have hospital to our ownselves. Dere de old people — dey are all above sixty — are all like noblemen, wid good clothes, plenty to eat, go where you like, and pipe of tobacco when you want. But I won't go in to hospital away from my old woman. I will get a bit of crust for her as long as I can stand — but I can hardly do that now. Every one got his feeling, and I will feel for her as long as I live. When dere is de weather I have de rheumatis — oh! very bad — sometimes I can scarcely stand or walk. I am seventy-tree, and it is a sad time for me now. I am merry sometime tho'. Everyting wid de pocket. When de pocket is merry, den I am merry too. Sometime I go home wid one shilling, and den I tink all gets worse and worse, and what will become of me I say — but dat is de Almighty's work, and I trust in him. Can I trust any better one? Sometime I say I wish I was back in my countree — and I tink of my poor moder wat is dead now, and den I am very sad. Oh yes, bless your heart, very sad indeed!"

The old man appears to sell excellent articles, and to be a very truthful, fair-dealing man.

AN IRISH STREET-SELLER

Of the causes which induced a good-looking Irish woman to become a street-seller I had the following account, which I give in its curious details:—

"'Deed thin, sir, it's more than 20 long years since I came from Dublin to Liverpool wid my father and mother, and brother William that's dead and gone, rest his soul. He died when he was fourteen. They was masons in Ireland. Was both father and mother masons, sir? Well, then, in any quiet job mother helped father, for she was a strong woman. They came away sudden. They was in some thrubble, but I never knew what, for they wouldn't talk to me about it. We thravelled from Liverpool to London, for there was no worruk at Liverpool; and he got worruk on buildings in London, and had 18s. a week; and mother cleaned and worruked for a greengrocer, as they called him—he sold coals more than anything—where we lodged, and it wasn't much she got, but she airned what is such a thrubble to poor people, the rint. We was well off, and I was sent to school; and we should have been better off, but father took too much to the dhrop, God save him. He fell onste and broke his leg; and though the hospital gintlemen, God bless them for good Christians, got him through it, he got little worruk when he came out again, and died in less than a year. Mother wasn't long afther him; and on her death-bed she said, so low I could hardly hear her, 'Mary, my darlint, if you starruve, be vartuous. Remimber poor Illen's funeral.'

"When I was quite a child, sir, I went wid mother to a funeral—she was a relation—and it was of a young woman that died after her child had been borrun a fortnight, and she wasn't married; that was Illen. Her body was brought out of the lying-in hospital—I've often heard spake of it since—and was in the churchyard to be buried; and her brother, that hadn't seen her for a long time, came and wanted to see her in her coffin, and they took the lid off, and then he currused her in her coffin afore him; she'd been so wicked. But he wasn't a good man hisself, and was in dhrink too; still nobody said anything, and he walked away. It made me ill to see Illen in her coffin, and hear him curruse, and I've remimbered it ever since.

"I was thin fifteen, I believe, and hadn't any friends that had any tie to me. I was lone, sir, But the neebours said, 'Poor thing, she's left on the shuckrawn' [homeless]; and they helped me, and I got a place. Mistress was very kind at first, that's my first mistress was, and I had the care of a child of three years old; they had only one, because mistress was busy making waistcoats. Master was a hatter, and away all day, and they was well off. But some women called on mistress once, and they had a deal of talkin', and blad-herin', and laughin', and I don't know how often I was sent out for quarterns of gin. Then they all went out together; and mistress came home quite tipsy just afore master, and went upstairs, and had just time to get into bed; she told me to tell master she had one of her sick head-aches and was forced to go to bed; she went on that way for three or four days, and master and she used to quarrel of a night, for I could hear them. One night he came home sooner than common, and he'd been drinking, or perhaps it might be thrubble, and he sent me to bed with the child; and sometime in the night, I don't know what time, but I could only see from a gas-lamp that shined into the room, he came in, for there was no fastenin' inside the door, it was only like a closet, and he began to ask me about mistress.

"When he larned she'd been drinking wid other women, he used dreadful language, and pulled me out of bed, and struck me with a stick that he snatched up, he could see it in the gas-light, it was little Frank's horse, and swore at me for not telling him afore. He only struck me onste, but I screamed ever so often, I was so frightened. I dressed myself, and lay down in my clothes, and got up as soon as it was light — it was summer time — and thought I would go away and complain to some one. I would ask the nee-bours who to complain to. When I was going out there was master walking up and down the kitchen. He'd never been to bed, and he says, says he, 'Mary, where are you going?' So I told him, and he begged my pardon, and said he was ashamed of what he'd done, but he was half mad; then he began to cry, and so I cried, and mistress came home just then, and when she saw us both crying ·

together, *she* cried, and said she wasn't wanted, as we was man and wife already. Master just gave her a push and down she fell, and he ran out. She seemed so bad, and the child began to cry, that I couldn't lave thin; and master came home drunk that night, but he wasn't cross, for he'd made out that mistress had been drinking with some neebours, and had got to her mother's, and that she was so tipsy she fell asleep, they let her stay till morning, and then some woman set her home, but she'd been there all night. They made it up at last, but I wouldn't stay. They was very kind to me when I left, and paid me all that was owing, and gave me a good pair of shoes, too; for they was well off.

"I had many places for seven years; after that, and when I was out of a place, I stayed wid a widder, and a very dacint woman she was, wid a daughter working for a bookbinder, and the old woman had a good pitch with fruit. Some of my places was very harrud, but shure, again, I met some as was very kind. I left one because they was always wanting me to go to a Methodist chapel, and was always running down my religion, and did all they could to hinder my ever going to mass. They would hardly pay me when I left, because I wouldn't listen to them, they said — the haythens! — when they would have saved my soul. *They* save my soul, indeed! The likes o' thim! Yes, indeed, thin, I had wicked offers sometimes, and from masters that should have known better. I kept no company wid young men. One mistress refused me a karackter, because I was so unhandy, she said; but she thought better of it. At last, I had a faver [fever], and wasn't expected for long [not expected to live]; when I was getting well, everything went to keep me. What wasn't good enough for the pawn went to the dolly [dolly-shop, generally a rag and bottle shop, or a marine store].

"When I could get about, I was so shabby, and my clothes hung about me so, that the shops I went to said, 'Very sorry, but can't recommend you anywhere;' and mistresses looked strange at me, and I didn't know what to do and was miserable. I'd been miserable sometimes in place, and had many a cry, and thought how 'lone' I was, but I never was so miserable as this. At last, the old woman I stayed along wid — O, yes, she was an Irishwoman — advised me to sill fruit in the streets, and I began on strawberries, and borrowed 2s. 6d. to do it wid. I had my hilth better than ever thin; and after I'd sold fruit of all kinds for two years, I got married. My husband had a potato can thin. I knew him because he lived near, and I saw him go in and out, and go to mass. After that he got a porter's place and dropped his can, and he porters when he has a chance still, and has a little work in sewing sacks for the corn-merchants. Whin he's at home at his sacks, as he is now, he can mind the children — we have two — and I sells a few oranges to make a thrifle. Whin there's nothing ilse for him to do, he sills fruit in the sthreets, and thin I'm at home. We do middlin', God be praised."

There is no doubt my informant was a modest, and, in her way a worthy woman. But it may be doubted if any English girl, after seven years of domestic service, would have so readily adapted herself to a street calling. Had an English girl been living among, and used to the society of women who supported themselves by street labour, her repugnance to such a life might have been lessened; but even then, I doubt if she, who had the virtue to resist the offers told of by my Irish informant, could have made the attempt to live by selling fruit. I do not mean that she would rather have fallen into immoral courses than honestly live upon the sale of strawberries, but that she would have struggled on and striven to obtain any domestic labour in preference to a street occupation.

TWO STREET BOYS

I NOW GIVE the answers I received from two boys. The first, his mother told me, was the best scholar at his school when he was there, and before he had to help her in street sale. He was a pale, and not at all forward boy, of thirteen or fourteen, and did not appear much to admire being questioned. He had not been to a Ragged School, but to an "academy" kept by an old man. He did not know what the weekly charge was, but when father was living (he died last autumn) the schoolmaster used to take it out in vegetables. Father was a costermonger; mother minded all about his schooling, and master often said she behaved to him like a lady. "God," this child told me, "was our Heavenly Father, and the maker of all things; he knew everything and everybody; he knew people's thoughts and every sin they committed if no one else knew it. His was the kingdom and the power, and the glory, for ever and ever, Amen. Jesus Christ was our Lord and Saviour; he was the son of God, and was crucified for our sins. He was a God himself." [The child understood next to nothing of the doctrine of the Trinity, and I did not press him.] "The Scriptures, which were the Bible and Testament, were the Word of God, and contained nothing but what was good and true. If a boy lied, or stole, or committed sins," he said, "he would be punished in the next world, which endured for ever and ever, Amen. It was only after death, when it was too late to repent, that people went to the next world." He attended chapel, sometimes.

As to mundane matters, the boy told me that Victoria was Queen of Great Britain and Ireland. She was born May 24, 1819, and succeeded his late Majesty, King William IV., July 20, 1837. She was married to his Royal Highness Prince Albert, &c., &c. France was a different country to this: he had heard there was no king or queen there, but didn't understand about it. You couldn't go to France by land, no more than you could to Ireland. Didn't know anything of the old times in history; hadn't been told. Had heard of the battle of Waterloo; the English licked. Had heard of the battle of Trafalgar, and of Lord Nelson; didn't know much about him; but there was his pillar at Charing-cross, just by the candlesticks [fountains]. When I spoke of astronomy, the boy at once told me he knew nothing about it. He had heard that the earth went round the sun, but from what he'd noticed, shouldn't have thought it. He didn't think that the sun went round the earth, it seemed to go more sideways. Would like to read more, if he had time, but he had a few books, and there was hundreds not so well off as he was.

I am far from undervaluing, indeed I would not indulge in an approach to a scoff, at the extent of this boy's knowledge. Many a man who piques himself on the plenitude of his breeches' pocket, and who attributes his success in life to the fulness of his knowledge, knows no more of Nature, Man, and God, than this poor street child.

Another boy, perhaps a few months older, gave me his notions of men and things. He was a thick-limbed, red-cheeked fellow; answered very freely, and sometimes, when I could not help laughing at his replies, laughed loudly himself, as if he entered into the joke.

Yes, he had heer'd of God, who made the world. Couldn't exactly recollec' when he'd heer'd on him, but he had, most sartenly. Didn't know when the world was made or how anybody could do it. It must have taken a long time. It was afore his time, "or yourn either, sir." Knew there was a book called the Bible; didn't know what it was about; didn't mind to know; knew of such a book to a sartinty, because a young 'oman took one to pop [pawn] for an old 'oman what was on the spree—a bran new 'un—but the cove wouldn't have it, and the old 'oman said he might be d—d. Never heer'd tell on the deluge; of the world having been drownded it couldn't, for there wasn't water enought to do it. He weren't a going to fret hisself for such things as that. Didn't know what happened to people after death, only that they was buried. Had seen a dead body laid out; was a little afeared at first; poor Dick looked so different, and when you touched his face, he was so cold! oh, so cold! Had heer'd on another world; wouldn't mind if he was there hisself, if he could do better, for things was often queer here. Had heered on it from a tailor—such a clever cove,

a stunner — as went to 'Straliar [Australia], and heer'd him say
he was going into another world.

Had never heer'd of France, but had heer'd of Frenchmen; there
wasn't half a quarter so many on 'em as of Italians, with their
earrings like flash gals. Didn't dislike foreigners, for he never saw
none. What was they? Had heer'd of Ireland. Didn't know where
it was, but it couldn't be very far, or such lots wouldn't come from
there to London. Should say they walked it, aye, every bit of the
way, for he'd seen them come in, all covered with dust. Had
heer'd of people going to sea, and had seen the ships in the river,
but didn't know nothing about it, for he was very seldom that way.
The sun was made of fire, or it wouldn't make you feel so warm.
The stars was fire, too, or they wouldn't shine. They didn't make
it warm, they was too small. Didn't know any use they was of.
Didn't know how far they was off; a jolly lot higher than the gas
lights some on 'em was. Was never in a church; had heer'd they
worshipped God there; didn't know how it was done; had heer'd
singing and playing inside when he'd passed; never was there, for
he hadn't no togs to go in, and wouldn't be let in among such
swells as he had seen coming out. Was a ignorant chap, for he'd
never been to school, but was up to many a move and didn't do
bad. Mother said he would make his fortin yet.

Had heer'd of the Duke of Wellington; he was Old Nosey; didn't
think he ever seed him, but had seed his statty. Hadn't heer'd of
the battle of Waterloo, nor who it was atween; once lived in Web-
ber-row, Waterloo-road. Thought he had heer'd speak of Bonaparte; didn't know what he was; thought he had heer'd of Shakespeare, but didn't know whether he was alive or dead, and didn't
care. A man with something like that name kept a dolly and did
stunning; but he was such a hard cove that if *he* was dead it
wouldn't matter. Had seen the Queen, but didn't recollec' her
name just at the minute; oh! yes, Wictoria and Albert. Had no
notion what the Queen had to do. Should think she hadn't such
power [he had first to ask me what 'power' was] as the Lord Mayor
or as Mr. Norton as was the Lambeth beak, and perhaps is still.
Was never once before a beak and didn't want to. Hated the
crushers; what business had they to interfere with him if he was
only resting his basket in a street? Had been once to the Wick, and

once to the Bower: liked tumbling better; he meant to have a little pleasure when the peas came in.

The knowledge and the ignorance of these two striplings represented that of street children generally. Those who may have run away from a good school, or a better sort of home as far as means constitute such betterness, of course form exceptions. So do the utterly stupid.

THE CRIPPLED STREET BIRD-SELLER

THE POOR man's deformity may be best understood by describing it in his own words: "I have no ankle." His right leg is emaciated, the bone is smaller than that of his other leg (which is not deformed), and there is no ankle joint. The joints of the wrists and shoulders are also defective, though not utterly wanting, as in the ankle. In walking this poor cripple seems to advance by means of a series of jerks. He uses his deformed leg, but must tread, or rather support his body, on the ball of the misformed foot, while he advances his sound leg; then, with a twist of his body, after he has advanced and stands upon his undeformed leg and foot, he throws forward the crippled part of his frame by the jerk I have spoken of. His arms are usually pressed against his ribs as he walks, and convey to a spectator the notion that he is unable to raise them from that position. This, however, is not the case; he can raise them, not as a sound man does, but with an effort and a contortion of his body to humour the effort. His speech is also defective, his words being brought out, as it were, by jerks; he has to prepare himself, and to throw up his chin, in order to converse, and then he speaks with difficulty. His face is sun-burnt and healthy-looking. His dress was a fustian coat with full skirts, cloth trousers somewhat patched, and a clean coarse shirt. His right shoe was suited to his deformity, and was strapped with a sort of leather belt around the lower part of the leg.

A considerable number of book-stall keepers, as well as coster-mongers, swag-barrowmen, ginger-beer and lemonade sellers, orange-women, sweet-stuff vendors, root-sellers, and others, have established their pitches — some of them having stalls with a cover, like a roof — from Whitechapel workhouse to the Mile End turn-pike-gate; near the gate they are congregated most thickly, and there they are mixed with persons seated on the forms belonging to adjacent innkeepers, which are placed there to allow any one to have his beer and tobacco in the open air. Among these street-sellers and beer-drinkers is seated the crippled bird-seller, generally motionless.

His home is near the Jew's burial-ground, and in one of the many "places" which by a misnomer, occasioned by the change in the character and appearance of what *were* the outskirts, are still called "Pleasant." On seeking him here, I had some little difficulty in finding the house, and asking a string of men, who were chopping firewood in an adjoining court, for the man I wanted, mentioning his name, no one knew anything about him; though when I spoke of his calling, "Oh," they said, "you want Old Billy." I then found Billy at his accustomed pitch, with a very small stock of birds in two large cages on the ground beside him, and he accompanied me to his residence. The room in which we sat had a pile of fire-wood opposite the door; the iron of the upper part of the door-latch being wanting was replaced by a piece of wood — and on the pile sat a tame jackdaw, with the inquisitive and askant look peculiar to the bird. Above the pile was a large cage, containing a jay — a bird seldom sold in the streets now — and a thrush in different compartments. A table, three chairs, and a hamper or two used in the wood-cutting, completed the furniture. Outside the house were cages containing larks, goldfinches, and a very fine starling, of whose promising abilities the bird-seller's sister had so favourable an opinion that she intended to try and teach it to talk, although that was very seldom done now.

The following is the statement I obtained from the poor fellow. The man's sister was present at his desire, as he was afraid I could not understand him, owing to the indistinctness of his speech; but that was easy enough, after awhile, with a little patience and attention.

"I was born a cripple, sir," he said, "and I shall die one. I was born at Lewisham, but I don't remember living in any place but London. I remember being at Stroud though, where my father had taken me, and bathed me often in the sea himself, thinking it might do me good. I've heard him say, too, that when I was very young he took me to almost every hospital in London, but it was of no use. My father and mother were as kind to me and as good parents as could be. He's been dead nineteen years, and my mother died before him. Father was poor, almost as poor as

I am. He worked in a brickfield, but work weren't regular. I couldn't walk at all until I was six years old, and I was between nine and ten before I could get up and down stairs by myself. I used to slide down before, as well as I could, and had to be carried up. When I could get about and went among other boys, I was in great distress, I was teased so. Life was a burthen to me, as I've read something about. They used to taunt me by offering to jump me" [invite him to a jumping match], "and to say, I'll run you a race on one leg. They were bad to me then, and they are now. I've sometimes sat down and cried, but not often. No, sir, I can't say that I ever wished I was dead. I hardly know why I cried, I suppose because I was miserable.

"I learned to read at a Sunday school, where I went a long time. I like reading. I read the Bible and tracts, nothing else; never a newspaper. It don't come in my way, and if it did I shouldn't look at it, for I can't read over well and it's nothing to me who's king or who's queen. It can never have anything to do with me. It don't take my attention. There'll be no change for me in this world. When I was thirteen my father put me into the bird trade. He knew a good many catchers. I've been bird-selling in the streets for six-and-twenty years and more, for I was 39 the 24th of last January. Father didn't know what better he could put me to, as I hadn't the right use of my hands or feet, and at first I did very well. I liked the birds and do still. I used to think at first that they was like me; they was prisoners, and I was a cripple. A first I sold birds in Poplar, and Limehouse, and Black-wall, and was a help to my parents, for I cleared 9s. or 10s. every week. But now, oh dear, I don't know where all the money's gone to. I think there's very little left in the country. I've sold larks, linnets, and goldfinches, to captains of ships to take to the West Indies. I've sold them, too, to go to Port Philip. O, and almost all those foreign parts. They bring foreign birds here, and take back London birds. I don't know anything about foreign birds. I know there's men dressed as sailors going about selling them; they're duffers — I mean the men. There's a neighbour of mine, that's very likely never been 20 miles out of London, and when he hawks birds he always dresses like a countryman, and duffs that way.

"When my father died," continued the man, "I was completely upset; everything in the world was upset. I was forced to go into the workhouse, and I was there between four and five months. O, I hated it. I'd rather live on a penny loaf a day than be in it again. I've never been near the parish since, though I've often had nothing to eat many a day. I'd rather be lamer than I am, and be oftener called silly Billy – and that sometimes makes me dreadful wild – than be in the workhouse. It was starvation, but then I know I'm a hearty eater, very hearty. Just now I know I could eat a shilling plate of meat, but for all that I very seldom taste meat. I live on bread and butter and tea, and sometimes bread without butter. When I have it I eat a quartern loaf at three meals. It depends upon how I'm off. My health's good. I never feel in any pain now; I did when I first got to walk, in great pain. Beer I often don't taste once in two or three months, and this very hot weather one can't help longing for a drop, when you see people drinking it all sides of you, but they have the use of their limbs."

[Here two little girls and a boy rushed into the room, for they had but to open the door from the outside, and, evidently to tease the poor fellow, loudly demanded "a ha'penny bird." When the sister had driven them away, my informant continued.] "I'm still greatly teased, sir, with children; yes, and with men too, both when they're drunk and sober. I think grown persons are the worst. They swear and use bad language to me. I'm sure I don't know why. I know no name they call me by in particular when I'm teased, if it isn't 'Old Hypocrite,' I can't say why they call me 'hypocrite.' I suppose because they know no better. Yes, I think I'm religious, rather. I would be more so, if I had clothes. I get to chapel sometimes." [A resident near the bird-seller's pitch, with whom I had some conversation, told me of "Billy" being sometimes teased in the way described. Some years ago, he believe it was at Limehouse, my informant heard a gentlemanly looking man, tipsy, d – n the street bird-seller for Mr. *Hobbler*, and bid him to go to the Mansion House, or to h – l. I asked the cripple about this, but he had no recollection of it; and, as he evidently did not understand the allusion to Mr. Hobbler, I was not surprised at his forgetfulness.]

"I like to sit out in the sunshine selling my birds," he said. "If it's rainy, and I can't go out, because it would be of no use, I'm moped to death. I stay at home and read a little; or I chop a little fire-wood, but you may be very sure, sir, it's little I can do that way. I never associate with the neighbours. I never had any pleasure, such as going to a fair, or like that. I don't remember having ever spent a penny in a place of amusement in my life. Yes I've often sat all day in the sun, and of course a deal of thoughts goes though my head. I think, shall I be able to afford myself plenty of bread when I get home? And I think of the next world sometimes, and feel quite sure, quite, that I shan't be a cripple there. Yes, that's a comfort, for this world will never be any good to me. I feel that I shall be a poor starving cripple, till I end, perhaps, in the workhouse. Other poor men can get married, but not such as me. But I never was in love in my life, never." [Among the vagrants and beggars, I may observe, there are men more terribly deformed than the bird-seller, who are married, or living in concubinage.] "Yes, sir," he proceeded, "I'm quite reconciled to my lameness, quite; and have been for years. O, no, I never fret about that now; but about starving, perhaps, and the work-house.

"Before father died, the parish allowed us 1s. 6d. and a quartern loaf a week; but after he was buried, they'd allow me nothing; they'd only admit me into the house. I hadn't a penny allowed to me when I discharged myself and came out. I hardly know how ever I *did* manage to get a start again with the birds. I knew a good many catchers, and they trusted me. Yes, they was all poor men. I did pretty tidy by bits, but only when it was fine weather, until these five years or so, when things got terrible bad. Particularly just the two last years with me. Do you think times are likely to mend, sir, with poor people? If working-men had only money, they'd buy innocent things like birds to amuse them at home; but if they can't get the money, as I've heard them say when they've been pricing my stock, why in course they can't spend it."

"Yes, indeed," said the sister, "trade's very bad. When my husband and I once earned 18s. at the fire-wood, and then 15s., we can't now earn 12s. the two of us, slave as hard as we will. I always dread the winter a-coming. Though there may be more fire-wood wanted, there's greater expenses, and it's a terrible time for such as us."

"I dream sometimes, sir," the cripple resumed in answer to my question, "but not often. I often have more than once dreamed I was starving and dying of hunger. I remember that, for I woke in a tremble. But most dreams is soon forgot. I've never seemed to myself to be a cripple in my dreams. Well, I can't explain how, but I feel as if my limbs was all free like — so beautiful. I dream most about starving, I think, than about anything else. Perhaps that's when I have to go to sleep hungry. I sleep very well, though, take it altogether. If I had only plenty to live upon there would be nobody happier. I'm happy enough when times is middling with me, only one feels it won't last. I like a joke as well as anybody when times is good; but that's been very seldom lately.

"It's all small birds I sell in the street now, except at a very odd time. That jackdaw there, sir, he's a very fine bird. I've tamed him myself, and he's as tame as a dog. My sister's a very good hand among birds, and helps me. She once taught a linnet to say 'Joey' as plain as you can speak it yourself, sir. I buy birds of different catchers, but haven't money to buy the better kinds, as I have to sell at 3d. and 4d. and 6d. mostly. If I had a pound to lay out in a few nice cages and good birds, I think I could do middling, this fine weather particler, for I'm a very good judge of birds, and know how to manage them as well as anybody. Then birds is rather dearer to buy than they was when I was first in the trade. The catchers have to go further, and I'm afeared the birds is getting scarcer, and so there's more time taken up. I buy of several catchers.

"The last whole day that I was at my pitch I sold nine birds, and took about 3s. If I could buy birds ever so cheap, there's always such losses by their dying. I've had three parts of my young linnets die, do what I might, but not often so many. Then if they die all the food they've had is lost. There goes all for nothing the rape and flax-seed for your linnets, canary and flax for your goldfinches, chopped eggs for your nightingales, and German paste for your sky-larks. I've made my own German paste when I've wanted a sufficient quantity. It's made of pea-meal, treacle, hog's-lard, and moss-seed. I sell more goldfinches than anything else. I used to sell a good many sparrows for shooting, but I haven't done anything that way these eight or nine years. It's a fash'nable sport still, I hear. I've reared nightingales that sung beautiful, and have sold them at 4s. a piece, which was very cheap. They often die when the time for their departure comes. A shopkeeper as supplied such as I've sold would have charged £1 a piece for them. One of my favouritest birds is redpoles, but they're only sold in the season. I think it's one of the most knowingest little birds that is; more knowing than the goldfinch, in my opinion.

"My customers are all working people, all of them. I sell to nobody else; I make 4s. or 5s.; I call 5s. a good week at this time of year, when the weather suits. I lodge with a married sister; her husband's a wood-chopper, and I pay 1s. 6d. a week, which is cheap, for I've no sticks of my own. If I earn 4s. there's only 2s. 6d. left to live on the week through. In winter, when I can make next to nothing, and must keep my birds, it is terrible—oh yes, sir, if you believe me, terrible!"

A STREET-ORDERLY

THE STREET-ORDERLY system forms part of the operations on be-half of the poor adopted by a society, of which Mr. Charles Coch-rane is the president, entitled the "National Philanthropic Asso-ciation," which is said to have for its object "the promotion of social and salutiferous improvements, street cleanliness, and the employment of the poor, so that able-bodied men may be pre-vented from burthening the parish-rate, and preserved inde-pendent of workhouse, alms, and degradation."

"The orderlies," says the Report of the Association, "keep the streets free from mud in winter, and dust in summer; and that with the least possible personal drudgery; adhering to the prin-ciple of operation laid down, viz., that of '*Cleansing and keeping Clean,*' they have merely, after each morning's sweeping and removal of dirt, to keep a vigilant look-out over the surface of street allotted to them; and to remove with the hand-brush and dust-pan, from any particular spot, whatever dirt or rubbish may fall upon it, *at the moment of its deposit.* Thus are the streets under their care kept constantly clean.

"But sweeping and removing dirt," continues the Report, "is not the only occupation of the street-orderly, whilst keeping up a careful inspection of the ground allotted to him. He is also the watchman of house-property and shop-goods; the guardian of reticules, pocket-books, purses, and watch-pockets;—the experi-enced observer and detector of pickpockets; the ever ready, though unpaid, auxiliary to the police constable. Nay, more;—he is always at hand, to render assistance to both equestrian and pedestrian; if a horse slip, stumble, or fall,—if a carriage break down, or vehicles come into collision,—the street-orderly darts forward to raise and rectify them: if foot-passengers be run over, or knocked down, or incautiously loiter on a crossing, the street-orderly rescues them from peril or death; or warns them of the approaching danger of carriages driving in opposite directions: if other accidents befall pedestrians,—if they fall on the pavement, from sudden illness, faintness, or apoplexy, the street-orderly is at hand to render assistance, or convey them to the nearest surgery or hospital. If strangers are at fault as to the localities of London, or the place of their destination, the orderly, in a civil and respectful manner, directs them on their way. If habitual or professional mendicants are importunate or troublesome, the street-orderly warns them off; or hands them to the care of the policeman. And if a *really* poor or starving fellow-creature wanders in search of food or alms, he leads them to a workhouse or soup-kitchen."

I now give the following account from one of the street-orderlies, a tall, soldierly-looking man:—

"I'm 42 now," he said, "and when I was a boy and a young man I was employed in *The Times* machine office, but I got into a bit of a row—a bit of a street quarrel and frolic, and was called on to pay £3, something about a street-lamp: that was out of the question; and as I was taking a walk in the park, not just knowing what I'd best do, I met a recruiting sergeant, and enlisted on a sudden—all on a sudden—in the 16th Lancers. When I came to the standard, though, I was found a little bit too short. Well, I was rather frolicsome in those days, I confess, and perhaps *had rather a turn for a roving life*, so when the sergeant said he'd take me to the East India Company's recruiting sergeant, I consented, and was accepted at once. I was taken to Calcutta, and served under General Nott all through the Afghan war. I was in the East India Company's artillery, 4th company and 2nd battalion. Why, yes, sir, I saw a little of a what you may call 'service.' I was at the fighting at Candahar, Bowlinglen, Bowling-pass, Clatigillsy, Ghuznee, and Caboul. The first real warm work I was in was at Candahar. I've heard young soldiers say that they've gone into action the first time as merry as they would go to a play. Don't believe them, sir. Old soldiers will tell you quite different. You *must* feel queer and serious the first time you're in action: it's not fear—it's nervousness. The crack of the muskets at the first fire you hear in real hard earnest is uncommon startling; you see the flash of the fire from the enemy's line, but very little else. Indeed, oft enough you see nothing but smoke, and hear nothing but balls whistling every side of you. And then you get excited, just as if

STREET ORDERLIES

you were at a hunt; but after a little service — I can speak for myself, at any rate — you go into action as you go to your dinner.

"I served during the time when there was the Afghanistan retreat; when the 44th was completely cut up, before any help could get up to them. We suffered a good deal from want of sufficient food; but it was nothing like so bad, at the very worst, as if you're suffering in London. In India, in that war time, if you suffered, you were along with a number in just the same boat as yourself; and there's always something to hope for when you're in army. It's different if you're walking the streets of London by yourself — I felt it, sir, for a little bit after my return — and if you haven't a penny, you feel as if there wasn't a hope. If you have friends it may be different, but I had none. It's no comfort if you know hundreds are suffering as you are, for you can't help and cheer one another as soldiers can.

"Well, sir, as I've told you, I saw a good deal of service all through that war. Indeed I served thirteen years and four months, and was then discharged on account of ill health. If I'd served eight months longer that would have been fourteen years, and I should have been entitled to a pension. I believe my illness was caused by the hardships I went through in the campaigns, fighting and killing men that I never saw before, and until I was in India had never heard of, and that I had no ill-will to; certainly not, why should I? they never did me any wrong. But when it comes to war, if you can't kill them they'll kill you. When I got back to London I applied at the East India House for a pension, but was refused. I hadn't served my time, though that wasn't my fault.

"I then applied for work in *The Times* machine office, and they were kind enough to put me on. But I wasn't master of the work, for there was new machinery, wonderful machinery, and a many changes. So I couldn't be kept on, and was some time out of work, and very badly off, as I've said before, and then I got work as a scavenger. O, I knew nothing about sweeping before that. I'd never swept anything except the snow in the north of India, which is quite a different sort of thing to London dirt. But I very soon got into the way of it. I found no difficulty about it, though some may pretend there is an art in it. I had 15s. a week, and when I was no longer wanted I got employment as a street-orderly. I never was married, and have only myself to provide for. I'm satisfied that the street-orderly is far the best plan for street-cleaning. Nothing else can touch it, in my opinion, and I thought so before I was one of them, and I believe most working scavengers think so now, though they mayn't like to say so, for fear it might go against their interest.

"Oh, yes, I'm sometimes questioned by gentlemen that may be passing in the streets while I'm at work, all about our system. They generally say, 'and a very good system, too.' One said once, 'It shows that scavengers can be decent men; they weren't when I was first in London, above 40 years ago.' Well, I sometimes get the price of a pint of beer given to me by gentlemen making inquiries, but very seldom."

THE MASTER SWEEPERS

I CAN supply the following account of two. The soot, I should observe, is seldom kept long, rarely a month, on the premises of a sweeper, and is in the best "concerns" kept in cellars.

The localities in which many of the sweepers reside are the "lowest" places in the district. Many of the houses in which I found the lower class of sweepers were in a ruinous and filthy condition. The "high-class" sweepers, on the other hand, live in respectable localities, often having back premises sufficiently large to stow away their soot.

I had occasion to visit the house of one of the persons from whom I obtained much information. He is a master in a small way, a sensible man, and was one of the few who are teetotallers. His habitation, though small — being a low house only one story high — was substantially furnished with massive mahogany chairs, table, chests of drawers, &c., while on each side of the fire-place, which was distinctly visible from the street over a hall door, were two buffets, with glass doors, well filled with glass and china vessels. It was a wet night, and a fire burned brightly in the stove, by the light of which might be seen the master of the establishment sitting on one side, while his wife and daughter occupied the other; a neighbour sat before the fire with his back to the door, and altogether it struck me as a comfortable-looking evening party. They were resting and chatting quietly together after the labour of the day, and everything betokened the comfortable circumstances in which the man, by sobriety and industry, had been able to place himself. Yet this man had been a climbing-boy, and one of the unfortunates who had lost his parents when a child, and was apprenticed by the parish to this business. From him I learned that his was not a solitary instance of teetotalism (I have before spoken of another); that, in fact, there were some more, and one in particular named Brown, who was a good speaker, and devoted himself during his leisure hours at night in advocating the principles which by experience he had found to effect such great good to himself; but he also informed me that the majority of the others were a drunken and dissipated crew, sunk to the lowest degree of misery, yet recklessly spending every farthing they could earn in the public-house.

Different in every respect was another house which I visited in the course of my inquiries, in the neighbourhood of H—— -street, Bethnal-green. The house was rented by a sweeper, a master on his own account, and every room in the place was let to sweepers and their wives or women, which, with these men, often signify one and the same thing. The inside of the house looked as dark as a coal-pit; there was an insufferable smell of soot, always offensive to those unaccustomed to it; and every person and every thing which met the eye, even to the caps and gowns of the women, seemed as if they had just been steeped in Indian ink. In one room was a sweep and his woman quarrelling. As I opened the door I caught the words, "I'm d—d if I has it any longer. I'd see you b—y well d—d first, and you knows it." The savage was intoxicated, and his red eyes flashed though his sooty mask with drunken excitement, and his matted hair, which looked as though it had never known a comb, stood out from his head like the whalebone ribs of his own machine. "B—y Bet," as he called her, did not seem a whit more sober than her man; and the shrill treble of her voice was distinctly audible till I turned the corner of the street, whither I was accompanied by the master of the house, to whom I had been recommended by one of the fraternity as an intelligent man, and one who knew "a thing or two." "You see," he said, as we turned the corner, "there isn't no use a talkin' to them ere fellows—they're all tosticated now, and they doesn't care nothink for nobody; but they'll be quiet enough to-morrow, 'cept they yarns somethink, and if they do then they'll be just as bad to-morrow night. They're a awful lot, and nobody ill niver do anythink with them." This man was not by any means in such easy circumstances as the master first mentioned. He was merely a man working for himself, and unable to employ any one else in the business; as is customary with some of these people, he had taken the house he had shown me to let to lodgers of his own class, making something by so doing; though, if his own account be correct, I'm at a loss to imagine how he contrived even to get his rent. From him I obtained the following statement: —

"Yes, I was a climbing-boy, and sarved a rigler printiceship for seven years. I was out on my printiceship when I was fourteen. Father was a silk-weaver, and did all he knew to keep me from being a sweep, but I would be a sweep, and nothink else." [This is not so very uncommon a predilection, strange as it may seem.] So father, when he saw it was no use, got me bound printice. Father's alive now, and near 90 years of age. I don't know why I wished to be a sweep, 'cept it was this — there was sweeps always lived about here, and I used to see the boys with lots of money a tossin' and gamblin', and wished to have money too. You see they got money where they swept the chimneys; they used to get 2d. or 3d. for theirselves in a day, and sometimes 6d. from the people of the house, and that's the way they always had plenty of money. I niver thought anythink of the climbing; it wasn't so bad at all as some people would make you believe. There are two or three ways of climbing. In wide flues you climb with your elbows and your legs spread out, your feet pressing against the sides of the flue; but in narrow flues, such as nine-inch ones, you must slant it; you must have your sides in the angles, it's wider there, and go up just that way." [Here he threw himself into position — placing one arm close to his side, with the palm of the hand turned outwards, as if pressing the side of the flue, and extending the other arm high above his head, the hand apparently pressing in the same manner.] "There," he continued, "that's slantin'. You just put yourself in that way, and see how small you make yourself. I niver got to stay stuck myself, but a many of them did; yes, and were taken out dead. They were smothered for want of air, and the fright, and a stayin' so long in the flue; you see the waistband of their trousers sometimes got turned down in the climbing, and in narrow flues, when not able to get it up, then they stuck. I had a boy once — we were called to sweep a chimney down at Poplar. When we went in he looked up the flues, 'Well, what is it like?' I said. 'Very narrow,' says he, 'don't think I can get up there;' so after some time we gets on top of the house, and takes off the chimney-pot, and has a look down — it was wider a' top, and I thought as how he could go down. 'You had better buff it, Jim,' says I.

I suppose you know what that means; but Jim wouldn't do it, and kept his trousers on. So down he goes, and gets on very well till he comes to the shoulder of the flue, and then he couldn't stir. He shouts down. 'I'm stuck.' I shouts up and tells him what to do. 'Can't move,' says he, 'I'm stuck hard and fast.' Well, the people of the house got fretted like, but I says to them, 'Now my boy's stuck, but for Heaven's sake don't make a word of noise; don't say a word, good or bad, and I'll see what I can do.' So I locks the door, and buffs it, and forces myself up till I could reach him with my hand, and as soon as he got his foot on my hand he begins to prize himself up, and gets loosened, and comes out at the top again. I was stuck myself, but I was stronger nor he, and I manages to get out again. Now I'll be bound to say if there was another master there as would kick up a row and a-worrited, that ere boy 'ud a niver come out o' that ere flue alive. There was a many o' them lost their lives in that way. Most all the printices used to come from the 'House' [workhouse]. There was nobody to care for them, and some masters used them very bad. I was out of my time at fourteen, and began to get too stout to go up the flues; so after knockin' about a year or so, as I could do nothink else, I goes to sea on board a man-o'-war, and was away four year. Many of the boys, when they got too big and useless, used to go to sea in them days — they couldn't do nothink else. Yes, many of them went for sodgers; and I know some who went for gipsies, and others who went for play-actors, and a many who got on to be swell-mobsmen, and thieves, and housebreakers, and the like o' that ere. There ain't nothink o'that sort a-goin' on now since the Ack of Parliament. When I got back from sea father asked me to larn his business; so I takes to the silk-weaving and larned it, and then married a weaveress, and worked with father for a long time. Father was very well off — well off and comfortable for a poor man — but trade was good then. But it got bad afterwards, and none on us was able to live at it; so I takes to the chimney-sweeping again. *A man might manage to live somehow at the sweeping, but the weaving was o' no use.* It was the furrin silks as beat us all up, that's the whole truth. Yet they tells us as how they was a-doin' the country good; but they may tell that to the marines — the sailors won't believe it — not a word on it. I've stuck to the sweeping ever since, and sometimes done very fair at it; but since the Ack there's so many leeks come to it that I don't know how they live—they must be eatin' one another up.

"Well, since you ask then, I can tell you that our people don't care much about law; they don't understand anythink about politics much; they don't mind things o' that ere kind. They only minds to get drunk when they can. Some on them fellows as you seed in there niver cleans their selves from one year's end to the other. They'll kick up a row soon enough, with Chartists or anybody else. I thinks them Chartists are a weak-minded set; they was too much a frightened at nothink,—a hundred o' them would run away from one blue-coat, and that wasn't like men. I was often at Chartist meetings, and if they'd only do all they said there was a plenty to stick to them, for there's somethink wants to be done very bad, for everythink is a-gettin' worser and worser every day. I used to do a good trade, but now I don't yarn a shilling a day all through the year. I may walk at this time three or four moles and not get a chimney to sweep, and then get only a sixpence or threepence, and sometimes nothink. It's a starvin', that's what it is; there's so much 'querying' a-goin' on. Querying? that's what we calls underworking.[1] If they'd all fix a riglar price we might do very well still. I'm 50 years of age or thereabouts."

Some years back the sweepers' houses were often indicated by an elaborate sign, highly coloured. A sweeper, accompanied by a "chummy" (once a common name for the climbing-boy, being a corruption of chimney), was depicted on his way to a red brick house, from the chimneys of which bright yellow flames were streaming. Below was the detail of the things undertaken by the sweep, such as the extinction of fires in chimneys, the cleaning of smoke-jacks, &c., &c. A few of these signs, greatly faded, may be seen still. A sweeper, who is settled in what is accounted a "genteel neighbourhood," has now another way of making his calling known. He leaves a card whenever he hears of a new comer, a tape being attached, so that it can be hung up in the kitchen, and thus the servants are always in possession of this address. The following is a customary style:—

---

[1] Querying means literally inquiring or asking for work at the different houses. The "queriers" among the sweeps are a kind of pedler operatives.

"Chimneys swept by the improved machine, much patronized by the Humane Society.

"W. H., Chimney Sweeper and Nightman, 1, —— Mews, in returning thanks to the inhabitants of the surrounding neighbourhood for the patronage he has hitherto received, begs to inform them that he sweeps all kinds of chimneys and flues in the best manner.

"W. H. attending to the business himself, cleans smoke-jacks, cures smoky coppers, and extinguishes chimneys when on fire, with the greatest care and safety; and, by giving the strictest personal attendance to business, performs what he undertakes with cleanliness and punctuality, whereby he hopes to ensure a continuance of their favours and recommendations.

"Clean cloths for upper apartments. Soot-doors to any size fixed. Observe the address, 1, —— Mews, near ——."

At the top of this card is an engraving of the machine; at the foot a rude sketch of a nightman's cart, with men at work. All the cards I saw reiterated the address, so that no mistake might lead the customer to a rival tradesman.

A CESSPOOL-SEWERMAN

I GIVE the following brief and characteristic statement, which is peculiar in showing the habitual *restlessness* of the mere labourer. My informant was a stout, hale-looking man, who had rarely known illness. All these sort of labourers (nightmen included) scout the notion of the cholera attacking *them!*

"Work, sir? Well, I think I *do* know what work is, and has known it since I was a child; and then I was set to help at the weaving. My friends were weavers at Norwich and, 26 years ago, until steam pulled working men down from being well paid and well off, it was a capital trade. Why, my father could sometimes earn £3 at his work as a working weaver; there was money for ever then; now 12s. a-week is, I believe, the tip-top earnings of his trade. But *I didn't like the confinement or the close air in the factories,* and so, when I grew big enough, I went to ground-work in the city [so he frequently called Norwich]; I call ground-work such as digging drains and the like. Then I 'listed in the Marines. *Oh, I hardly know what made me;* men does foolish things and don't know why; it's human nature. I'm sure it wasn't the bounty of £3 that tempted me, for I was doing middling, and sometimes had night-work as well as ground-work to do. I was then sent to Sheerness and put on board the *Thunderer* man-of-war, carrying 84 guns, as a marine. She sailed through the Straits [of Gibraltar], and was three years and three months blockading the Dardanelles, and cruising among the islands. I never saw anything like such fortifications as at the Dardanelles; why, there was mortars there as would throw a ton weight. No, I never heard of their having been fired.

"Yes, we sometimes got leave for a party to go ashore on one of the islands. They called them Greek islands, but I fancy as how it was Turks near the Dardanelles. O yes, the men on the islands was civil enough to us; they never spoke to us, and we never spoke to them. The sailors sometimes, and indeed the lot of us, would have bits of larks with them, laughing at 'em and taking sights at 'em and such like. Why, I've seen a fine-dressed Turk, one of their grand gentlemen there, when a couple of sailors has each been taking a sight at him, and dancing the shuffle along with it, make each on 'em a low bow, as solemn as could be. Perhaps he thought it was a way of being civil in our country! I've seen some of the head ones stuck over with so many knives, and cutlasses, and belts, and pistols, and things, that he looked like a cutler's shop-window. We were ordered home at last, and after being months in barracks, which I didn't relish at all, were paid off at Plymouth. Oh, a barrack life's anything but pleasant, but I've done with it. After that I was eight years and a quarter a gentleman's servant, coachman, or anything [in Norwich], and then got tired of that and came to London, and got to ground and new sewer-work, and have been on the sewers above five years.

"Yes, I prefer the sewers to the Greek islands. I was one of the first set as worked a pump. There was a great many spectators; I dare say as there was 40 skientific gentlemen. I've been on the sewers, flushing and pumping, ever since. The houses we clean out, all says it's far the best plan, ours is. 'Never no more night-men,' they say. You see, sir, our plan's far less trouble to the people in the house, and there's no smell — least I never found no smell, and it's cheap, too. In time the nightmen'll disappear; in course they must, there's so many new dodges comes up, always some one of the working classes is a being ruined. If it ain't steam, it's something else as knocks the bread out of their mouths quite as quick."

THE BEARDED CROSSING-SWEEPER
AT THE EXCHANGE

SINCE the destruction by fire of the Royal Exchange in 1838, there has been added to the curiosities of Cornhill a thickset, sturdy, and hirsute crossing-sweeper — a man who is as civil by habit as he is independent by nature. He has a long flowing beard, grey as wood smoke, and a pair of fierce moustaches giving a patriarchal air of importance to a marked and observant face, which often serves as a painter's model. After half-an-hour's conversation, you are forced to admit that his looks do not all belie him, and that the old mariner (for such was his profession formerly) is worthy in some measure of his beard.

He wears an old felt hat — very battered and discoloured; around his neck, which is bared in accordance with sailor custom, he has a thick blue cotton neckerchief tied in a sailor's knot; his long iron-grey beard is accompanied by a healthy and almost ruddy face. He stands against the post all day, saying nothing, and taking what he can get without solicitation.

When I first spoke to him he wanted to know to what purpose I intended applying the information that he was prepared to afford, and it was not until I agreed to walk with him as far as St. Mary-Axe that I was enabled to obtain his statement, as follows:

"I've had this crossing ever since '38. The Exchange was burnt down in that year. Why, sir, I was wandering about trying to get a crust, and it was very sloppy, so I took and got a broom; and while I kept a clean crossing, I used to get ha'pence and pence. I got a dockman's wages — that's half-a-crown a-day; sometimes only a shilling and sometimes more. I have taken a crown — but that's very rare. The best customers I had is dead. I used to make a good Christmas, but I don't now. I have taken a pound or thirty shillings, then in the old times.

"I smoke, sir; I *will* have tobacco, if I can't get grub. My old woman takes cares that I have tobacco.

"I have been a sailor, and the first ship as ever I was in was the Old Colossus, 74, but we was only cruising about the Channel then, and took two prizes. I went aboard the Old Remewa guard-ship—we were turned over to her—and from her I was drafted over to the Escramander frigate. We went out chasing Boney, but he gived himself up to the Old Impregnable. I was at the taking of Algiers, in 1816, in the Superb. I was in the Rochfort, 74, up the Mediterranean (they call it up the Mediterranean, but it was the Malta station) three years, ten months, and twenty days, until the ship was paid off.

"Then I went to work at the Dockyard. I had a misfortune soon after that. I fell out of a garret window, three stories high, and that kept me from going to the Docks again. I lost all my top teeth by that fall. I've got a scar here, one on my chin but I warn't in the hospital more than two weeks.

"I was afeard of being taken up solicitin' charity, and I knew that sweeping was a safe game; they couldn't take me up for sweeping a crossing.

"Sometimes I gets insulted, only in words; sometimes I get chaffed by sober people. Drunken men I don't care for; I never listen to 'em, unless they handle me, and then, although I am sixty-three this very day, sir, I think I could show them some-thing. I *do* carry my age well; and if you could ha' seen how I have lived this last winter through, sometimes one pound of bread between two of us, you'd say I was a strong man to be as I am.

"Those who think that sweepin' a crossing is idle work, make a great mistake. In wet weather, the traffic that makes it gets slop-py as soon as it's cleaned. Cabs and 'buses, and carriages contin-ually going over the crossing must scatter the mud on it, and you must look precious sharp to keep it clean; but when I once get in the road, I never jump out of it. I keeps my eye both way, and if I gets in too close quarters, I slips round the wheels. I've had them almost touch me.

"No, sir, I never got knocked down. In foggy weather, of course, it's no use sweeping at all.

"Parcels! it's very few parcels I get to carry now; I don't think I get a parcel to carry once in a month: there's 'buses and rail-ways so cheap. A man would charge as much for a distance as a cab would take them.

"I don't come to the same crossing on Sundays; I go to the

The Bearded Crossing-Sweeper at the Exchange

corner of Finch-lane. As to regular customers, I've none — to say regular; some give me sixpence now and then. All those who used to give me regular are dead.

"I was a-bed when the Exchange was burnt down.

"I have had this beard five years. I grew it to sit to artists when I got the chance; but it don't pay expenses — for I have to walk four or five miles, and only get a shilling an hour: besides, I'm often kept nearly two hours, and I get nothing for going and nothing for coming, but just for the time I am there.

"Afore I wore it, I had a pair of large whiskers. I went to a gentleman then, an artist, and he *did* pay me well. He advised me to grow mustarshers and the beard, but he hasn't employed me since.

"They call me 'Old Jack' on the crossing, that's all they call me. I get more chaff from the boys than anyone else. They only say, 'Why don't you get shaved?' but I take no notice on 'em.

"Old Bill, in Lombard Street; I knows him; he used to make a good thing of it, but I don't think he makes much now.

"My wife — I am married, sir — doesn't do anything. I live in a lodging-house, and I pay three shillings a-week.

"I tell you what we has, now, when I go home. We has a pound of bread, a quarter of an ounce of tea, and perhaps a red herring.

"I've had a weakness in my legs for two years; the veins comes down, but I keep a bandage in my pocket, and when I feels' em coming down, I puts the bandage on 'till the veins goes up again — it's through being on my legs so long (because I had very strong legs when young) and want of good food. When you only have a bit of bread and a cup of tea — no meat, no vegetables — you find it out; but I'm as upright as a dart, and as lissom as ever I was.

"I gives threepence for my brooms. I wears out three in a week in the wet weather. I always leans very hard on my broom, 'specially when the mud is sticky — as it is after the roads is watered. I am very particular about my brooms; I gives 'em away to be burned when many another would use them."

THE CROSSING-SWEEPER WHO HAD BEEN
A SERVANT-MAID

SHE IS to be found any day between eight in the morning and
seven in the evening, sweeping away in a convulsive, jerky sort of
manner, close to —— square, near the Foundling. She may be
known by her pinched-up straw bonnet, with a broad, faded, almost colourless ribbon. She has weak eyes, and wears over them
a brownish shade. Her face is tied up, because of a gathering
which she has on her head. She wears a small, old plaid cloak, a
clean checked apron, and a tidy printed gown.

She is rather shy at first, but willing and obliging enough withal;
and she lives down Little —— Yard, in Great —— street. The
"yard" that is made like a mousetrap — small at the entrance, but
amazingly large inside, and dilapidated though extensive.

Here are stables and a couple of blind alleys, nameless, or bearing the same name as the yard itself, and wherein are huddled
more people than one could count in a quarter of an hour, and
more children than one likes to remember, — dirty children, list-
lessly trailing an old tin baking-dish, or a worn-out shoe, tied to
a piece of string; sullen children, who turn away in a fit of sleepy
anger if spoken to; screaming children, setting all the parents in
the "yard" at defiance; and quiet children, who are arranging
banquets of dirt in the reeking gutters.

The "yard" is devoted principally to costermongers.

The crossing-sweeper lives in the top-room of a two-storied
house, in the very depth of the blind alley at the end of the yard.
She has not even a room to herself, but pays one shilling a-week
for the privilege of sleeping with a woman who gets her living
by selling tapes in the streets.

"Ah!" says the sweeper, "poor woman, she ̄has a hard time of
it; her husband is in the hospital with a bad leg, — in fact, he's
scarcely ever out. If you could hear that woman cough, you'd
never forget it. She would have had to starve to-day if it hadn't

been for a person who actually lent her a gown to pledge to raise her stock-money, poor thing."

The room in which these people live has a sloping roof, and a small-paned window on each side. For furniture, there were two chairs and a shaky, three-legged stool, a deal table, and a bed rolled up against the wall—nothing else. In one corner of the room lay the last lump remaining of the seven pounds of coals. In another corner there were herbs in pans, and two water-bottles without their noses. The most striking thing in that little room was some crockery the woman had managed to save from the wreck of her things; among this, curiously enough, was a soup-tureen, with its lid not even cracked.

There *was* a piece of looking-glass—a small three-cornered piece—forming an almost equilateral triangle,—and the oldest, and most rubbed and worn-out piece of a mirror that ever escaped the dust-bin.

The fireplace was a very small one, and on the table were two or three potatoes and about one-fifth of a red herring, which the poor street-seller had saved out of her breakfast to serve for her supper. "Take my solemn word for it, sir," said the sweeper, "and I wouldn't deceive you, that is all she will get besides a cup of weak tea when she comes home tired at night."

The statement of this old sweeper is as follows:—

"My name is Mary ——. I live in —— yard. I live with a person of the name of ——, in the back attic; she gets her living by selling flowers in pots in the street, but she is now doing badly. I pay her a shilling a-week.

"My parents were Welsh. I was in service, or maid-of-all-work, till I got married. My husband was a seafaring man when I married him. After we were married, he got his living by selling memorandum-almanack books, and the like, about the streets. He was driven to that because he had no trade in his hand, and he was obliged to do something for a living. He did not make much, and over-exertion, with want of nourishment, brought on a para-lytic stroke. He had the first fit about two years before he had the second; the third fit, which was the last, he had on the Monday and died on the Wednesday week. I have two children still living. One of them is married to a poor man, who gets his living in the streets; but as far as lays in his power he makes a good husband and father. My other daughter is living with a niece of mine, for I can't keep her, sir; she minds the children.

"My father was a journeyman shoemaker. He was killed; but I cannot remember how — I was too young. I can't recollect my mother. I was brought up by an uncle and aunt till I was able to go to service. I went out to service at five, to mind children under a nurse, and I was in service till I got married. I had a great many situations; you see, sir, I was forced to keep in place, because I had nowhere to go to, my uncle and aunt not being able to keep me. I was never in noblemen's families, only tradespeople's. Service was very hard, sir, and so I believe it continues.

"I am fifty-five years of age, and I have been on the crossing fourteen years; but just now it is very poor work indeed. Well, if I wishes for bad weather, I'm only like other people, I suppose. I have no regular customers at all; the only one I had left has lost his senses, sir. Mr. H ——, he used to allow us sixpence a-week; but he went mad, and we don't get it now. By us, I mean the three crossing-sweepers in the square where I work.

"Indeed, I like the winter-time, for the families is in. Though the weather is more severe, yet you *do* get a few more ha'pence. I take more from the staid elderly people than from the young. At Christmas, I think I took about eleven shillings, but certainly not more. The most I ever made at that season was fourteen shillings. The worst about Christmas is, that those who give much then generally hold their hand for a week or two.

"A shilling a-day would be as much as I want, sir. I have stood in the square all day for a ha'penny, and I have stood here for nothing. One week with another, I make two shillings in the seven days, after paying for my broom. I have taken threepence ha'penny to-day. Yesterday — let me see — well, it was threepence ha'penny, too; Monday, I don't remember; but Sunday I recollet — it was fippence ha'penny. Years ago I made a great deal more — nearly three times as much.

"I come about eight o'clock in the morning, and go away about six or seven; I am here every day. The boys used to come at one time with their brooms, but they're not allowed here now by the police.

"I should not think crossings worth purchasing, unless people made a better living on them than I do."

I gave the poor creature a small piece of silver for her trouble, and asked her if that, with the threepence halfpenny, made a good day. She answered heartily —

"I should like to see such another day to-morrow, sir.

"Yes, winter is very much better than summer, only for the trial of standing in the frost and snow, but we certainly *do* get more then. The families won't be in town for three months to come yet. Ah! this neighbourhood is nothing to what it was. By God's removal, and by their own removal, the good families are all gone. The present families are not so liberal nor so wealthy. It is not the richest people that give the most. Tradespeople, and 'specially gentlefolks who have situations, are better to me than the nobleman who rides in his carriage.

"I always go to Trinity Church, Gray's-inn-road, about two doors from the Welsh School — the Rev. Dr. Witherington preaches there. I always go on Sunday afternoon and evening, for I can't go in the morning; I can't get away from my crossing in time. I never omit a day in coming here, unless I'm ill, or the snows is too heavy, or the weather too bad, and then I'm obliged to resign.

"I have no friends, sir, only my children; my uncle and aunt have been dead a long time. I go to see my children on Sunday, or in the evening, when I leave here.

"After I leave I have a cup of tea, and after that I go to bed; very frequently I'm in bed at nine o'clock. I have my cup of tea if I can anyway get it; but I'm forced to go without *that* sometimes.

"When my sight was better, I used to be very partial to reading; but I can't see the print, sir, now. I used to read the Bible, and the newspapers. Story-books I have read, too, but not many novels. Yes, *Robinson Crusoe* I know, but not the *Pilgrim's Progress*. I've heard of it; they tell me it is a very interesting book to read, but I never had it. We never have any ladies or Scripture-readers come to our lodgings; you see, we're so out, they might come a dozen times and not find us at home.

"I wear out three brooms in a week; but in the summer one will last a fortnight. I give threepence ha'penny for them; there are twopenny-ha'penny brooms, but they are not so good, they are liable to have their handles come out. It is very fatiguing standing so many hours; my legs aches with pain, and swells. I was once in Middlesex Hospital for sixteen weeks with my legs. My eyes have been weak from a child. I have got a gathering in my head from catching cold standing on the crossing. I had the fever this time twelvemonth. I laid a fortnight and four days at home, and seven weeks in the hospital. I took the diarrhoea after that, and was six weeks under the doctor's hands. I used to do odd jobs, but my health won't permit me now. I used to make two or three shillings a-week by 'em, and get scraps and things. But I get no broken victuals now.

"I never get anything from servants; they don't get more than they know what to do with.

"I don't get a drop of beer once in a month.

"I don't know but what this being out may be the best thing, after all; for if I was at home all my time, it would not agree with me."

JIMMY SHAW

THE PROPRIETOR of one of the largest sporting public-houses in London, who is celebrated for the rat-matches which come off weekly at his establishment, was kind enough to favour me with a few details as to the quality of those animals which are destroyed in his pit. His statement was certainly one of the most curious that I have listened to, and it was given to me with a readiness and a courtesy of manner such as I have not often met with during my researches. The landlord himself is known in pugilistic circles as one of the most skilful boxers among what is termed the "light weights."

His statement is curious, as a proof of the large trade which is carried on in these animals, for it would seem that the men who make a business of catching rats are not always employed as "exterminators," for they make a good living as "purveyors" for supplying the demands of the sporting portion of London.

"The poor people," said the sporting landlord, "who supply me with rats, are what you may call barn-door labouring poor, for they are the most ignorant people I ever come near. Really you would not believe people could live in such ignorance. Talk about Latin and Greek, sir, why English is Latin to them – in fact, I have a difficulty to understand them myself. When the harvest is got in, they go hunting the hedges and ditches for rats. Once the farmers had to pay 2*d*. a-head for all rats caught on their grounds, and they nailed them up against the wall. But now that the rat-ketchers can get 3*d*. each by bringing the vermin up to town, the farmers don't pay them anything for what they ketch, but merely give them permission to hunt them in their stacks and barns, so that they no longer get their 2*d*. in the country, though they get their 3*d*. in town.

"I have some twenty families depending upon me. From Clavering, in Essex, I suppose I have hundreds of thousands of rats sent to me in wire cages fitted into baskets. From Enfield I have a great quantity, but the ketchers don't get them all there, but

185

travel round the country for scores of miles, for you see 3*d*. a-head is money; besides, there are some liberal farmers who will still give them a halfpenny a-head into the bargain. Enfield is a kind of headquarters for rat-ketchers.

"It's dangerous work, though, for you see there is a wonderful deal of difference in the specie of rats. The bite of sewer or water-ditch rats is very bad. The water and ditch rat lives on filth, but your barn-rat is a plump fellow, and he lives on the best of everything. He's well off. There's as much difference between the barn and sewer-rats as between a brewer's horse and a costermonger's. Sewer-rats are very bad for dogs, their coats is poisonous.

"Some of the rats that are brought to me are caught in the warehouses in the City. Wherever there is anything in the shape of provisions, there you are sure to find Mr. Rat an intruder. The ketchers are paid for ketching them in the warehouses, and then they are sold to me as well, so the men must make a good thing of it. Many of the more courageous kind of warehousemen will take a pleasure in hunting the rats themselves.

"I should think I buy in the course of the year, on the average, from 300 to 700 rats a week." [Taking 500 as the weekly average, this gives a yearly purchase of 26,000 live rats.] "That's what I kill taking all the year round, you see. Some first-class chaps will come here in the day-time, and they'll try their dogs. They'll say, 'Jimmy, give the dog 100.' After he's polished them off they'll say, perhaps, 'Hang it, give him another 100.' Bless you!" he added in a kind of whisper, "I've had noble ladies and titled ladies come here to see the sport—on the quiet, you know. When my wife was here they would come regular, but now she's aeay they don't come so often.

"The largest quantity of rats I've bought from one man was five guineas' worth, or thirty-five dozen at 3*d*. a-head, and that's a load for a horse. This man comes up from Clavering in a kind of cart, with a horse that's a regular phenomena, for it ain't like a beast nor nothing. I pays him a good deal of money at times, and I'm sure I can't tell what he does with it; but they *do* tell me that he deals in old iron, and goes buying it up, though he don't seem to have much of a head-piece for that sort of fancy neither.

"During the harvest time the rats run scarcer, you see, and the

THE CROSSING-SWEEPER WHO HAD BEEN A SERVANT-MAID

ketcher turns up rat-ketching for harvest work. After the harvest rats gets plentiful again.

"I've had as many as 2,000 rats in this very house at one time. They'll consume a sack of barley-meal a week, and the brutes, if you don't give 'em good stuff, they'll eat one another, hang 'em!

"I'm the oldest canine fancier in London, and I'm the first that started ratting; in fact, I know I'm the oldest caterer in rat-killing in the metropolis. I began as a lad, and I had many noble friends, and was as good a man then as I am now. In fact, when I was seventeen or eighteen years of age I was just like what my boy is now. I used at that time to be a great public character, and had many liberal friends — very liberal friends. I used to give them rat sports, and I have kept to it ever since. My boy can handle rats now just as I used to then.

"Have I been bit by them? Aye, hundreds of times. Now, some people will say, 'Rub yourself over with caraway and stuff and then rats won't bite you.' But I give you my word and honour it's all nonsense, sir.

"As I said, I was the first in London to give rat sports, and I've kept to it ever since. Bless you, there's nothing that a rat won't bite through. I've seen my lads standing in the pit with the rats running about them, and if they haven't taken the precaution to tie their trousers round with a bit of string at the bottom, they'd have as many as five or six rats run up their trouser-legs. They'll deliberately take of their clothes and pick them out from their shirts, and bosoms, and breeches. Some people is amused, and others is horror-struck. People have asked them whether they ain't rubbed? They'll say 'Yes,' but that's as a lark; 'cos, sometimes when my boy has been taking the rats out of the cage, and somebody has taken his attention off, talking to him, he has had a bite, and will turn to me with his finger bleeding and say, 'Yes, I'm rubbed, ain't I, father? look here!'"

"A rat's bite is very singular, it's a three-cornered one, like a leech's, only deeper, of course, and it will bleed for ever such a time. My boys have sometimes had their fingers go dreadfully bad from rat-bites, so that they turn all black and putrid like — aye, as black as the horse-hair covering to my sofa. People have said to me, 'You ought to send the lad to the hospital and have his finger took off;' but I've always left it to the lads, and they've said, 'Oh, don't mind it, father; it'll get all right by and by.' And so it has.

"The best thing I ever found for a rat-bite was the thick bottoms of porter casks put on as a poultice. The only thing you can do is to poultice, and these porter bottoms is so powerful and draws so, that they'll actually take thorns out of horses' hoofs and feet after steeplechasing.

"In handling rats, it's nothing more in the world but nerve that does it. I should faint now if a rat was to run up my breeches, but I have known the time when I've been kivered with 'em.

"I generally throw my dead rats away now; but two or three years since my boys took the idea of skinning them into their heads, and they did about 300 of them, and their skins was very promising. The boys was, after all, obliged to give them away to a furrier, for my wife didn't like the notion, and I said. 'Throw them away;' but the idea strikes me to be something, and one that is lost sight of, for the skins are warm and handsome-looking —a beautiful grey.

'There's nothing turns so quickly as dead rats, so I am obleeged to have my dustmen come round every Wednesday morning; and regularly enough they call too, for they know where there is a bob and a pot. I generally prefers using the authorised dustmen, though the others come sometimes—the flying dustmen they call 'em—and if they're first, they has the job.

"It strikes me, though, that to throw away so many valuable skins is a good thing lost sight of.

"The rats want a deal of watching, and a deal of sorting. Now you can't put a sewer and a barn-rat together, it's like putting a Roosshian and a Turk under the same roof.

"I can tall a barn-rat from a ship-rat or a sewer-rat in a minute, and I have to look over my stock when they come in, or they'd fight to the death. There's six or seven different kinds of rats, and if we don't sort 'em they tear one another to pieces. I think when I have a number of rats in the house, that I am a lucky man if I don't find a dozen dead when I go up to them in the morning; and when I tell you that at times—when I've wanted to make up my number for a match—I've given 21*s*. for twenty rats, you may think I lose something that way every year. Rats, even now, is occasionally 6*s*. a-dozen; but that, I think, is most inconsistent.

"If I had my will, I wouldn't allow sewer ratting, for the rats in the shores eats up a great quantity of sewer filth and rubbish, and is another specie of scavenger in their own way."

After finishing his statement, the landlord showed me some very curious specimens of tame rats—some piebald, and others quite white, with pink eyes, which he kept in cages in his sitting-room. He took them out of their cages, and handled them without the least fear, and even handled them rather rudely, as he showed me the peculiarities of their colours; yet the little tame creatures did not once attempt to bite him. Indeed, they appeared to have lost the notion of regaining their liberty, and when near their cages struggled to return to their nests.

In one of these boxes a black and white rat were confined together, and the proprietor, pointing to them, remarked. "I hope they'll breed, for though white rats is very scarce, only occurring in fact by a freak of nature, I fancy I shall be able, with time and trouble, to breed 'em myself. The old English rat is a small jet-black rat; but the first white rat as I heard of come out of a burial-ground. At one time I bred rats very largely, but now I leaves that fancy to my boys, for I've as much as I can do continuing to serve my worthy patrons."

AN OLD STREET SHOWMAN

A SHORT, thick-set man, with small, puckered-up eyes, and dressed in an old brown velveteen shooting-jacket, gave me an account of some bygone exhibitions of the galantee show.

"My father was a soldier," he said, "and was away in foreign parts, and I and a sister lived with my mother in St. Martin's workhouse. I was fifty-five last New-year's-day. My uncle, a boot-maker in St. Martin's-lane, took my mother out of the workhouse, that she might do a little washing, and pick up a living for herself; and we children went to live with my grandfather, a tailor. After his death, and after many changes, we had a lodging in the Dials, and there——, the sweep, coaxed me with pudding one day, and encouraged me so well, that I didn't like to go back to my mother; and at last I was 'prenticed to him from Hatton-Garden on a month's trial, and I liked chimley-sweeping for that month; but it was quite different when I was regularly indentured. I was cruelly treated then, and poorly fed, and had to turn out bare-footed between three and four many a morning in frost and snow. In first climbing the chimleys, a man stood beneath me and pushed me up, telling me how to use my elbows and knees, and if I slipped, he was beneath me and ketched me, and shoved me up again. The skin came off my knees and elbows; here's the marks now, you see. I suffered a great deal, as well as Dan Duff, a fellow-sweep, a boy that died. I've been to Mrs. Montague's dinner in the Square on the 1st of May, when I was a boy-sweep. It was a dinner in honour of her son having been stolen away by a sweep." [The man's own words.] "I suppose there were more than three hundred of us sweeps there in a large green, at the back of her house. I run away from my master once, but was carried back, and was rather better used. My master then got me knee and ankle-pads, and bathed my limbs in salt and water, and I managed to drag on seven sorrowful years with him. I was glad to be my own man at last, and I cut the sweep trade, bought pandean pipes, and started with an organ-man, as his mate. I saved money with the organ-man and then bought a drum. He gave me five shillings a-week and my wittles and drink, washing and lodging, but there wasn't so much music afloat then.

"I left the music-man and went out with 'Michael,' the Italy bear. Michael was the man's name that brought over the bear from somewhere abroad. He was a Italy man; and he used to beat the bear, and manage her; they called her Jenny; but Michael was not to say roughish to her, unless she was obstropelous. If she were, he showed her the large mop-stick, and beat her with it—hard sometimes—specially when she wouldn't let the monkey get a top on her head; for that was a part of the performance. The monkey was dressed the same as a soldier, but the bear had no dress but her muzzle and chain. The monkey (a clever fellow he was, and could jump over sticks like a Christian) was called Billy. Hr jumped up and down the bear, too, and on his master's shoulders, where he set as Michael walked up and down streets. The bear had been taught to roll and tumble. She rolled right over her head, all round a stick, and then she danced round about it. She did it at the word of command. Michael said to her. 'Round and round again.' We fed her on bread, a quartern-loaf every night after her work in a half-a-pail of water, the same every morning; never any meat—nothing but bread, boiled 'tatoes, or raw carrots: meat would have made her savage. The monkey was fed upon nuts, apples, gingerbread, or anything. Besides them we had two dancing-dogs. The bear didn't like them, and they were kept on one side in performing. The dogs jumped through hoops, and danced on their hind legs; they're easyish enough trained.

"Sometimes the butchers set bull-dogs, two or three at a time, at Jenny; and Michael and me had to beat them off as well as the two other men that we had with us. Those two men collected the money, and I played the pipes and drum, and Michael minded the bear and the dogs and monkey. In London we did very well. The West-end was the best. Whitechapel was crowded for us, but only with ha'pence. I don't know what Michael made, but I had seven shillings a-week, with my wittles and lodging. Michael done well. We generally had twenty to thirty shillings every night in ha'-pence, and used to give twenty-one shillings of it for a one-pound note; for they was in then. When we've travelled in the country,

ONE OF THE FEW REMAINING CLIMBING SWEEPS

we've sometimes had trouble to get lodgings for the bear. We've had to sleep in outhouses with her, and have sometimes frightened people that didn't know as we was there, but nothing serious. Bears is well-behaved enough if they ain't aggravated. Perhaps no one but me is left in England now what properly understands a dancing-bear.

"Jenny wasn't ever baited, but offers was made for it by sporting characters.

"The country was better than London, when the weather allowed; but in Gloucester, Cheltenham, and a good many places, we weren't let in the high streets.

"The gentlefolk in the balconies, both in town and country, where they had a good sight, were our best friends.

"It's more than thirty years ago — yes, a good bit more now; at Chester races, one year, we were all taken, and put into prison: bear, and dogs, and musicianer, and all — every one — because we played a day after the races; that was Saturday.

"We were all in quod until Monday morning. I don't know how the authorities fed the bear. We were each in a separate cell, and I had bread and cheese, and gruel.

"On Monday morning we were discharged, and the bear was shot by the magistrate's orders. They wanted to hang poor Jenny at first but she was shot, and sold to the hairdressers.

"I couldn't stay to see her shot, and had to go into an alehouse on the road. I don't know what her carcase sold for. It wasn't very fat.

"Michael and me then parted at Chester, and he went home rich to Italy, taking his monkey and dogs with him, I believe.

"He lived very careful, chiefly on rice and cabbage, and a very little meat with it, which he called 'manesta.' He was a very old man. I had 'manesta' sometimes, but I didn't like it much. I drummed and piped my way from Chester to London, and there took up with another foreigner, named Green, in the clock-work-figure line.

"The figures were a Turk called Bluebeard, a sailor, a lady called Lady Catarina, and Neptune's car, which we called Nelson's car as well; but is was Neptune's car by rights.

"These figures danced on a table, when taken out of a box. Each had its own dance when wound up.

"First came my Lady Catarina. She, and the others of them, were full two feet high. She had a cork body, and a very handsome silk dress, or muslin, according to the fashion, or the season. Black in Lent, according to what the nobility wore.

"Lady Catarina, when wound up, danced a reel for seven minutes, the sailor a hornpipe, and Bluebeard shook his head, rolled his eyes, and moved his sword, just as natural as life. Neptune's car went either straight or round the table, as it was set.

"We often showed our performances in the houses of the nobility, and would get ten or twelve shillings at a good house, where there were children.

"I had a third share, and in town and country we cleared fifty shilling a-week, at least, every week, among the three of us, after all our keep and expenses were paid.

"At Doncaster races we have taken three pounds in a-day, and four pounds at Lincoln races.

"Country, in summer, is better than town. There's now no such exhibition, barring the one I have; but that's pledged. It cost twenty pounds at Mr.——'s for the four figures without dress. I saved money, which went in an illness of rheumatic gout. There's no bears at all allowed now. Times are changed, and all for the worser. I stuck to the clock-work concern sixteen years, and knows all parts of the country—Ireland, Scotland, Guernsey, Jersey, and the Isle of Wight.

"A month before Christmas we used to put the figures by, for the weather didn't suit; and then we went with a galantee show of a magic lantern. We showed it on a white sheet, or on the ceiling, big or little, in the houses of the gentlefolk, and the schools where there was a breaking-up. It was shown by way of a treat to the scholars. There was Harlequin, and Billy Button, and suchlike. We had ten and sixpence and fifteen shillings for each performance, and did very well indeed, I have that galantee show now, but it brings in very little.

"Green's dead, and all in the line's dead, but me. The galantee show don't answer, because magic lanterns are so cheap in the shops. When we started, magic lanterns wasn't so common; but we can't keep hold of a good thing in these times. It was a reg'lar thing for Christmas once—the galantee shows.

"I can make, in a holiday time, twenty shillings a-week; but that's only a holiday times, and is just a mere casualty a few times a year.

"I do other jobs, when I can get 'em — at other times, I delivers bills, carries boards, and helps at funerals."

THE CHINESE SHADES

"THE PROPER name of my exhibition," said a showman of this class to me, "is *Lez Hombres*, or the shades; that's the proper name for it, for Baron Rothschild told me so when I performed before him. We calls it the Chinese galantee show. It was invented over there with the Chinese, and some travellers went over there and see them doing it, and they come over here and tell us about it. They didn't do it as we do, you know. As for doing pieces, we lick them, out of the field. Them only did the shadows, we do a piece with 'em.

"I should say, sir,—let me calculate—it is about twenty-six years since the ombres first come out. Reduce it if you like, but that's the time. Thomas Paris was the first as come out with them. Then Jim Macklin, and Paul Herring the celebrated clown, and the best showman of Punch in the world for pantomime tricks— comic business, you know, but not for showing in a gentleman's house—was the next that ever come out in the streets with the Chinese galantee show. I think it was his own ingenuity that first gave him the notion. It was thoughts of mind, you know,—you form the opinion in your own mind, you know, by taking it from the Chinese. They met a friend of theirs who had come from China, and he told him of the shadows. One word is as good as fifty, if it's a little grammatical—sound judgment. When it first come out, he began with the scene called 'Mr. Jobson the Cobbler,' and that scene has continued to be popular to the present day, and the best scene out. He did it just equally the same as they do it now in a Punch-and-Judy frame, with a piece of calico stretch- ed in front, and a light behind to throw the shadows on the sheet.

"Paul Herring did excellent well with it—nothing less than 30*s*. or £2 a-night. He didn't stop long at it, because he is a stage clown, and had other business to attend to. I saw him the first time he performed. It was in the Waterloo-road, and the next night I were out with one of my own. I only require to see a thing once to be able to do it; but you must have ingenuity, or it's no use whatsumdiver. Every one who had a Punch-and-Judy frame took to it; doing the regular business in the day and at night turning to the shadows. In less than a week there were two others out, and then Paul Herring cut it. He only done it for a lark. He was hard up for money and got it.

"I was the first that ever had a regular piece acted in his show. I believe there's nobody else as did, but only them that's copied me. They come and follow me, you understand, and copied me. I am the author of 'Cobbler Jobson,' and 'Kitty biling the Pot, or the Woodchopper's Frolic.' There's 'Billy Button's journey to Brentford on horseback, and his favourite servant, Jeremiah Stitchem, in want of a situation.' I'm the author of that, too. It's adapted from the equestrian piece brought out at Astley's. I don't know who composed 'the Broken Bridge.' It's too far gone by to trace who the first author is, but it was adapted from the piece brought out formerly at Drury-lane Theatre. Old ancient gentlemen has told me so who saw it, when it was first brought out, and they're old enough to be my grandfather. I've new revised it.

"We in general goes out about 7 o'clock, bedause we gets away from the noisy children — they place them to bed, and we gets respectable audiences. We choose our places for pitching; Leicester-square is a very good place, and so is Islington, but Regent-street is about the principal. There's only two of us about now, for it's dying away. When I've a mind to show, I can show, and no mistake, for I'm better now than I was twenty years ago.

" 'Kitty biling the Pot, or the Woodchopper's Frolic,' is this. The shadow of the fireplace is seen with the fire alight, and the smoke is made to go up by mechanism. The woodchopper comes in very hungry and wants his supper. He calls his wife to ask if the leg of mutton is done. He speaks in a gruff-voice. He says, 'My wife is very lazy, and I don't think my supper's done. I've been chopping wood all the days of my life, and I want a bullock's head and a sack of potatoes.' The wife comes to him and speaks in a squeaking voice, and she tells him to go and chop some more wood, and in half-an-hour it will be ready. Exaunt.

"Then the wife calls the daughter Kitty, and tells her to see that the pot don't boil over; and above all to be sure and see that the cat don't steal the mutton out of the pot. Kitty says, 'Yes mother, I'll take particular care that the mutton don't steal the cat out of the pot.' Cross-questions, you see — comic business. Then mother says, 'Kitty, bring up the broom to sweep up the room,' and Kitty replies, 'Yes, mummy, I'll bring up the room to sweep up the broom.' Exaunt again. It's regular stage business and cross-questions. She brings up the broom, and the cat's introduced whilst she is sweeping. The cat goes Meaw! meaw! meaw! and Kitty gives it a crack with the broom. Then Kitty gets the bellows and blows up the fire. It's beautiful representation, for you see her working the bellows, and the fire get up, and the sparks fly up the chimney. She says, 'If I don't make haste the mutton will be sure to steal the cat out of the pot.' She blows the fire right out, and says, 'Why, the fire's blowed the bellows out! but I don't mind, I shall go and play at shuttlecock.' Childlike, you see. Then the cat comes in again, and says, Meaw! meaw! and then gets up and steals the mutton. You see her drag it out by the claw, and she burns herself and goes, spit! spit! Then the mother comes in and sees the fire out, and says. 'Where's my daughter? Here's the fire out, and my husband's coming home, and there isn't a bit of mutton to eat!' She calls, 'Kitty Kitty!' and when she comes, asks where she's been. 'I've been playing at shuttlecock.' The mother asks, 'Are you sure the cat hasn't stolen the mutton.' 'Oh, no, no, mother', and exaunt again. Then the mother goes to the pot. She's represented with a squint, so she has one eye up the chimney and another in the pot. She calls out, 'Where's the mutton? It must be down at the bottom, or it has boiled away.' Then the child comes in and says, 'Oh! mother, mother, here's a great he-she-tom cat been and gone off with the mutton'. Then the mother falls down, and calls out, 'I shall faint, I shall faint! Oh! bring me a pail of gin.' Then she revives, and goes and looks in the pot again. It's regular stage business, and if it was only done on a large scale would be wonderful.

"Then comes the correction scene. Kitty comes to her, and her mother says, 'Where have you been?' and Kitty says, 'Playing at shuttlecock, mummy;' and then the mother says, 'I'll give you some shuttlecock with the gridiron,' and exaunt, and comes back with the gridiron; and then you see her with the child on her knee correcting of her. Then woodchopper comes in and wants his supper, after chopping wood all the days of his life. 'Where's supper?' 'Oh, a nasty big he-she-tom cat has been and stole the mutton out of the pot.' 'What?' passionate directly, you see. Then she says, 'You must put up with bread and cheese.' He answers, 'That don't suit some people,' and then comes a fight. Then Spring-heeled Jack is introduced, and he carries off the fireplace and pot and all. Exaunt. That's the end of the piece, and a very good one it was. I took it from Paris, and improved on it. Paris had no workable figures. It was very inferior. He had no fire. It's a dangerous concern the fire is, for it's done with a little bit of the snuff off a candle, and if you don't mind you go alight. It's a beautiful performance.

"Our exhibition generally begins with a sailor doing a hornpipe, and then the tight-rope dancing, and after that the Scotch horn-pipe dancing. The little figures regularly move their legs as if dancing, the same as on the stage, only it's more cleverer, for they're made to do it by ingenuity. Then comes the piece called 'Cobbler Jobson.' We call it 'the laughable, comic, and interesting scene of old Father Jobson, the London cobbler; or, the old Lady disappointed of her Slipper.' I am in front, doing the speaking and playing the music on the pandanean pipe. That's the real word for the pipe, from the Romans, when they first invaded England. That's the first music ever introduced into England, when the Romans first invaded it. I have to do the dialogue in four different voices. There is the child, the woman, the countryman, and myself, and there's not many as can do it besides me and another.

"The piece called Cobbler Jobson is this. It opens with the shadow of a cottage on one side of the sheet, and a cobbler's stall on the other. There are boots and shoes hanging up in the windows of the cobbler's stall. Cobbler Jobson is supposed at work inside, and heard singing:

> *'An old cobbler I am,*
> *And live in my stall;*
> *It serves me for house,*
> *Parlour, kitchen, and all.*
> *No coin in my pocket,*
> *No care in my pate,*

200

I sit down at my ease,
And get drunk when I please.
Hi down, hi derry down.'

"Then he sings again:

'Last night I took a wife,
And when I first did woo her,
I vower I'd stick through life
Like cobbler's wax unto her.
Hi down, derry down down down.'

"Then the figure of a little girl comes in and raps at the door:
'Mr. Jobson, is my mamma's slipper done?' 'No, miss, it's not
done; but if you'll call in half-an-hour it shall be well done, for
I've taken the soles off and put the upper leathers in a pail to
soak.' 'What, in a pail?' 'Yes, my dear, without fail.' 'Then you
won't disappint.' 'No, my dear, I'd sooner a pot than a pint.'
'Then I may depend?' 'Yes, and you won't have it.' He says this
aside, so the girl don't hear him. Then Jobson begins to sing
again. He comes in front and works. You see his lapstone and the
hammer going. He begins to sing:

'T'other morning for breakfast on bacon and spinnage,
Says I to my wife, 'I'm going to Greenwich;'
Says she, 'Dicky Hall, then I'll go too!'
Says I, 'Mrs. Hall, I'll be dished if you do.
Hi down, hi derry down.'

"Then the little girl comes in again to know if the slipper is
done, and as it isn't, it's 'My dear, you must go without it.' Then
she gets impertinent, and says, 'I shan't go with it, you nasty old
waxy, waxy, waxy, waxy, waxy! Oh, you nasty old ball of bristles
and bunch of wax!' Then he tries to hit her, and she runs into the
house, and as soon as he's at work she comes out again: 'Ah, you
nasty cobbler! who's got a lump of wax on his breeches? who sold
his wife's shirt to buy a ha'porth of gin?' Then the cobbler is
regularly vexed, and he tries to coax her into the stall to larrup
her. 'Here, my dear, here's a lump of pudden and a farden.' 'Oh
yes, you nasty old cobbler! you only want to give me a lump of

pudden on my back.' 'Here's a penny, my dear, if you'll fetch it.'
'Chuck it here, and I'll fetch it.' At last she goes into stall, and
she gets a hiding with the hammer. She cries out. 'You nasty old
cobbler waxy! waxy! waxy! I'll go and tell my mother all about
it.' That's what we call the aggriwating scene; and next comes the
passionate scene.

"He begins singing one of his songs. He thinks he's all right
now he's got rid of the girl.

"Then comes in the old lady, shaking with rage. 'How dare you
to strike my child in this here kind of a manner! Come out of the
stall, or I'll pull you out neck and crop!' Then Jobson is in a
funk, and expects a hiding. 'Oh, mum! I'm very sorry, but your
child said, I skinned a cat for ninepence, and called me cobbler
waxy, waxy, waxy.' 'I won't believe a word of it, Mr. Jobson.'
'Yes, mum, your child's very insulting.' 'How dare you strike the
chick? You nasty old villain! I'll tear the cyes out of you.'

"A fight then commences between them, and the old lady gets
the worst of it. Then they make it up, and they'll have some gin.
'I'll be a penny to your threepence,' says the cobbler; and the old
lady says, 'Oh, I can always treat myself.' Then there's another
fight, for there's two fights in it. The old lady gets the worst of it,
and runs into the cottage, and then old Jobson cries, 'I'd better be
off, stall and all, for fear she should come back with the kitchen
poker.' That finishes up the scene, don't you see, for he carries off
the stall with him.

"Cobbler Jobson is up to the door, I think. It's first rate; it only
wants elaborating. 'Billy Button' is a very laughable thing, and
equally up to the door. There's another piece called 'Billy Waters,
the celebrated London Beggar;' and that's a great hit. There's the
'Bull-baiting.' That's all the scenes I known of. I believe I am the
only man that knows the words all through. 'Kitty biling the pot'
is one of the most beautifullest scenes in the world. It wants
expounding, you know; for you could open in the whole length
of the theatre. I wanted to take Ramsgate Theatre, and do it
there; but they wanted £2 a night, and that was too much for
me. I should have put a sheet up, and acted in with real figures,
as large as life.

"When I was down at Brighton, acting with the Chinese

Flushing The Sewers

galantee show, I was forced to drop performing of them. Oh dear! oh dear! don't mention it. You'd have thought the town was on fire. You never saw such an uproar as it made; put the town in such an agitation, that the town authorities forced me to desist. I filled the whole of North-street, and the people was pressing upon me so, that I was obliged to run away. I was lodging at the Clarence Hotel in North-street, at the time. I ran off down a side-street. The next day the police come up to me and tell me that I mustn't exhibit that performance again.

"I shall calculate it at 5*s.* a-night, when I exhibit with the ombres. We don't go out every night, for it's according to the weather; but when we do, the calculation is 5*s.* every night. Some times it is 10*s.* or it may be only 2*s.* 6*d.*; but 5*s.* is a fair balance. Take it all the year round, it would come to 9*s.* a-week, taking the good weather in the bad. It's no use to exaggerate, for the shoe is sure to pinch somewhere if you do.

"We go out two men together, one to play the pipes and speak the parts, and the other to work the figures. I always do the speaking and the music, for that's what is the most particular. When we do a full performance, such as at juvenile parties, it takes one about one hour and a quarter. For attending parties we generally gets a pound, and, perhaps, we may get three or four during the Christmas holiday-time, or perhaps a dozen, for it's according to the recommendation from one to another. If you goes to a gentleman's house, it's according to whether you behave yourself in a superior sort of manner, but if you have any vulgarity about you you must exaunt, and there's no recommendation.

"Tom Paris, the first man that brought out the ombres in the streets, was a short, stout man, and very old. He kept at it for four or five years, I believe, and he made a very comfortable living at it, but he died poor; what became of him I do not know. Jim Macklin I've very little knowledge of. He was a stage performer, but I'm not aware what he did do. I don't know when he died, but he's dead and gone; all the old school is dead and gone—all the old ancient performers. Paul Herring is the only one that's alive now, and he does the clown. He's a capital clown for tricks; he works his own tricks: that's the beauty of him.

"When we are performing of an evening, the boys and children will annoy us awful. They follow us so that we are obliged to go miles to get away from them. They will have the best places; they give each other raps on the head if they don't get out of each other's way. I'm obliged to get fighting myself, and give it them with the drumsticks. They'll throw a stone or two, and then you have to run after them, and swear you're going to kill them. There's the most boys down at Spitalfields, and St. Luke's, and at Islington; that's where there's the worst boys, and the most audaciousest. I dare not go into St. Luke's; they spile their own amusement by making a noise and disturbance. Quietness is everything; they haven't the sense to know that. If they give us any money it's very trifling, only, perhaps, a farden or a half-penny, and then it's only one out of a fifty or a hundred. The great business is to keep them quiet. No; girls ain't better behaved than boys; they was much wus. I'd sooner have fifty boys round me than four girls. The impertinence of them is above bearing. They come carrying babies, and pushing, and crowding, and tearing one another to pieces. 'You're afore me — I was fust — No you wasn't — Yes I was' — and that's the way they go on. If a big man comes in front I'm obliged to ask him to go backwards, to let the little children to see. If they're drunk, perhaps they won't, and then there's a row, and all the children will join in. Oh, it's dread-ful erksome!

"I was once performing on Islington-green, and some drunken people, whilst I was collecting my money, knocked over the con-cern from wanton mischief. They said to me 'We haven't seen nothing, master.' I said, 'I can see you; and haven't you got a brown?' Then they begun laughing, and I turned round, and there was the show in a blaze, and my mate inside a kicking. I think it was two or three drunken men did it, to injure a poor man from gaining his livelihood from the sweat of his brow. That's eighteen years ago.

"I was up at Islington last week, and I was really obliged to give over on account of the children. The moment I put it down there was thousands round me. They was sarcy and impertinent. There was a good collection of people, too. But on account of the theatrical business we want quiet, and they're so noisy there's no being heard. It's morals is everything. It's shameful how parents lets their children run about the streets. As soon as they fill their bellies off they are, till they are hungry again.

"The higher class of society is those who give us the most money. The working man is good for his penny or halfpenny, but the higher class supports the exhibition. The swells in Regent-street ain't very good. They comes and looks on for a moment, and then go on, sometimes they exempt themselves with 'I'm sorry, but I've no pence.' The best is the gentlemen; I can tell them in a minute by their appearance.

"When we are out performing, we in generally burn three candles at once behind the curtain. One is of no utility, for it wants expansion, don't you see. I don't like naphtha or oil-lamps, 'cos we're confined there, and it's very unhealthy. It's very warm as it is, and you must have a eye like a hawk to watch it, or it won't throw the shadows. A brilliant light and a clean sheet is a great attaction, and it's the attraction is everything. In the course of the evening we'll burn six penny candles; we generally use the patent one, 'cos it throws a clear light. We cut them in half. When we use the others I have to keep a look-out, and tell my mate to snuff the candles when the shadows get dim. I usually say, 'Snuff the candles!' out loud, because that's a word for the outside and the inside too, 'cos it let the company know it isn't all over and leads them to expect another scene or two."

A STREET CONJURER

"IN LONDON I had a great quantity of parlours where I was known and allowed to perform. One night I'd take the West-end, and another the East-end. Sometimes I have done four or five houses of an evening, and I have had to walk miles for that — to Woolwich and back for instance, or to Edmonton and back — and occasionally I'd only come home with 1s. 6d. I have also had 8s. from one parlour only, and then I'd consider that a night's performance, and come home again.

"I remember one very peculiar circumstance which happened to me whilst I was out busking. There is a house at the bottom of York-street, Westminster, where they wouldn't allow any other conjurer but me. I was very friendly with the landlord, and I went there regularly every week, and I'd invariably take such a thing as 2s. or 3s. out of the room. If I found only a small muster in the parlour, I'd say, 'I'll come another evening,' and go off to another parlour in Pimlico. One night the company in the parlour said, after I had been performing, 'What a pity it is that one of your talent doesn't take a large room somewhere, and we'd patronise you.' 'Why,' says the landlord, 'he can have my large room upstairs if he likes.' I agreed to it, and says, 'Well, gentlemen, we'll have it next Wednesday evening, if you think proper.' The landlord didn't tell his wife that there was a performance to take place on the Wednesday evening. When I went to this house to the appointment, there were about thirty assembled.

"The landlord was out. When we asked the landlady for the room, she wouldn't, and we had all the difficulty in the world before we got the apartment. I wanted a large table-cloth to dress up my stand, for I have, in order to perform some of my tricks, to make a bag with the end of the table-cloth to drop things into. We sent the waiter to ask for this cloth, and says she, 'I ain't going to lend no conjurers table-cloths.' Then a gentleman says, 'Oh, nonsense, I'll soon get you a table-cloth. She'll lend me one in a minute.' He goes to the bar, but the reply she made was, 'I'm surprised at Mr. W. having such a performance up there, and no table-cloth shall you have from me.' He came up-stairs, and said he had been grossly insulted at the bar; and then another gentleman said, 'Well, this young man shan't be disappointed, and we'll see if we can't find another house down the street, and move it to there, and we'll all go.' One went out, and came back and said he'd not only got a very large room and everything required, but the landlord had four friends in the bar who'd join our company. I made altogether about £1 that night, for I made no charge, and it was altogether contribution. None of that company ever returned to that house again, so he lost the whole of his parlour customers. I could never go into that house again, and I really was sorry for the landlord, for it wasn't his fault. This is a very good proof that it is to the advantage of landlords to allow respectable performers to visit their parlours.

"At other times I have sometimes gone into a parlour and found the customers talking politics. If it was a very good company, and I saw good business, I'd try to break the thread of the discussion by saying when there was a pause in the debate, 'Gentlemen, would you like to see some of my performances, such as walking round the ceiling with my head down?' Then they'd say, 'Well, that's very curious; let's see you.' Of course I couldn't do this, and I only said it to attact notice. Then I'd do my card-tricks, and make a collection, and after that, remark that as the ceiling-walking performance was a dangerous one, I must have a sovereign; of course they wouldn't give this, and I'd take my leave.

"One night, in Oxford-street, I met a singer and he says, 'Where are you going?' I told him I was hunting for a good parlour, and he told me he had just left a good company at such and such a house. I thanked him, and I went there. It was up a long passage, and I entered the room without asking the landlord's permission, and I called for a glass of porter. As soon as I saw the waiter out of the room I made my appeal to the company. They were all of them agreeable and most happy to see my performances. After I'd done my performance I went to make a collection, and they said. 'Oh, certainly not; we thought you'd done it for your own amusement; we never give anything to anybody.' I lost one hour of the best time of the night. I said, 'Very good, gentlemen, I'm satisfied if you are.' It was an agreed plan with the landlord, for he came into the room; and he says, 'What, another one!' and he seized me by the neck and pushed me out. As soon as I got outside I met another conjurer, and he asked me where I'd been. I thought I'd let him be served the same as I was, so I showed him the house, and told him he could make a second 'nobbings' as we term it. I stopped outside peeping over the glass, and presently I see him being pushed out by the landlord as I had been. We had a hearty laugh, and then we started off to Regent-street, to one of out principal houses, but there wasn't a soul in the room. It was a house in a back-street, where none but grooms and footmen resort to. But we was determined to have some money that night, as both our families wanted it—both him and me did.

"Passing a tobacconist's shop in Regent-street, we saw three gents conversing with the lady behind the counter. I told him I'll go in, get a pickwick here, and see if I can't have a performance in the front of this counter. These things only wants an introduction; so I looks at my pickwick, and says I, 'This is a pickwick? why I swallows such as these;' and I apparently swallowed it. One of them says, 'You don't mean to say you swallowed it?' 'Certainly I did, sir,' I replied; and then he makes me do it again. Then I told them I'd show them something more wonderful still, so I said, 'Have you gentlemen such a thing as a couple of half-crowns about you?' they gave me the money, and I did the trick of passing the money from hand to hand. I said to them, 'Can you tell me which hand the money's in?' says he, 'Why, anybody can see it's in that one.' 'No, sir,' says I, 'I think not.' 'If it ain't says he, 'you may keep 'em.' Then I opened both hands, and they were in neither, and he asked where they was then; so I told him I'd given him them back again, which of course he denied, and appeared much surprised. Then I took 'em out of his cravat. It's a very clever trick, and appears most suprising, though its's as simple as possible, and all done by the way in which you take them out of the cravat; for you keep them palmed, and have to work 'em up into the folds. Of course I returned the half-crowns to him, but when I heard him say you may keep them I did feel comfortable, for that was something to the good. My friend outside was looking through the window, and I could see him rubbing his hands with glee; I got another half-crown out of them gentlemen before I'd done with them, for I showed 'em a trick with some walking-sticks which were lying on the counter, and also cut the tape in two and made it whole again, and such-like performances.

"When a fellow is on his beam-ends, as I was then, he must keep his eyes about him, and have impudence enough for anything or else he may stop and starve. The great art is to be able to do tricks with anything that you can easily get hold of. If you take up a bit of string from a counter, or borrow a couple of shillings of a gentleman, your tricks with them startles him much more than if you had taken them out of your own pocket, for he sees there's been no preparation. I got ten shillings out of these two gents I spoke of, and then I and my mate went and busked in a parlour, and got fivepence more; so that we shared five and twopence-ha'-penny each.

"I have often made a good deal of money in parlours by showing how I did my little tricks, such as cutting the tape and passing the half-crowns. Another thing that people always want to know is the thimble-rig trick. Of course it doesn't matter so much showing how these tricks are done, because they depend upon the quickness and dexterity of handling. You may know how an artist paints a picture, but you mayn't be able to paint one yourself.

"I never practised thimble-rigging myself, for I never approved of it as a practice. I've known lots of fellows who lived by it. Bless you! they did well, never sharing less than their £4 or £5 every day they worked. This is the way it's done. They have three thimbles, and they put a pea under two of 'em, so that there's only one without the pea. The man then begins moving them about and saying. 'Out of this one into that one,' and so on, and winds up by offering to 'lay anything, from a shilling to a pound,' that nobody can tell which thimble the pea is under. Then he turns round to the crowd, and pretends to be pushing them back, and whilst he's saying. 'Come, gentlemen, stand more back-warder,' one of the confederates, who is called 'a button,' lifts up one of the thimbles with a pea under it, and laughs to those around, as much as to say, 'We've found it out.' He shows the pea two or three times, and the last time he does to, he removes it, either by taking it up under his forefinger nail or between his thumb and finger. It wants a great deal of practice to do this nicely, so as not to be found out. When the man turns to the table again the button says, 'I'll bet you a couple of sovereigns I know where the pea is. Will any gentleman go me halves?' Then, if there's any hesitation, the man at the table will pretend to be nervous and offer to move the thimbles again, but the button will seize him by the arm, and shout as if he was in a passion. 'No, no, none of that! It was a fair bet, and you shan't touch 'em.' He'll then again ask if anybody will go him halves, and there's usually somebody flat enough to join him. Then the stranger is asked to lift the thimble, so that he shouldn't suspect anything, and of course there's no pea there.

"He is naturally staggered a bit, and another confederate standing by will say calmly, 'I knew you was wrong; here's the pea;' and he lifts up the thimble with the second pea under it. If nobody will go shares in the button's bet, then he lifts up the thimble and replaces the pea as he does so, and of course wins the stake, and he takes good care to say as he pockets the sovereign, 'I knew it was there; what a fool you was not to stand in.' The second time they repeat the trick there's sure to be somebody lose his money. There used to be a regular pitch for thimble-riggers opposite Bedlam, when the shows used to put up there. I saw a brewer's collector lose £7 there in less than half-an-hour. He had a bag full of gold, and they let him win the three first bets as a draw. Most of these confederates are fighting-men and if a row ensues they're sure to get the best of it.

"A very good place where I used to go busking was at Mother Emmerson's in Jermyn-street. There used to be all sorts of characters there, jugglers, and singers, and all sorts. It was a favourite house of the Marquis of Waterford, and he used to use it nearly every night. I've seen him buy a pipe of port, and draw tumblers of it for any body that came in, for his great delight was to make people drunk. He says to Mrs. Emmerson, 'How much do you want for that port, mother?' and then he wrote a cheque for the amount and had it tapped. He was a good-hearted fellow, was my Lord; if he played any tricks upon you, he'd always square it up. Many a time he's given me half-a-pint of brandy, saying. 'That's all you'll get from me.' Sometimes I'd say to him, 'Can I show you a few tricks, my Lord?' and then, when I'd finished, I knew he never gave money if you asked him for it, so I'd let him abuse me and order me out of the house as a humbug; and then, just as I'd got to the door, he'd call me back and give me half-a-sovereign. I've seen him do some wonderful things. I've seen him jump into an old woman's crockeryware-basket, while she was carrying it along, and smash everything. Sometimes he'd get seven or eight cabs and put a lot of fiddlers and other musicians on the roofs, and fill 'em with anybody that liked, and then go off in procession round the streets, he driving the first cab as fast as he could and the bands playing as loud as possible. It's wonderful the games he'd be up to. But he always paid handsomely for whatever damage he did. If he swept all the glasses off a counter, there was the money to make 'em good again. Whenever I did any tricks before him, I took good care not to produce any apparatus that I cared for, or he'd be sure to smash it.

"One night I hadn't a penny in the world, and at home I knew they wanted food; so I went out to busk, and I got over in the Old Kent-road, and went to a house there called the Green Man. I walked into the parlour; and though I hadn't a penny in my pocket, I called for four pen'orth of rum and water. I put my big dice down upon the table by the side of me, and begun sipping my rum, and I could see everybody looking at this dice, and at last, just as I expected, somebody asked what it was. So I says 'Gentlemen, I get my living this way, and if you like, I shall be happy to show you a few of my deceptions for your entertainment.' They said 'Certainly, young man, we are perfectly agreeable.' Ah! I thought to myself, thank heaven that's all right, for I owed for the rum and water you see, and if they'd refused, I don't know what I should have done. I pulled out my nice clean cloth and laid it upon the table, and to work I went. I had only done one or two tricks, when in comes the waiter, and directly he sees me he cries out, 'We don't allow no conjurers or anything of that kind here,' and I had to pack up again. When he'd gone the company said, 'Go on, young man, it's all right now;' so I out with my cloth again; then in came the landlord, and says he,

'You've already been told we don't allow none of you conjurer fellows here,' and I had to put up a second time.

"When he'd gone, the gents told me to begin again. I had scarcely spread my cloth when in comes the landlord again, in a towering rage, and shouts out, 'What, at it again! Now you be off;' so I said, 'I only did it to oblige the company present, who were agreeable, and that I hand't yet finished my rum and water, which wasn't paid for.' 'Not, paid for?' says he; 'No,' says I; 'but I'm waiting here for a friend, and he'll pay for it.' You may imagine my feelings, without a penny in my pocket. 'Don't let me catch you at it again, or I'll give you in charge,' says he. Scarcely had he left again when the company began talking about it, and saying it was too bad to stop me; so one of them rings the bell, and when the landlord comes in he says, 'Mr. Landlord, this young person has been very civil, and conducted himself in a highly respectable manner, and has certainly afforded us a great deal of amusement; now why should you object to his showing us some tricks?' 'Thank heavens,' thought I to myself. 'I'm saved, and the rum will be paid for.' The landlord's manner altered all of a sudden, and says he. 'Oh, certainly, gentlemen! certainly! if it's your wish, I don't mind the young man's being here; though I make it a rule to keep my parlour select.'

"Then I set to work and did all my tricks comfortably, and I made a collection of 7s. 6d. Then I rang the bell like a lord, and I put down a shilling to pay for the rum and water, and saying, 'Gentlemen, I'm very much obliged to you for your patronage,' to which they replied, 'Not at all, young man', I walked past the bar to leave. Then the landlord comes up to me and says, shaking his fist, and blue in the face with rage, 'If ever I catch you here again, you d——rogue, I'll give you to a policeman.' So, without more ado, I walks round to the other door, and enters the parlour again and tells the company, and they had in the landlord and blowed him well up. This will just show you the risks we have to run when out busking for a living, and what courage is wanted to speculate upon chances.

"There are very few conjurers out busking now. I don't know above four; one of 'em has had the best chances in the world of getting on; but he's a very uneducated man, and that has stood in his way, though he's very clever, and pr'aps the best hand at the cups and balls of any man in England. For instance, once he was at a nobleman's party, giving his entertainment, and he says such a thing as this: — 'You see, my lords and ladies, I have a tatur in this hand, and a tatur in that; now I shall pass 'em into this handkercher.' Of course the nobleman said to himself, 'Tatur! handkercher! why, who's this feller?' You may depend upon it he was never asked there any more; for every thing in a wizard's business depends upon graceful action, and his style of delievry, so that he may make himself agreeable to the company.

"When a conjurer's out busking, he may reckon upon making his 20s. a-week, taking the year round; pr'aps, some weeks, he won't take more than 12s. or 15s.; but then, at other times, he may get 6s. or 8s. in one parlour alone, and I have taken as much as £1 by teaching gentlemen how to do the tricks I had been performing. I have sometimes walked my twenty miles a-day, and busked at every parlour I came to (for I never enter tap-rooms), and come home with only 1s. 6d. in my pocket. I have been to Edmonton and back only and earned 1s., and then pr'haps, at eleven the same night, when I was nearly done up, and quite dispirited with my luck, I've turned into one of the parlours in town and earned my 6s. in less than an hour, where I'd been twelve only earning one."

THE STREET FIRE-KING, OR SALAMANDER

THIS PERSON came to me recommended by one of my street ac-
quaintances as the "pluckiest fire-eater going," and that as he was
a little "down at heel," he should be happy for a consideration to
give me any information I might require in the "Salamader line."

He was a tall, gaunt man, with an absent-looking face, and so
pale that his dark eyes looked positively wild.

I could not help thinking, as I looked at his bony form, that fire
was not the most nutritious food in the world, until the poor fellow
explained to me that he had not broken his fast for two days.

He gave the following account of himself: —

"My father was a barber — a three-ha'penny one — and doing a
good business, in Southwark. I used to assist him, lathering up the
chins and shaving 'em — torturing, I called it. I was a very good
light hand. You see, you tell a good shaver by the way he holds
the razor, and the play from the wrist. All our customers were
tradesmen and workmen, but father would never shave either
coalheavers or fishermen, because they always threw down a penny, and said there was plenty of penny barbers, and they wouldn't
give no more. The old man always stuck up for his price to the
day of his death. There was a person set up close to him for a
penny, and that injured us awful. I was educated at St. George's
National and Parochial School, and I was a national lad, and wore
my own clothes; but the parochials wore the uniform of blue bob-
tailed coats, and a badge on the left side. When they wanted to
make an appearance in the gallery of the church on charity-ser-
mon days, they used to make all the nationals dress like the
parochials, so as to swell the numbers up.

"I was too fond of entertainments to stick to learning, and I
used to step it. Kennington-common was my principal place. I
used, too, to go to the outside of the Queen's-bench and pick up the
racket-balls as they was chucked over, and then sell them for
three-ha'pence each. I got promoted from the outside to the inside;
for, from being always about, they took me at threepence a-day,

and gave me a bag of whitening to whiten the racket-balls. When I used to hop the wag from school I went there, which was three times a-week, which was the reg'lar racket-days. I used to spend my threepence in damaged fruit—have a pen'orth of damaged grapes or plums—or have a ha'porth of wafers from the confectioner's. Ah, I've eat thousands and thousands of ha'porths. It's a kind of paste, but they stick like wafers—my father's stuck a letter many a time with 'em. They goes at the bottom of the russetfees cake—ah, ratafees is the word.

"I got so unruly, and didn't attend to school, so I was turned out, and then I went to help father and assist upon the customers. I was confined so in the shop, that I only stopped there three-months, and then I run away. Then I had no home to go to, but I found a empty cart, situated in Red-cross-street, near the Borough-market, and there I slept for five nights. Then Greenwich fair came on. I went round the fair, and got assisting a artist as was a likeness-cutter, and had a booth, making black profiles. I assisted this man in building his booth, and he took a great fancy to me, and kept me as one of his own. He was a shoemaker as well, and did that when fair was over. I used to fetch his bristles and leather, and nuss the child. He lived near the Kent-road; and one day as I was going out for the leather, I fell upon mother, and she solaced me, and took me home; and then she rigged me out and kept me, till I run away again; and that was when Greenwich fair came on again, for I wanted to go back then. At the fair I got to be doorsman and grease-pot boy inside a exhibition, to let the people out and keep the lamps.

"I got a shilling a-day for my attendance during fair time, and I travelled with them parties for five months. That was Peterson's, the travelling comedian, or what we call a 'mumming concern.' When we got to Bexley, I thought I should like to see a piece called 'Tricks and Trials,' then being performed at the Surrey Theatre, so I cut away and come up to London again. There I got employment at a japanner, builing up the stuff. I made a little bit of an appearance, and then I went home. I had learnt three or four comic songs, and I used to go singing at consart-rooms. I was a reg'lar professional. I went a busking at the free consart-rooms, and then go round with the cap. I principally sing

'The Four-and-Nine,' or 'The Dark Arches,' or 'The Ship's Carpenter,' and 'The Goose Club.'

"It was at one of these free consart-rooms that I first saw a chap fire-eating. You see, at a free consart-room the professionals ain't paid, no more do the audience to come in, but the performers are allowed to go round with a cap for their remuneration. They are the same as the cock-and-hen clubs. This fire-eater was of the name of West, and I know'd him afore, and he used to ask me to prepare the things for him. His performance was, he had a link a-light in his hand, and he used to take pieces off with a fork and eat it. Then he would get a plate with some sulphur, light it, place it under his nose, and inhale the fumes that rose from it; and then he used to eat it with a fork whilst a-light. After that he'd get a small portion of gunpowder, put it in the palm of his hand, and get a fusee to answer for a quick-match, to explode the powder, and that concluded the performance – only three tricks. I was stunned the first time I see him do it; but when I come to prepare the things for him, I got enlightened into the business. When his back was turned, I used to sniff at the sulphur on the sly. I found it rather hard, for the fumes used to get up your head, and reg'lar confuse you, and lose your memory. I kept on the singing at the consarts, but I practised the fire-eating at home. I tried it for the matter of two months, before I found the art of it. It used to make me very thick in my voice; and if I began it before breakfast it used to make you feel ill: but I generally began it after meals. I tried the link and sulphur till I got perfect in these two. It blistered my mouth swallowing the fire, but I never burnt myself seriously at it.

"After I learnt those, I got travelling again with a man that swallowed a poker, of the name of Yates. One of his tricks was with tow. He'd get some, and then get a frying-pan, and he'd put the tow in the fire-pan, and he'd get some ground rosin and brimstone together and put them on top of the tow in the pan. Then, when he'd set light to it he used to bring it on the outside of the show and eat it with a knife and fork, while I held the pan. I learnt how to do the trick; this was when he had done with it, and I'd take it away. Then I used to eat the portion that was left in the pan, till I became the master of that feat.

"When I left Yates I practised again at home until I was perfect, and then I went about doing the performance myself. The first place that I attempted was at the Fox and Cock, Gray's-inn-lane, and I was engaged there at three shillings a-night, and with collections of what people used to throw to me I'd come away with about seven shillings and sixpence. I was very successful indeed, and I stopped there for about seven months, doing the fire-business; and I got another job at the same place, for one of the potmen turned dishonest, and the master gave me eight shillings a-week to do his work as well. I have continued ever since going to different consart-rooms, and giving my performances. My general demand for a night's engagement is four shillings and six pen'orth of refreshment. When I perform I usually have a decanter of ale and two glasses upon the table, and after every trick I sit down whilst an overture is being done and wash my mouth out, for it gets very hot. You're obliged to pause a little, for after tasting one thing, if the palate doesn't recover, you can't tell when the smoke is coming.

"I wore a regular dress, a kind of scale-armour costume, with a red lion on the breast. I do up my moustache with cork, and rouge a bit. My tights is brown, with black enamel jack-boots. On my head I wears a king's coronet and a ringlet wig, bracelets on my wrists, and a red twil petticoat under the armour dress, where it opens on the limps.

"For my performances I begin with eating the lighted link, an ordinary one as purchased at oil-shops. There's no trick in it, only confidence. It won't burn you in the inside, but if the pitch falls on the outside, of course it will hurt you. If you hold your breath the moment the lighted piece is put in your mouth, the flame goes out on the instant. Then we squench the flame with spittle. As we takes a bit of link in the mouth, we tucks it on one side of the cheek, as a monkey do with nuts in his pouch. After I have eaten sufficient fire I take hold of the link, and extinguish the lot by putting the burning end in my mouth. Sometimes, when I makes a slip, and don't put it in careful, in makes your moustache fiz up. I must also mind how I opens my mouth, 'cos the tar sticks to the lip wherever it touches, and pains sadly. This sore on my hand is caused by the melted pitch droppin on my fingers, and the sores is liable to be bad for a week or eight days. I don't spit out my bits of link; I always swallow them. I never did spit 'em out, for they are very wholesome, and keeps you from having any sickness. Whilst I'm getting the next trick ready I chews them up and eats them. It tastes rather roughish, but not nasty when you're accustomed to it. It's only like having a mouthful of dust, and very wholesome.

"My next trick is with a piece of tow with a piece of tape rolled up in the interior. I begin to eat a portion of this tow—plain, not a-light—till I find a fitting opportunity to place the tape in the mouth. Then I pause for a time, and in the meantime I'm doing a little pantomime business—just like love business, serious —till I get the end of this tape between my teeth, and then I draws it out, supposed to be manufactured in the pit of the stom-ach. After that—which always goes immensely—I eat some more tow, and inside this tow there is what I call the fire-ball— that is, a lighted fusee bound round with tow and placed in the centre of the tow I'm eating—which I introduce at a fitting opportunity. Then I blows out with my breath, and that sends out smoke and fire. That there is a very hard trick, for it's ac-cording how this here fite-ball bustes. Sometimes it bustes on the side, and then it burns all the inside of the mouth, and the next morning you can take out pretty well the inside of your mouth with your finger; but if it bustes near the teeth, then it's all right, for there's vent for it. I also makes the smoke and flame—that is sparks—come down my nose, the same as coming out of a black-smith's chimney. It makes the eyes water, and there's a tingling; but it don't burn or make you giddy.

"My next trick is with the brimstone. I have a plate of lighted sulphur, and first inhale the fumes, and then devour it with a fork and swallow it. As a costermonger said when he saw me do it. 'I say, old boy, your game ain't all brandy.' There's a kind of acid, nasty, sour taste in this feat, and at first it used to make me feel sick; but now I'm used to it, and it don't. When I puts it in my mouth it clings just like sealing-wax and forms a kind of dead ash. Of a morning, if I haven't got my breakfast by a certain time, there's a kind of retching in my stomach, and that's the only in-convenience I feel from swallowing the sulphur for that there feat.

"The next is, with two sticks of sealing-wax and the same plate. They are lit by the gas and dropped on one another till they are bodily a-light. Then I borrow either a ring of the company, or a pencil-case, or a seal. I set the sealing-wax a-light with a fork, and I press the impression of whatever article I can get with the tongue, and the seal is passed round to the company. Then I finish eating the burning wax. I always spits that out after, when no one's looking. The sealing-wax is all right if you get it into the interior of the mouth, but if it is stringy, and it falls, you can't get it off, without it takes away skin and all. It has a very pleasant taste, and I always prefer the red, as its flavour is the best. Hold your breath and it goes out, but still the heat remains, and you can't get along with that so fast as the sulphur. I often burn myself, especially when I'm bothered in my entertainment; such as any person talking about me close by, then I listen to 'em perhaps, and I'm liable to burn myself. I haven't been able to perform for three weeks after some of my burnings. I never let any of the audience know anything of it, but smother up the pain, and go on with my other tricks.

"The other trick is a feat which I make known to the public as one of Ramo Samee's, which he used to perform in public-houses and tap-rooms, and made a deal of money out of. With the same plate and a piece of dry tow placed in it, I have a pepper-box, with ground rosin and sulphur together. I light the tow, and with a knife and fork I set down to it and eat it, and exclaim, 'This is my light supper.' There isn't no holding the breath so much in this trick as in the others, but you must get it into the mouth any how. It's like eating a hot beef-steak when you are ravenous. The rosin is apt to drop on the flesh and cause a long blister. You se, we have to eat it with the head up, full-faced; and really, without it's seen, nobody would believe what I do.

"There's another feat, of exploding the gunpowder. There's two ways of exploding it. This is my way of doing it, though I only does it for my own benefits and on grand occasions, for it's very dangerous indeed to the frame, for it's sure to destroy the hair of the head; or if anything smothers it, it's liable to shatter a thumb or a limb.

"I have a man to wait on me for this trick, and he unloops

STREET CONJURER PERFORMING

my dress and takes it off, leaving the bare back and arms. Then I gets a quarter of a pound of powder, and I has an ounce put on the back part of the neck, in the hollow, and I holds out each arm with an orange in the palm of each hand, with a train along the arms, leading up to the neck. Then I turns my back to the audience, and my man fires the gunpowder, and it blew up in a minute, and ran down the train and blew up that in my hands. I've been pretty lucky with this trick, for it's only been when the powder's got under my bracelets, and then it hurts me. I'm obliged to hold the hand up, for if it hangs down it hurts awful. It looks like a scurvy, and as the new skin forms, the old one falls off.

"That's the whole of my general performance for concert business, when I go busking at free concerts or outside of shows (I generally gets a crown a-day at fairs). I never do the gunpowder but only the tow and the link.

"I have been engaged at the Flora Gardens, and at St. Helena Gardens, Rotherhithe, and then I was Signor Salamander, the great fire-king from the East-end theatres. At the Eel-pie-house, Peckham, I did the 'terrific flight through the air,' coming down a wire surrounded by fire-works. I was called Herr Alma, the flying fiend. There was four scaffold-poles placed at the top of the house to form a tower, just large enough for me to lie down on my belly, for the swivels on the rope to be screwed into the cradle round my body. A wire is the best, but they had a rope. On this cradle were places for the fire-works to be put in it. I had a helmet of fire on my head, and the three spark cases (they are made with steel-filings, and throw out sparks) made of Prince of Wales feathers. I had a sceptre in my hand of two serpents, and in their open mouths they put fireballs, and they looked as if they was spitting fiery venom. I had wings, too, formed from the ankle to the waist. They was netting, and spangled, and well sized to throw of the fire. I only did this two nights, and I had ten shillings each performance. It's a momentary feeling coming down, a kind of suffocation like, so that you must hold your breath. I had two men to cast me off. There was a gong first of all, knocked to attract the attention, and then I made my appearance. First, a painted pigeon, made of lead, is sent down the wire as a pilot. It has moveable wings. Then all the fire-works are lighted up.

and I come down right through the thickest of 'em. There's a trap-door set in the scene at the end, and two men is there to look after it. As soon as I have passed it, the men shut it, and I dart up against a feather-bed. The speed I come down at regularly jams me up against it, but you see I throw away this sceptre and save myself with my hands a little. I feel fagged for want of breath. It seems like a sudden fright, you know. I sit down for a few minutes, and then I'm all right.

"I'm never afraid of fire. There was a turner's place that took fire, and I saved that house from being burned. He was a friend of mine, the turner was, and when I was there, the wife thought she heard the children crying, and asked me to go up and see what it was. As I went up I could smell fire worse and worse, and when I got in the room it was full of smoke, and all the carpet, and bed-hangings, and curtains smouldering. I opened the window, and the first burst out, so I ups with the carpet and throw'd it out of the window, together with the blazing chairs, and I rolled the linen and drapery up and throw'd them out. I was as near suf-focated as possible. I went and felt the bed, and there was two children near dead from the smoke; I brought them down, and a medical man was called, and he brought them round.

"I don't reckon no more than two other fire-kings in London beside myself. I only know of two, and I should be sure to hear of 'em if there were more. But they can only do three of the tricks, and I've got novelties enough to act for a fortnight, with fresh performances every evening. There's a party in Drury-lane is willing to back me for five, fifteen or twenty pounds, against anybody that will come and answer to it, to perform with any other man for cleanness and cleverness, and to show more variety of performance.

"I'm always at fire-eating. That's how I entirely get my living, and I perform five nights out of the six. Thursday night is the only night, as I may say, I'm idle. Thursday night everybody's fagged, that's the saying—Got no money. Friday, there's many large firms pays their men on, especially in Bermondsey.

"I'm out of an engagement now, and I don't make more than eleven shillings a-week, because I'm busking; but when I'm in an engagement my money stands me about thirty-five shillings a-week, putting down the value of the drink as well—that is, what's allowed for refreshment. Summer is the worst time for me, 'cos people goes to the gardens. In the winter season I'm always engaged three months out of six. You might say, if you counts the overplus at one time, and minus at other times, that I makes a pound a-week. I know what it is to go to the treasury on a Saturday, and get my thirty shillings, and I know what it is to have the landlord come with his 'Hallo! hallo! here's three weeks due, and another week running on.'

"I was very hard up at one time—when I was living in Friar-street—and I used to frequent a house kept by a betting-man, near the St. George's Surrey Riding-school. A man I knew used to supply this betting-man with rats. I was at this public-house one night when this rat-man comes up to me, and says he, 'Hallo! my pippin; here, I want you; I want to make a match. Will you kill thirty rats against my dog?' So I said, 'Let me see the dog first;' and I looked at his mouth, and he was an old dog; so I says, 'No, I won't go in for thirty; but I don't mind trying at twenty.' He wanted to make it twenty-four, but I wouldn't. They put the twenty in the rat-pit, and the dog went in first and killed his, and he took a quarter of an hour and two minutes. Then a fresh lot were put in the pit, and I began; my hands were tied behind me. They always make an allowance for a man, so the pit was made closer, for you see a man can't turn round like a dog; I had half the space of the dog. The rats lay in a cluster, and then I picked them off where I wanted 'em, and bit 'em between the shoulders It was when they came to one or two that I had the work, for they cut about. The last one made me remember him, for he gave me a bite, of which I've got the scar now. It festered, and I was obliged to have it cut out. I took Dutch drops for it, and poulticed it by day, and I was bad for three weeks. They made a subscription in the room of fifteen shillings for killing these rats. I won the match, and beat the dog by four minutes. The wager was five shillings, which I had. I was at the time so hard up, I'd do anything for some money; though, as far as that's concerned, I'd go into a pit now, if anybody would make it worth my while."

STROLLING ACTORS

WHAT ARE called strolling actors are those who go about the country and play at the various fairs and towns. As long as they are acting in a booth they are called canvas actors; but supposing they stop in a town a few days after a fair, or build up in a town where there is no fair, that constitutes what is termed private business.

"We call strolling actors 'mumming,' and the actors 'mummers.' All spouting is mumming. A strolling actor is supposed to know something of everything. He doesn't always get a part given to him to learn, but he's often told what character he's to take, and what he's to do, and he's supposed to be able to find words capable of illustrating the character; in fact, he has to 'gag,' that is, make up words.

"When old Richardson was alive, he used to make the actors study their parts regularly; and there's Thorne and Bennett's, and Douglas's, and other large travelling concerns, that do so at the present time; but where there's one that does, there's ten that don't. I was never in one that did, not to study the parts, and I have been mumming, on and off, these ten years.

"There's very few penny gaffs in London where they speak; in fact, I only know one where they do. It ain't allowed by law, and the police are uncommon sewere. They generally play ballets and dumb acting, singing and dancing, and such-like.

"I never heard of such a thing as a canvas theatre being prosecuted for having speaking plays performed, so long as a fair is going on, but if it builds at other times I have known the mayor to object to it, and order the company away. When we go to pitch in a town, we always, if it's a quiet one, ask permission of the mayor to let us build.

"The mummers have got a slang of their own, which parties connected with the perfession generally use. It is called 'mummers' slang,' and I have been told that it's a compound of broken Italian and French. Some of the Romanee is also mixed up with

it. This, for instance, is the slang for 'Give me a glass of beer,' —
'Your nabs sparkle my nabs,' 'a drop of beware.' 'I have got no
money' is, 'My nabs has nanti dinali.' I'll give you a few sentences.

" 'Parni' is rain; and 'toba' is ground.

" 'Nanti numgare' is — No food.

" 'Nanti fogare' is — No tobacco.

" 'Is his nabs a bona pross?' — Is he good for something to
drink?

" 'Nanti, his nabs is a keteva homer' — No, he's a bad sort.

" 'The casa will parker our nabs multi' means, — This house
will tumble down.

" 'Vada the glaze' is — Look at the window.

"These are nearly all the mummers' slang words we use; but
they apply to different meanings. We call breakfast, dinner, tea,
supper, all of them 'numgare;' and all beer, brandy, water, or
soup, are 'beware.' We call everybody 'his nabs' or 'her nabs.' I
went among the penny-ice men, who are Italian chaps, and I
found that they were speaking a lot of mummer's slang. It is a
good deal Italian. We think it must have originated from Italians
who went about doing pantomimes.

"Now, the way we count money is nearly all of it Italian; from
one farthing up to a shilling is this: —

" 'Patina, nadsa, oni soldi, duey soldi, tray soldi, quatro soldi,
chinqui soldi, say soldi, seter soldi, otter soldi, navra soldi, deshra
soldi, lettra soldi, and a biouk.' A half-crown is a 'metsa carroon;'
a 'carroon' is a crown; 'metsa punta' is half-a-sovereign; a 'punta'
is a pound. Even with these few words, by mixing them up with
a few English ones, we can talk away as fast as if we was using
our own language.

"Mumming at fairs is harder than private business, because you
have to perform so many times. You only wear one dress, and
all the actor is expected to do is to stand up to the dances outside
and act in. He'll have to dance perhaps sixteen quadrilles in the
course of the day, and act about as often inside. The company
generally work in shares, or if they pay by the day, it's about four
or five shillings a-day. When you go to get engaged, the first question is, 'What can you do?' and the next, 'Do you find your own
properties, such as russet boots, your dress, hat and feathers, &c?'

Of course they like your dress the better if it's a showy one; and it don't much matter about its corresponding with the piece. For instance, Henry the Second in 'Fair Rosamond,' always comes on with a cavalier's dress, and nobody notices the difference of costume. In fact, the same dresses are used over and over again for the same pieces. The general dress for the ladies is a velvet skirt with a satin stomacher, with a gold band round the waist and a pearl band on the forehead. They, too, wear the same dresses for all the pieces. A regular fair show has only a small compass of dresses, for they only goes to the same places once in a-year, and of course their costumes ain't remembered.

"The principal fair pieces are 'Blue Beard,' 'Robert, duke of Normandy,' and 'Fair Rosamond, or the Bowers of Woodstock.' I recollect once they played 'Maria Martin,' at a fair, in a company I was with, and we played that in cavalier costume; and so we did 'The Murder at Stanfield Hall,' Rush's affair, in dresses of the time of Charles the Second.

"An actor's share will average for the fair at five shillings a-day, if the fair is anything at all. When we don't work we don't get paid, so that if we only do one fair a-week, that's fifteen shillings, unless we stop to do a day or two private business after the fair.

" 'Fair Rosamond' isn't so good a piece as 'Blue Beard,' for that's a great fair piece, and a never-failing draw. Five years ago I was with a company — Star and Lewis were the acting managers. Then 'Blue Beard' was our favourite piece, and we played it five fairs out of six. 'Fair Rosamond' is too sentimental. They like a comedy man, and the one in 'Fair Rosamond' isn't nothing. They like the secret-chamber scene in 'Blue Beard.' It's generally done by the scene rolling up and discovering another, with skeletons painted on the back, and blue fire. We always carried that scene with us wherever we went, and for the other pieces the same scenes did. At Star's, our scenes were somewhat about ten feet wide and eight feet high. They all rolled up, and there were generally about four in working order, with the drop curtain, which made five.

"You may put the price of a good fair theatrical booth down at from fifty pounds to two hundred and fifty pounds. There's some of them more expensive still. For instance, the paintings alone on the front of Douglas's Shakesperian theatre, must have cost seventy pounds; and his dress must have cost a deal, for he's got a private theatre at Bolton, and he works them there as well as at fairs.

" 'The Bottle Imp' is a very effective fair piece. It opens with a scene of Venice, and Willebald and Albert, which is the comedy man and the juvenile. The comic man's principal line is, 'I'll tell your mother,' every time Alberts wants to go and see his sweetheart, or if he's doing anything that he thinks improper. In the first act Albert goes to his sweetheart's house, and the father consents to their union, provided he can gain so many ducats. Albert then finds out a stranger, who is Nicolo, who asks him to gamble with him at dice: Albert says he is poor. Nicolo says he once was poor, but now he has great wealth. He then tells Albert, that if he likes he can be rich too. He says, 'Have you not heard of imps and bottle imps?' 'Stuff!' says Albert! 'me, indeed! a poor artist; I have heard of such things, but I need them not.' 'But, boy,' says Nicolo, 'I have that in my possession will make you rich indeed; a drop of the elixir in this bottle, rubbed on the outside, will give you all you require; and if ever you wish to part with it, you must sell it for less than you gave.' He gives three ducats for it, and as he gives the money the demon laughs from the inside, 'Ha! ha! ha! mine, mine!' Albert looks amazed. Nicolo says, 'Ah, youth! may you know more happiness than I have whilst I had that in my possession:' and then he goes off. Albert then tries the power of the bottle. He says, 'What, ho! I wish for wine,' and it's shoved on from the side. As he is drinking, Willebald exclaims, 'O dear, O dear! I've been looking for my master. O that I were only safe back again in Threadneedle-street, I'll never go hunting pretty girls again. Oh, won't I tell his mother!' 'How now, caitiff! — Leave me!' says Albert. 'All right,' says Willebald; 'I'll leave you — won't I tell your mother!'

"When Willebald goes, Albert wishes for sleep, and the Bottle Imp replies, 'All your wishes shall be gratified, excepting one. Sleep you cannot have while I am in your possession.' The demon then seizes him by the throat, and Albert falls on stage, demon exulting over him. Enter Willebald, who seeing the demon, cries 'Murder! murder! Oh, won't I tell their mothers!' and that ends the first act.

"In the second and last act, Albert gives Willebald instructions to sell the bottle; 'but it is to be for less than three ducats.' Willebald says, 'No marine-storekeeper would give three ducats for an old bottle;' but he goes off shouting out, 'Who'll buy a bottle? Who'll buy a bottle?' In the next scene, Willebald is still shouting his bottle for sale, with folks laughing off stage and dogs barking. He says, 'Ah! laugh away. It's well to be merry, but I'm obliged to cry — Who'll buy a bottle?' He then says he's 'not going walking about all day selling a bottle;' and then he says he's got two ducats, and he'll buy the bottle himself, sooner than trudge about Venice. Then he says, 'Oh, Mr. Bottle, here are the ducats; now you are mine.' Then the demon cries, 'Mine, mine!' He says it was only the wind. Then he says, 'Oh, how I wish I was at home again, and heard my little brothers and sisters singing!' And instantly from the sides you hear, 'Boys and girls come out to play!' Then Willebald says, 'I wish you'd hold your tongues, you little brutes!' and they cease. Next he complains that he's so poor, and he wishes it would rain gold on him, and then down comes a shower. Then in comes Albert, who asks whether the bottle has been sold; and Willebald replies that it's all right. 'Thank heavens,' cries Albert; 'but yet I pity the miserable wretch who has bought it.' 'What do you mean? O dear, O dear! to frighten one so! I'll tell your mother!' 'Know ye not, caitiff!' continues Albert, 'that that bottle contains a demon? O what a weight hast thou removed from my heart!' As Willebald is deploring his lot, enter a poor man, who asks for a drink of water; and Willebald tells him he can't give him any water, but he has an elixir he shall have very cheap. The old man replies that he hasn't got more than a petani, which is the sixtieth part of a farthing. However, Willebald sells him the bottle; and as it's the smallest coin in the world, and the bottle can't go no cheaper, the demon rushes in and seizes the beggar, who turns out to be Nicolo, the first who sold the bottle. As he is being carried off, Willebald cries out, 'For shame, you ugly devil to treat the old gentleman like that! Won't I tell your mother!' and down comes the curtain.

"The 'Bottle Imp' is a very successful romantic drama. There's plenty of blue fire in it. The 'Bottle Imp' have it at every entrance that fellow do. There is some booths that are fonder of the 'Bottle

Imp' than any other piece. We played it at Bill Weale's theatre
more than any other drama. The imp is always acted by a man
in a cloak with a mask on. You can see his cavalier boots under his
cloak, but that don't matter to holiday folk when once they know
it's intended to be a demon.

"It's a very jolly life strolling, and I wouldn't leave it for any
other if I had my choice. At times it's hard lines; but for my
part I prefer it to any other. It's about fifteen shillings a-week for
certain. If you can make up your mind to sleep in the booth, it
ain't such bad pay. But the most of the men go to lodgings, and
they don't forget to boast of it. 'Where do you lodge?' one'll ask.
'Oh, I lodged at such a place,' says another; for we're all first-
rate fellows, if you can get anybody to believe us.

"Mummers' feed is a herring, which we call a pheasant. After
performance we generally disperse, and those who have lodgings
go to 'em; but if any sleep in the booth, turn in. Perhaps there's a
batch of coffee brought forwards, a subscription supper of three.
The coffee and sugar is put in a kettle and boiled up, and then
served up in what we can get; either a saucepan lid, or a cocoa-nut
shell, or a publican's pot, or whatever they can get. Mummers is
the poorest, flashest, and most independent race of men going. If
you was to offer some of them a shilling they'd refuse it, though
the most of them would take it. The generality of them is cobblers'
lads, and tailors' apprentices, and clerks, and they do account for
that by their having so much time to study over their work.

"Private business is a better sort of acting. There we do nearly
the entire piece, with only the difficult parts cut out. We only do
the outline of the story, and gag it up. We've done various plays
of Shakespeare in this way, such as 'Hamlet' or 'Othello,' but
only on benefit occasions. Then we go as near as memory will let
us, but we must never appear to be stuck for words. Our prices
of admission in the country for private business is theepence and
sixpence, or sometimes sixpence or one shilling, for it all depends
upon the town, but in London it's oftener one penny and twopence. We only go to the outskirts and act there, for they won't
allow us in the streets. The principal parts for pitching the booth
for private business in London, is about Lock's-field, Walworth.
We opened there about six years ago last Easter.

"Our rehearsals for a piece are the funniest things in the world. Perhaps we are going to play 'The Floating Beacon, or The Weird Woman of the Wreck.' The manager will, when the night's performance is over, call the company together, and he'll say to the low-comedyman, 'Now, you play Jack Junk, and this is your part; you're supposed to fetch Frederick for to go to sea. Frederick gets capsized in the boat, and gets aboard of the floating beacon. You go to search for him, and the smugglers tell you he's not aboard, and they give you the lie; then you say, 'What, the lie to a English sailor!' and you chuck your quid in his eye, saying, 'I've had it for the last fourteen days, and now I scud it with a full sail in your lubberly eye.' Then you have to get Frederick off.'

"Then the manager will turn to the juvenile, and say, 'Now, sir, you'll play Frederick. Now then, Frederick, you're in love with a girl, and old Kinslade, the father, is very fond of you. You get into the boat to go to the ship, and you're wrecked and get on to the beacon. You're very faint, and stagger on, and do a back fall. You're picked up by the weird woman, and have some dialogue with her; and then you have some dialogue with the two smugglers, Ormaloff and Augestoff. You pretend to sleep, and they're going to stab you, when the wild woman screams, and you awake and have some more dialogue. Then they bring a bottle, and you begin drinking. You change the cups. Then there's more dialogue, and you tackle Ormaloff. Then you discover your mother and embrace. Jack Junk saves you. Form a picture with your mother, the girl, and old Winslade, and Jack Junk over you.'

"That's his part, and he's got to put it together and do the talk.

"Then the manager turns to Ormaloff and Augerstoff, and says: 'Now, you two play the smugglers, do you hear? You're to try and poison the young fellow, and you're defeated.'

"Then he says to the wild woman: 'You're kept as a prisoner aboard the beacon, where your husband has been murdered. You have refused to become the wife of Ormaloff. Your child has been thrown overboard. You discover him in Frederick, and you scream when they are about to stab him, and also when he's about to drink. Make as much of it as you can, please; and don't forget the scream.'

" 'Winslade, you know your part. You've only got to follow Junk.'

" 'You're to play the lady, you Miss. You're in love with Frederick. You know the old business: 'What! to part thus? Alas! alas! never to this moment have I confessed I love you!'

"That's a true picture of a mumming rehearsal, whether it's fair or private business. Some of the young chaps stick in their parts. They get the stage fever and knocking in the knees. We've had to shove them on to the scene. They keep on asking what they're to say. 'Oh, say anything!' we tell 'em, and push 'em on to the stage.

"If a man's not gifted with the gab, he's no good at a booth. I've been with a chap acting 'Mary Woodbine', and he hasn't known a word of his part. Then, when he's stuck, he has seized me by the throat, and said, 'Caitiff! dog! be sure thou provest my wife unfaithful to me.' Then I saw his dodge, and I said. 'Oh, my lord!' and he continued – 'Give me the proof, or thou hadst best been born a dog.' Then I answered. 'My lord, you wrong your wife, and torture me;' and he said, 'Forward, then, liar! dog!' and we both rushed off.

"We were acting at Lock's-fields, Walworth, once, doing private business, when we got into trouble, and were all put into prison for playing without a licence. We had built up in a piece of private ground – in a dust-yard known as Calf's – and we had been there eleven months doing exceedingly well. We treated the policeman every night, and gave him as much, with porter and money, that was equal to one shilling a-night, which was taken up from the company. It was something like a penny a-piece for the policeman, for we were rather afraid of something of the kind happening.

"It was about the time that 'Oliver Twist' was making such a success at the other theatres, and so we did a robbery from it, and brought out our version as 'The Golden Farmer.' Instead of having an artful dodger, we called our comic character Jimmy Twitcher, and made him do all the artful-dodgery business. We had three performance a-night in those days. We was in our second performance, and Jimmy Twitcher was in the act of getting through the window, and Hammer, the auctioneer, was asleep, saying in his sleep, 'Knock 'em down! going! going! gone!' when I saw the police in private clothes rising from the front seats, and coming towards the stage. They opened the side door, and let the other police in, about forty of them. Then the inspector said, 'Ladies and gentlemen, I forbid any of you to move, as I arrest those people for performing without a licence.' Nobody moved. Three policemen took hold of me, one at each arm, and one at the back of the neck. They wouldn't allow us to change our dresses, nor to take our other clothes, though they were close by. They marched us off to the Walworth station, along with about a hundred of the spectators, for some of them got away. My wife went to fetch my clothes for me, and they took her, too, and actually locked her up all night, though she was so near her pregnancy that the doctor ordered her pillows to sleep on. In the morning they took us all before the magistrate. The audience were fined one shilling a-head, or seven days; but they paid the shilling. We were all fined twenty shillings, or fourteen days. Some paid, but I couldn't raise it, so I was walked off.

"We were all in an awful fright when we found ourselves in the police-cell that night. Some said we should get six months, others twelve, and all we could say was, 'What on earth will our old women do?'

"We were all in our theatrical costumes. I was Hammer, the auctioneer, dressed in a long white coat, with the swallow-tails touching the ground, and blue bottoms. I had a long figured chintz waistcoat, and a pair of drab knee-breeches, grey stockings, and low shoes, and my hat was a white one with a low crown and broad brim, like a Quaker's. To complete it, I wore a full bushy wig. As we were being walked off from Walworth to Kennington-lane, to go before the magistrate, the tops of the houses and the windows were full of people, waiting to see us come along in our dresses. They laughed more than pitied us. The police got pelted, and I caught a severe blow by accident, from a turnip out of a greengrocer's shop.

"I served all the time at Kingston, in my theatrical dress. I had nothing but bread and water all the time, with gruel for breakfast and supper. I had to pick oakum and make mats. I was only there two days before I was made deputy-wardsman, for they saw I was a decent sort of fellow. I was very much cut up, thinking of the wife so near her confinement. It was very hard, I thought, putting us in prison for getting our bread, for we never had any warning, whatever our master may have had. I can tell you, it was a nail in my coffin, these fourteen days, and one of us, of the name of Chau, did actually die through it, for he was of a very delicate constitution, and the cold laid hold of him. Why, fellows of our life and animation, to be shut up like that, and not allowed to utter a word, it was dreadful severe.

"At this time a little penny work came out, entitled the 'Groans of the Gallows.' I was working at an establishment in Whitechapel and it was thought that something fresh would be a draw, and it was suggested that we should play this 'Groans of the Gallows,' for everything about hanging was always a hit. There was such a thing as ten people in the piece, and five was prominent characters. We got it written by one of the company, and it was called 'The Groans of the Gallows, or The Hangman's Career, illustrated with pictures.' This is how we brought it out. After an overture, the curtain rose and discovered a group on the stage, all with pots and pipes, gin measures, &c. They sing, 'We won't go home till morning,' and 'Kightly's a jolly good fellow.' Here the hangman is carousing with them, and his wife comes in and upbraids him with his intoxicating habits, and tells him that he spends all the money instead of purviding food for the children. A quarrel ensues, and he knocks her down with a quart pot and kills her. I was hangman. There is then a picture of amazement from all, and he's repenting of what he's done. He then says, 'This comes of a little drinking. From the half-pint to the pint, from the pint to the pot, and so on, till ruin stares me in the face. Not content with starving my children, I have murdered my wife. Oh that this may be a moral to all!'

"The officers come in and arrest him, when enters the sheriff, who tells him that he has forfeited his life; but that there is a vacancy for the public executioner, and that if he will accept the office his life shall be spared. He accepts the office, and all the characters groan at him. This ends the first scene. In the second enters Kightly and two officers, who have got him and accuse him of murder. He is taken off proclaiming his innocence. Scene the third. Kightly discovered at table in condemned cell, a few months supposing to have elapsed. The bell is tolling, and the hour of seven is struck. Enter sheriffs with hangman, and they tell him to do his duty. They then leave him, and he speaks thus: 'At length, then, two little months only have elapsed, and you, my friend, and pot-companion, aye, and almost brother, are the first victim that I have to execute for murder,' — and I shudder you know — 'which I know you are innocent of. Am *I* not a murderer, and do I not deserve hanging more than you? but the law will have its way, and I, the tool of that law, must carry it into force. It now becomes my painful duty to pinion your arms.' Then I do so, and it makes such a thrill through the house. 'I now take you from this place to your execution, where you will be suspended for one hour, and then it is my duty to cut you down. Have you any request to make?' He cries 'None!' and I add, 'Then follow me.' I always come on to that scene with a white night-cap and a halter on my arm. All the audience was silent as death as I spoke, and with tears in their eyes. Scene the fourth. Gallows being erected by workmen. That's picture, you know, our fixing the top beam with a hammer, another at the bottom, and a third arranging the bolt at the top. The bell still tolling, you know. Ah, it brought it home to one or two of them, I can tell you. As soon as the workmen have finished they go off. Enter procession of sheriff, parson, hangman, and the victim, with two officers behind. The parson asks the victim if he has any request to make, and he still says 'None', only he is innocent. The sheriffs then tell the hangman to do his duty. He then places the white cap over the man's head, and the noose about his neck, and is about leaving to draw the bolt, when I exclaim, 'Something here tells me that I ought not to hang this man. He is innocent, and I know it. I cannot, and I will not take his life.' Enter officer in haste, with pardon for Kightly. I then say, 'Kightly, you are free; live and be happy, and I am——' Here the sheriff adds, 'Doomed to the galleys for life.' That's because I refused to kill him, you know. I then exclaim, 'Then I shall be happy, knowing that I have not taken this man's life, and be thus enabled to give up the office of executioner and its most horrid paraphernalia.' Then there's blue fire and end of piece.

"That piece was very successful, and run for three weeks. It
drewn in a deal of money. The boys used to run after me in the
streets and call me Calcraft, so great was the hit I made in the
part. On one occasion a woman was to be hung, and I was going
along Newgate, past the prison, on the Sunday evening. There
was a quantity of people congregated, and some of the lads then
recognised me from seeing me act in the 'Groans from the Gallows,' and they sung out 'Here comes Calcraft!' Every eye was
turned towards me. Some said, 'No, no; that ain't him; but the
boys replied, 'Oh, yes it is; that's the man that played it at the
gaff.' Of course I mizzled for fear of a stone or two.

"The pay of an actor in private business varies from two shillings and sixpence to three shillings, and each man is also supposed
to sing two songs in each performance, which makes three performances a night besides performing a sketch. Your engagement
lasts as long as you suit the audience; for if you're a favourite
you may have such a thing as nine months at a time. Whenever
we have a benefit it's a ticket one, which amounts to two hundred
tickets and your night's salary, which generally brings you in a
pound, with your pay included. There's one in the company
generally has a benefit every Thursday, so that your turn comes
once in about six months, for the musicians, and the checktakers,
and all has their turn.

"The expense of putting a new piece on the stage is not more
than a pound, and that includes new scenery. They never do such
a thing as buy new dresses. Perhaps they pay such a thing as six
shillings a-week for their wardrobe to hire the dresses. Some gives
as much as ten shillings; but then, naturally, the costume is more
showy. All that we are supposed to find is russet boots, a set of
fleshings, a ballet shirt, and a wig.

"Town work is the more quiet and more general-business like.
There's no casualty in it, for you're not in shares, but on salaries,
and after your work there's your money, for we are paid nightly.
I have known as much as thirty-five shillings a-week given at one
of these theatres, when the admission is only a penny and twopence. Where I was at it would hold from six to seven hundred
people, and there was three performances a-night; and, indeed,
on Saturdays and Mondays generally four. We have no extra pay

for extra performances. The time allowed for each representation is from one hour to an hour and three-quarters. If we find there is a likelihood of a fourth house, we leave out a song each singer, and that save half an hour. As soon as one house is turned out another comes in, for they are always waiting outside the doors, and there is a rush immediately the house is empty. We begin at six and are over by a few minutes before twelve. When we do speaking pieces we have to do it on the sly, as we should be stopped and get into trouble."

THE GUN-EXERCISE
EXHIBITOR—ONE-LEGGED ITALIAN

"I AM an Italian, domiciled at Genoa, and I speak very little French, only just enough to ask for things—to get my life with, you know. Genoa is the most rich town in Piedmont, but it is not the most jolie. Oh no! no! no! Turin is the most beautiful, oh yes! It is a long street of palaces. You know Turin is where the King of Sardinia, with the long moustaches, lives. Has Monsieur been to Turin? No! Ah, it is a great sight! Perhaps Monsieur has seen Genoa? No! Ah, you have a great pleasure to come. Genoa is very rich, but Turin is very beautiful. I prefer Turin.

"I was a soldier in my country. Oh, not an officer. I was in the 2nd battalion of the Bassolein, nearly the same as the Chasseurs de Vincennes in France. It is the first regiment in Piedmont. We had a green uniform with a roll collar, and a belt round one shoulder, and a short rifle. We had a feather one side of our hats, which are of felt. Ah, c'était bien joli ça! We use long bullets, Minié ones. All the army in my country are under four brothers, who are all generals, and Ferdinando Marmora is the commander-in-chief—the same that was in the Crimea. Nearly all my companions in the Bassolein regiment were from the Tyrol. Ah, they shoot well! They never miss. They always kill. Sacré Dieu!

"I was wounded at the bataille de Pescare, against the Austrians. We gained the battle and entered the town. The General Radetzky was against us. He is a good general, but Ferdinando Marmora beat him. Ferdinando was wounded by a ball in the cheek. It passed from left to right. He has the mark now. Ah, he is a good general. I was wounded. Pardon! I cannot say if it was a bal de canon or a bal de fusil. I was on the ground like one dead. I fell with with my leg bent behind me, because they found me so. They tell me, that as I fell I cried, 'My God! my God!' but that is not in my memory. After they had finished the battle they took up the wounded. Perhaps I was on the ground twelve hours, but I do not know exactly. I was picked up with others and taken to the hospital, and then one day after my leg decomposed, and it was cut directly. All the bone was fracassé, vairy beaucoup. I was in the hospital for forty days. Ah! it was terrible. To cut the nerves was terrible. They correspond with the head. Ah, horrible! They gave me no chloroform. Rien! rien! No, nor any dormitore, as we call it in Italian, you know,—something in a glass to drink and make you sleep. Rien! rien! If I had gone into the Hôpital des Invalides, I should have had 20 sous a-day; but I would not, and now my pension is 12 sous a-day. I am paid that now; whether I am here or there, it is the same. My wife receives the 12 sous whilst I am here. I shall not stop here long. The language is too difficult. No, I shall not learn it, because at the house where I lodge we speak Italian, and in the streets I speak to no one.

"I have been to France, but there the policemen were against me. They are bêtes, the policemen français. The gentlemen and ladies are all good. As I walked in the streets with my crutch, one would say, 'Here, poor fellow, are two sous'; or, 'Come with me and have some wine.' They are good hearts there. Whilst I was going to Paris I walk on my leg. I also even now and then find good occasions for mounting in a voiture. I say to them, 'Monsieur, accord me the relief of a ride?' and they say, 'Yes, come, come.'

"In England no police interfere with me. Here it is good. If the police say to me 'Go on, go on,' I say, 'Pardon, Monsieur,' and move away. I never ask any body for money. I work in the streets, and do my gun exercise, and then I leave it to the Bon Dieu to make them give me something. I never ask.

"I have been very unfortunate. I have a tumour come under the arm where I rest on my crutch. It is a tumour, as they call it in France, but I do not know what it is named in English. I went to the hospital of San Bartolommeo and they cut it for me. Then I have hurt my stomach, from the force of calling out the differing orders of commanding, whilst I do my gun exercises in the streets. I was two months in my bed with my arm and my stomach being bad. Some days I cannot go out, I am so ill. I cannot drink beer, it is too hot for me, and gets to my head, and it is bad for my stomach. I eat fish: that is good for the voice and the stomach. Now I am better, and my side does not hurt me when I cry out my commanding orders. If I do it for a long time it is painful.

"Ah, pauvre diable! to stop two months in my bed, June, August! The most beautiful months. It was ruin to me.

"After I have gone out for one day, I am forced to rest for the next one. Monday, I go out, because I repose on the Sunday. Then all goes well, I am strong in my voice. But I cannot travailler two days following. It is not my leg, that is strong. It is my stomach, and the pains in my side from crying out my commandements. When I go out I make about 10s. a-week. Yes, it comes to that. It is more than 1s. a-day.

"I have a cold. I go out one day when it blew from the north, and the next day I was ill. It makes more cold than at Genoa, but at Turin in the winter it is more cold than here. It is terrible, terrible. A servant brings in a jug of water, and by-and-by it has ice on its top. I find the bourgeois and not the militaires give the most money. All the persons who have voyagé in France and Italy will give me money—not much, you know, but to me a fortune, fortune! If I see a foreigner in the crowd I speak to him. I know the face of an étranger tout-de-suite. Some say to me, 'Vous parlez Francais?' 'Oui Monsieur.' Others ask me, 'You speak Italian?' 'Si, Signor.' I never, when I go through my exercise, begin by addressing the people. If I told them I had been a soldier in the army of Sardinia, they would not understand me. Yes, some of the words sound the same in French and English, such as army and soldat, but I have not the heart to beg. I have been soldier, and I cannot take off my cap and beg. I work for what they give me. They give me money and I give them my exercise. I sometimes have done my exercise before a great crowd of people, and when it is done nobody will give me money, and my heart sinks within me. I stand there honteux. One will then in pity throw a sou, but I cannot pick it up, for I will not sell my pride for a penny. If they hand it to me, then I take it, and am pleased with their kindness. But I have only one leg, and to throw the penny on the ground is cruel, for I cannot bend down, and it hurts my pride to put such money in my pocket.

"The little children do not annoy me in the streets, because I never do my exercise until they are at school. Between one and two I never do my exercise, because the little children they are going back to their lessons. They never mock me in the streets,

241

for I have been unfortunate to lose my legs, and nobody will mock a miserable fortuné. The carts of the butchers and the bakers, which carry the meat and the bread, and go so fast in the streets, they frighten me when I do my exercises. They nearly écrasé the gens. Tenez! Yesterday I go to the chemin de fer de Birmingham, to the open space before the station, and then I do my exercise. All the people come to their windows and collect about to see me. I walk about like a soldier—but only on my one leg, you know, hopping—and I do my exercise with my crutch for my gun. I stand very steady on one leg. There was a coachman of a cab, and he continued to drive his horse at me, and say, 'Go on! go on!' There was no policeman, or he would not have dared to do it, for the policemen protect me. Le bête! I turn upon him and cry, 'Bête! take care, bête!' But he still say, 'Get on.' The cheval come close to my back whilst I hop on my one leg to avoid him. At last I was very tired, and he cried out always, 'Get on! get on!' So cried out for help, and all the ladies run out from their houses and protect me. They said, 'Poor fellow! poor fellow!' and all gave me half a sou. If I had had five shillings in my pocket, I would have gone to a journal and reported that bête, and had the fellow exposed; but I had not five shillings, so I could not go to a journal.

"When I do my exercise, this what I do. I first of all stand still on one leg, in the position of a militaire, with my crutch shouldered like a gun. That is how I accumulate the persons. Then I have to do all. It makes me laugh for I have to be the general, the capitaines, the drums, the soldiers, and all. Pauvre diable! I must live. It is curious, and makes me laugh.

"I first begin my exercises by doing the drums. I beat my hands together, and make a noise like this—'hum, hum! hum, hum! hum, hum! hum, hum! hu-u-u-m!' and then the drums go away and I do them in the distance. You see I am the drummers then. Next I become the army, and make a noise with my foot, resembling soldiers on a march, and I go from side to side to imitate an army marching. Then I become the trumpeters, but instead of doing the trumpets I whistle their music, and the sound comes nearer and nearer, and gets louder and louder, and then gradually dies away in the distance, as if a bataillon was marching in front of its general. I make a stamping with my foot, like men marching past. After that I become the officers, the capitaines and the lieutenants, as if the general was passing before them, and my crutch becomes my sword instead of my gun. Then I draw it from my side, and present it with the handle pointed to my breast. Then I become the general, and I gives this order: 'Separate bataillons three steps behind—un, deux, trois!' and I instantly turn to the army again and give three hops to the side, so that the general may walk up and down before me and see how the soldiers are looking. Then I in turn become the officer who gives the commands, and the soldiers who execute them. In hurts my voice when I cry out these commands. They must be very loud or all the army would not hear them. I can be heard a long way off when I call them out. I begin with a 'PORTEZ AR-R-RMES!' that is, 'Carry arms,' in England. Then I lift my crutch up on my left side and hold it there. Then comes 'PRESENT AR-R-RMES!' and then I hold the gun—my crutch, you know—in front of me, straight up. The next is, 'REPOSE AR-R-RMES!' and I put to my hip, with the barrel leaning forwards. When I say, barrel, it's only my crutch, you understand. Then I shout, 'Un, deux, trois! GROUND AR-R-RMS!' and let the top of my crutch slide on to the road, and I stamp with my toes to resemble the noise. Afterwards I give the command, 'PORTEZ AR-R-RMES!' and then I carry my arms again in my left hand, and slap my other hand hard down by my right side, like a véritable soldier, and stand upright in position. Whilst I am so I shout, 'SEPARATE THE COLUMNS! UN, DEUX, TR-R-ROIS!' and instantly I hop on my one leg three times backwards, so as to let the general once more walk down the ranks and inspect the men. As soon as he is supposed to be near to me, I shout 'PRESENT AR-R-RMES!' and then I hold my gun—the crutch, you comprehend—in front of me. Then, as soon as the general is supposed to have passed, I shout out, 'REPOSE AR-R-RMES!'' and I let the crutch slant from the right hip, waiting until I cry again 'GROUND AR-R-R-RMES! UN, DEUX, TR-R-ROIS!' and then down slides the crutch to the ground.

"Next I do the other part of the review. I do the firing, now only, you comprehend, I don't fire, but only imitate it with my crutch. I call out 'GROUND AR-R-RMS!' and let the top of my crutch fall to the earth. After that I shout, 'LOAD AR-R-RMS! UN, DEUX, TR-R-ROIS!' and I pretend to take a cartouche from my side and bite off the end, and slip it down the barrel of my crutch. Next I give the command, 'DRAW RAM-RODS! UN. DEUX, TR-R-ROIS!' and then I begin to ram the cartridge home to the breech of the barrel. Afterwards I give the command, 'COCK AR-R-RMS!' and then I pretend to take a percussion cap from my side-pocket, and I place it on the nipple and draw back the hammer. Afterwards I shout, 'POINT AR-R-RMS!' and I pretend to take aim. Next I shout, 'RECOVER AR-R-RMS!' that is, to hold the gun up in the air, and not to fire. Then I give orders, such as 'POINT TO THE LEFT,' or 'POINT TO THE RIGHT,' and, whichever way it is, I have to twist myself round on my one leg, and take an aim that way. Then I give myself the order to 'FIRE!' and I imitate it by a loud shout, and then rattling my tongue as if the whole line was firing. As quickly as I can call out I shout, 'RECOVER AR-R-RMS!' and I put up my gun before me to resist with my bayonet any charge that may be made. Then I shout out, 'DRAW UP THE RANKS AND RECEIVE THE CAVALRY!' and then I work myself along on my one foot, but not by hopping; and then I am waiting for the enemy's horse, and ready to receive them. After I have fired, I call out, 'CHAR-R-RGE!' and then I hop forward as fast as I can, as if I was rushing down upon the enemy, like this. Ah! I was nearly charging through your window; I only stopped in time, or I should have broken the squares in reality. Such a victory would have cost me too dear. After I have charged the enemy and put them to flight, then I draw myself up again, and give the order to 'FORM COLUMNS!' And next I 'CARRY AR-R-RMS,' and then 'PRESENT AR-R-RMS,' and finish by 'GROUNDING AR-R-RMS, UN, DEUX, TR-R-ROIS.'

"Oh, I have forgotten one part. I do it after the charging. When I have returned from putting the enemy to flight, I become the general calling his troops together. I shout, 'AR-R-RMS ON THE SHOULDER!' and then I become the soldier, and let my gun rest on my shoulder, the same as when I am marching. Then I shout, 'MARCH!' and I hop round on my poor leg, for I cannot march, you comprehend, and I suppose myself to be defiling be-

fore the general. Next comes the order 'HALT!' and I stop still.
"It does not fatigue me to hop about on one leg. It is strong as
iron. It is never fatigued. I have walked miles on it with my
crutch. It only hurts my chest to holloa out the commands, for
if I do not do it with all my force it is not heard far off. Besides,
I am supposed to be ordering an army, and you must shout out
to be heard by all the men; and although I am the only one, to be
sure, still I wish to make the audience believe I am an army.

"One day I was up where there is the Palace of the Regina,
by the park, with the trees—a very pretty spot, with a park
corner, you know. I was there, and I go by a street where the
man marks the omnibus which pass, and I go down a short street,
and I come to a large place where I do my exercises. A gentleman
say to me, 'Come, my friend,' and I go into his house, and he
give me some bread, and some meat, and some beer, and a shilling,
and I do my exercises for him. That is the only house where I
was called to perform inside. He spoke Italian, and French, and
English, so that I not know which country he belongs to. Another
day I was doing my exercises and some little children, called to
their mamma. 'Oh, look! look! come here! the soldier! the soldier!'
and the dame said to me, 'Come here and perform to my little
boys'; and she gave me sixpence. Those are my fortunes, for to-
day I may take two or three shillings, and to-morrow nothing but
a few miserable sous; or perhaps I am ill in my stomach with
shouting, and I cannot come out to work for my living.

"When it is cold it makes the end of my leg, where it's cut off,
begin to tremble, and then it almost shakes me with its shivering,
and I am forced to go home, for it is painful.

"I have been about fourteen months. They wanted 4s. to bring
me from Boulogne to London; but I had no money; so at the
bureau office they gave me a ticket for nothing. Then I came
straight to London. When I came to London I couldn't speak
English, and I knew no one, had no money, and didn't know where
to lodge. That is hard—bien dur. I bought some bread and eat it
and then in the evening I met an Italian who plays on the organ,
you know; and he said, 'Come with me;' and he took me to his
lodgings, and there I found Italians and Frenchmen, and I was
happy. I began to work the next day at my exercises.

"One day I was in the quarter of the palaces, by the park, you know, and I began my exercises. I could not speak English, and a policeman came to me and said, 'Go on!' What's that? I thought. He said, 'Go on!' again, and I couldn't comprehend, and asked him, 'Parlate Italiano?' and he kept on saying. 'Go on!' This is drole, I thought; so I said, 'Vous parlez Francais?' and he still said, 'Go on!' What he meant I couldn't make out, for I didn't know English, and I had only been here a week. I thought he wanted to see my exercises, so I began, 'Portez ar-r-r-mes!' and he still said, 'Go on!' Then I laughed, and made some signs to follow him. Oh, I thought, it is some one else who wants to see my exercises; and I followed him, enchanted with my good fortune. But, alas! he took me to a police office. There I had an interpreter, and I, was told I must not do my exercises in the street. When I told them I was a soldier in the army of the ally of England, and that I had been wounded in battle, and lost my leg fighting for my country, they let me go; and since the policemen are very kind to me, and always say, 'Go on,' with much politeness. I told the magistrate in Italian. 'How can England, so rich and so powerful, object to a pauvre diable like me earning a sou, by showing the exercises of the army of its ally?' The magistrate laughed, and so did the people, and I said, 'Good day,' and made my reverence and left. I have never been in a prison. Oh, no! no! no! no! no! What harm could I do? I have not the power to be a criminal, and I have the heart to be an honest man, and live by my exercises.

'I have travelled in the country. I went to Cheltenham and Bristol. I walked very little of the way. I did my exercises at one place, and then I got enough to go to another town. Ah, it is beautiful country out there. I went to Bristol. I made 7s. in two days there. But I don't like the country. It does not suit me. I prefer London.

"I one day did my exercises by—what do you call it? where the people go up—high, high—no, not St. Paul's—no, by a bridge, where there is an open space. Yes, the monument of Nelson; and then, Oh! what a crowd! To the right and the left, and to the front and behind, an immense crowd to see my exercises. I made a good deal of money that day. A great deal. The most that I ever did.

"I make about 8s. a-week regularly; I make more than that some weeks, but I often don't go out for a week, because in the rain nobody will come to see my exercises. Some weeks I make 15s., but others not 5s. But I must make 8s. to be able to pay for lodgings, and food, and washing, and clothes, and for my shoe; for I only want one. I give 3d. a-day for my lodgings; but then we have a kitchen, and a fire in it, where we go and sit. There are a great many paysans there, a great many boys, where I lodge, and that gives me pain to see them; for they have been brought over from their country, and here they are miserable, and cannot speak a word of English, and are made to work for their master, who takes the money. Oh! it's make me much pain.

"I cannot say if there are any others who do their exercises in the streets; but I have never seen any. I am, I think, the only stranger who does his exercises. It was my own idea. I did it in France whilst I was travelling; but it was only once or twice, for it was défendu to do it; and the policemen are very severe. Ils sont bêtes, les policemen en France. The gentlemens and ladies very good heart, and give a poor diable des sous, or offer wine to pauvre diable qui a perdu sa jambe en combattant pour sa patrie; mais les policemen sont bêtes. Ah, bêtes! so bêtes I can't tell you."

ITALIAN PIPERS AND CLARIONET PLAYERS

"THE COMPANION I got about with me, is with me from Naples, not the city, but in the country. His is of my family; no, not my cousin, but my mother was the sister of his cousin. Yes! yes! yes! my cousin. Some one told me he was my nephew, but it's cousin. Naples is a pretty city. It is more pretty than Paris, but not so big. I worked on the ground at Naples, in the country, and I guarded sheep. I never was a domestic; but it was for my father. It was ground of his. It was not much. He worked the earth for yellow corn. He had not much of sheep, only fifteen. I go out with the sheep I carry my bagpipes always with me. I play on them when I was sixteen years of age. I play them when I guard my sheep. In my country they call my instrument de 'zampogna.' All the boys in my country play on it, for there are many masters there who teach it. I taught myself to play it. I bought my own instrument. I gave the money myself for that affair. It cost me seven francs. The bag is made of a skin of goat. There are four clarionets to it. There is one for the high and one for the bass. I play them with different hands. The other two clarionets make a noise to make the accord; one makes high and the other the low. They drone to make harmony. The airs I play are the airs of my country. I did not invent them. One is 'La Tarentule Italien,' and another is what we call 'La Badend,' but I not know what you call it in French. Another is the 'Death of the Roi de France.' I know ten of these airs. The 'Pastorelle Neapolitan' is very pretty, and so is the 'Pastorelle Romaine.'

"When I go out to guard my sheep I play my zampogna, and I walk along and the sheep follow me. Sometimes I sit down and the sheep eat about me, and I play on my instrument. Sometimes I go into the mountains. There are plenty of mountains in my country, and with snow on them. I can hear the guardians of sheep playing all around me in the mountains. Yes, many at once, —six, ten, twelve, or fifteen, on every side. No, I did not play my instrument to keep my sheep together, only to learn the airs.

249

I was a good player, but there were others who played much better than me. Every night in my village there are four or six who play together instruments like mine, and all the people dance. They prefer to dance to the 'Tarentule Italien'. It is a pretty dance in our costume. The English do not dance like nous autres. We are not paid for playing in the village, only at fêtes, when gentlemen say, 'Play;' and then they give 20 sous or 40 sous, like that. There is the one only for singing chansons, and another for singing 'La prière de la Vierge.' Those that play the zampogna go to the houses, and the candles are lighted on the altar, and we play while the bourgeois sing the prière.

"I am aged 23 years next March. I was sixteen when I learnt my instrument. The twelfth of this month I shall have left my country nine months. I have traversed the states of Rome and of France to come to England. I marched all the distance, playing my zampogna. I gain ten sous French whilst I voyage in the states of France. I march from Marseilles to Paris. To reach Marseilles by the boat it cost 15 frs. by head.

"The reason why we left our native land is this:—One of our comrades had been to Paris, and he had said he gained much money by painters by posing for his form. Then I had envy to go to Paris and gain money. In my country they pay 20 sous for each year for each sheep. I had 200 to guard for a monsieur, who was very rich. There were four of us left our village at the same time. We all four played de zampogna. My father was not content that I voyage the world. He was very sorry. We got our passport arranged tout de suite, two passport for us four. We all began to play our instruments together, as soon as we were out of the village. Four of our friends accompanied us on our road, to say adieu. We took bread of corn with us to eat for the first day. When we had finished that we played at the next village, and they give us some more bread.

"At Paris I posed to the artists, and they pay me 20 sous for the hour. The most I pose is four hours for the day. We could not play our instruments in the street, because the serjeant-de-ville catch us, and take us directly to prison. I go to play in the courts before the houses. I asked the concierge at the door if he would give me permission to play in the court. I gain 15 sous or 1 franc par jour. For all the time I rest in Paris I gain 2 francs for the day. This is with posing to artists to paint, and for playing. I also play at the barriere outside Paris, where the wine is cheap. They gave us more there than in the courts; they are more generous where they drink the wine.

"When I arrive at Paris my comrades have leave me. I was alone in Paris. There an Italian proposed to me to go to America as his servant. He had two organs, and he had two servants to play them, and they gave him the half of that which they gained. He said to me that he would search for a piano organ for me, and I said I would give him the half of that which I gained in the streets. He made us sign a card before a notary. He told us it would cost 150 francs to go to America. I gave him the money to pay from Paris to Folkestone. From there we voyaged on foot to Londres. I only worked for him for eight days, because I said I would not go to Amérique. He is here now, for he has no money to go in Amérique.

"I met my cousin here in Londres. I was here fifteen days before I met him. We neither of us speak Anglais, and not French either, only a little very bad; but we understand it. We go out together now, and I play the zampogna, and he the 'biforc Italien,' or what the French call flageolet, and the English pipes. It is like a flageolet. He knows all the airs that I play. He play well the airs—that he does. He wears a cloak on his shoulders, and I have one, too; but I left it at home to-day. It is a very large cloak, with three yards of étoffe in it. He carry in his hat a feather of what you call here peacock, and a French lady give him the bright ribbon which is round his hat. I have also plume de peacock and flowers of stuff, like at the shops, round my hat. In my country we always put round our hat white and red flowers.

"Sometimes we go to pose to the artists, but it is not always. There are plenty of artists near Newman-street, but in other quarters there are none at all. It is for our costume they paint us. The colours they put on the pictures are those of our costume I have been three times to a gentleman in a large street, where they took our portraits photographique. They gave a shilling. I know the houses where I go to be done for a portrait, but I don't know the names of the messiers, or the streets where they reside.

At the artists' they pay 1s. par heure, and we pose two or three heures, and the most is four heures. When we go together we have 1s. each for the hour. My cousin is at an artist's to-day. They paint him more than me, because he carries a sash of silk round his waist with ornaments on it. I haven't got one, because I want the money to buy one.

"We gain 1s. each the day. Ah! pardon, monsieur, not more than that. The artists are not for every day, perhaps one time for the week. When we first come here, we take 5s. between the two, but now it makes cold, and we cannot often play. Yesterday we play in the ville, and we take 7d. each. Plenty of persons look at us, but when my comrade touch his hat they give nothing. There is one month we take 2s. each the day, but now it is 1s. For the three months that we have been here, we have gained 12s. the week each, that is, if we count what we took when first we arrived. For two months we took always a crown every day—always, always; but now it is only 1s., or 2s., or 7d. I have saved 72s., and I had it in my bourse, which I place under my head when I sleep. We sleep three in a bed—myself, my cousin and another Italian. In the night this other take my bourse and run away. Now I have only 8s. in my bourse. It nearly broke the heart when I was robbed.

"We pay 2d. for each for our bed every night. We live in a house held by a Mossieu Italian. There are three who sleep in one bed—me, and my comrade, and another. We are not large. This mossieu let us lodge cheaper than others, because we are miserable, and have not much money. For breakfast we have a half-loaf each one. It is a loaf that you must pay 4d. or 4¹/₂d. We pay 2¹/₂d. each for that, and ¹/₂d. each for a cup of tea or coffee. In the day we eat 2d, or 3d. between both for some bread, and we come home the night at half-past eight, and we eat supper. It is of macaroni, or potatoes boiled, and we pay 2¹/₂d. each. It costs us 9d. each the day to live. There are twenty-four Italians in the house where we live, and they have three kitchens. When one is more miserable than the others, then he is helped; and at another time he assists in his turn. We pay 2d. a-week to wash our shirt. I always share with my cousin what he makes in the day. If he goes to work and I stop at home, it is the same thing, and the same with me. He carries the money always, and pays for what we have want to eat; and then, if I wish to go back to my own country, then we share the money when we separate.

"The gentlemen give us more money than the ladies. We have never had anything to eat given to us. They have asked us to sing, but we don't know how. Only one we have sung to an Italian mossieu, who make our portraits. We sang the 'Prayer of the Sainte Vierge.' They have also asked us to dance, but we did not, because the serjeant-de-ville, if we assemble a great mob, come and defend us to play.

"We have been once before the magistrate, to force the mossieu who brought us over to render the passport of my native village. He has not rendered to me my card. We shall go before a magistrate again some day.

"I can read and write Italian. I did not go much to the school of my native village, but the master taught me what I know. I can read better than I write, for I write very bad and slow. My cousin cannot read and write. I also know my numbers, I can count quickly. When we write a letter, we go to an Italian mossieu, and we tell him to say this and that, and he puts it down on the paper. We pay 1s. for the letter, and then at the post they make us pay 2s. 2d. When my parents get a letter from me, they take it to a mossieu, or the schoolmaster of the village, to read for them, because they cannot read. They have sent me a letter. It was well written by a gentleman who wrote it for them. I have sent my mother five pieces of five fancs from Paris. I gave the money, and they gave me a letter; and then my mother went to the consul at Naples, and they gave her the money. Since I have been here I could send no money, because it was stolen. If I had got it, I should have sent some to my parents. When I have some more, I shall send it.

"I love my mother very much, and she is good, but my father is not good. If he gain a piece of 20 sous, he goes on the morrow to the marchand of wine, and play the cards, and spend it to drink. I never send my money to my father, but to my mother."

AN ITALIAN WITH MONKEY

AN ITALIAN, who went about with trained monkeys, furnished me with the following account.

He had a peculiar boorish, and yet good-tempered expression, especially when he laughed, which he did continually.

He was dressed in a brown, ragged, cloth jacket, which was buttoned over a long, loose, dirty, drab waistcoat, and his trousers were of broad-ribbed corduroy, discoloured with long wearing. Round his neck was a plaid handkerchief, and his shoes were of the extreme "strong-men's" kind, and grey with dust and want of blacking. He wore the Savoy and broad-rimmed felt hat, and with it on his head had a very picturesque appearance, and the shadow of the brim falling on the upper part of his brown face gave him almost a Murillo-like look. There was, however, an odour about him,—half monkey, half dirt,—that was far from agreeable, and which pervaded the apartment in which he sat.

"I have got monkey," he said, "but I mustn't call in London. I goes out in countree. I was frightened to come here. I was frightened you give me months in prison. Some of my countrymen is very frightened what you do. No, sir, I never play de monkey in de town. I have been out vare dere is so many donkey, up a top dat village—vat you call—I can't tell de name. Dey goes dere for pastime,—pleasure,—when it makes fine weather. Dere is two church, and two large hotel,—yes, I tink it is Blackheath! I goes dere sometime vid my monkey. I have got only one monkey now,—sometime I have got two;—he is dressed comme un soldat rouge, like one soldier, vid a red jacket and a Bonaparte's hat. My monkey only pull off his hat and take a de money. He used to ride a de dog; but dey stole a de dog,—some of de tinkare, a man vid de umbrella going by, stole a him. Dere is only tree months dat I have got my monkey. It is my own. I have dirty-five shillings for dis one I got.

"He did not know no tricks when he come to me first. I did

teach a him all he know. I teach a him vid de kindness, do you see. I must look rough for tree or four times, but not to beat him. He can hardly stir about; he is afraid dat you go to hit him, you see. I mustn't feed him ven I am teaching him. Sometimes I buy a happorth of nuts to give him, after he has done what I want him to do. Dis one has not de force behind; he is weak in de back. Some monkey is like de children at de school, some is very hard to teash, and some learn de more quick, you see. De one I had before dis one could do many tings. He had not much esprit pas grande chose; but he could play de drum,—de fiddle, too,—Ah! but he don't play de fiddle like de Christian, you know; but like de monkey. He used to fight wid de sword,—not exatly like de Christian, but like de monkey too,—much better. I beg your pardon to laugh, sir! He used to move his leg and jomp,—I call it danse,—but he could not do polka like de Christian.—I have seen the Christian though what can't danse more dan de monkey! I beg your pardon to laugh. I did play valtz to him on de organ. Non! he had not moosh ear for de musick, but I force him to keep de time by de jerk of de string. He commence to valtz well when he die. He is dead the vinter dat is passed, at Sheltenham. He eat some red-ee paint. I give him some castor-oil, but no good: he de in great deal pain, poor fellow! I rather lose six pounds that lose my monkey. I did cry!—I cry because I have no money to go and buy anoder monkey! Yes! I did love my monkey! I did love him for the sake of my life! I give de raisins, and bile dem for him. He have every ting he like. I am come here from Parma about fourteen or fifteen year ago. I used to work in my countree. I used to go and look at de ship in de montagnes: non! non! pas des vaisseaux, mais des moutons! I beg your pardon to laugh. De master did bring me up here,—dat master is gone to America now,—he is come to me and tell me to come to Angleterre. He has tell me I make plenty of money in dis country.

"Ah! I could get plenty of money in dat time in London, but now I get not moosh. I vork for myself at present. My master give me nine-ten shilling each week, and my foot, and my lodging —yes! everything ven I am first come here. I used to go out vid de organ,—a good one,—but I did get two, tree, and more shillan for my master each day. It was chance-work: sometimes I did get

noting at all. De organ was my master's. He had no one else
but me vid him. We used to travel about together, and he took
all de money. He had one German piano, and play de moosick.
I can't tell how moosh he did make,— he never tell to me,—but
I did sheat him sometimes myself. Sometime when I take de two
shillan I did give him de eighteen-pence! I beg your pardon to
laugh! De man did bring up many Italians to dis country, but now
it is difficult to get de passports for my countrymen.

"I was eighteen months with my master; after dat I vent to
farm-house. I run away from my master. He gave me a slap
of de face, you know, von time, so I don't like it, you know, and
run away! I beg your pardon to laugh! I used to do good many
tings at de farm-house. It was in Yorkshire. I used to look at de
beasts, and take a de vater. I don't get noting for my vork, only
for de sake of de belly I do it. I was dere about tree year. Dey
behave to me very well. Dey give me de clothes and all I want.
After dat I go to Liverpool, and I meet some of my countrymen
dere, and dey lend me de monkey, and I teash him to danse,
fight, and jomp, mush as I could, and I go wid my monkey about
de country.

"Some day I make tree shillan wid my monkey, sometime only
sixpence, and sometime noting at all. When it rain or snow I can
get noting. I gain peut-etre a dozen shillan a week wid my monkey,
sometime more, but not often. Dere is long time I have been in de
environs of London; but I don't like to go in de streets here.
I don't like to go to prison. Monkey is defended,—*défendu,*—what
you call it, in London. But dere is many monkey in London still.
Oh, non! not a dozen. Dere is not one dozen monkey wot play
in Angleterre. I know dere is two monkey at Saffron hill, and one
go in London; but he do no harm. I don't know dat de monkey
was train to go down de area and steal a de silver spoons out of
de kitchen. Dey would be great fool to tell dat; but every one
must get a living de best dey can. Wot I tell you about de monkey
I'm frightened vill hurt me!

"I tell you dey is defended in de streets, and dey take me up.
I hope not. My monkey is very honest monkey, and get me de
bread. I never was in prison, and I would not like to be. I play
de moosick, and please de people, and never steal noting. Non!

non! me to steal, nor my monkey too. Dey policeman never say noting to me. I am not beggar, but artiste!—every body know dat—and my monkey is artiste too! I beg your pardon to laugh."

AN ETHIOPIAN SERENADER

"It must be eight years ago," he commenced, "since the Ethiopian serenading come up—aye, it must be at least that time, because the twopenny boats was then running to London-bridge, and it was before the 'Cricket' was blown up. I know that, because we used to work the boats serenading. I used to wear a yellow waistcoat, in imitation of them at the St. James's Theatre.

"The first came out at St. Jame's Theatre, and they made a deal of money. There was five of them—Pell was bones, Harrington was concertina, I think, White was violin, Stanwood the banjo, and Germain the tambourine. I think that's how it was, but I can easy ascertain. After them sprang up the 'Lantum Serenaders' and the 'Ohio Serenaders,' the 'South Carolina Serenaders,' the 'Kentucky Minstrels,' and many other schools of them; but Pell's gang was at the top of the tree. Juba was along with Pell. Juba was a first class—a regular A I—he was a regular black, and a plendid dancer in boots.

"As soon as I could get in to vamp the tunes on the banjo a little, I went at it, too. I wasn't long behind them, you may take your oath. We judged it would be a hit, and it was fine. We got more money at it then than we do at any game now. First of all we formed a school of three—two banjos and a tambourine, and after that we added a bones and a fiddle. We used to dress up just the same then as now. We'd black our faces, and get hold of a white hat, and put a black band round it, or have big straw hats and high collars up to the ears. We did uncommonly well. The boys would follow us for miles, and were as good as advertisements, for they'd shout 'Here's the blacks!' as if they was trumpeting us. The first songs we came out with were 'Old Joe,' 'Dan Tucker,' and 'Going ober de Mountain,' and 'O come along, you sandy boys.' Our opening chorus was 'The Wild Racoon Track,' and we finished up with the 'Railway Overture,' and it was more like the railway than music, for it was all thumping and whistling, for nobody knowed how to play the banjo then.

"When I went out pitching first I could sing a good song; but it has ruined my voice now, for I used to sing at the top—tenor is the professional term.

"It wasn't everybody as could be a nigger then. We was thought angels then. It's got common now, but still I've no hesitation in saying that, keep steady and sober, and it works well to the present day. You can go and get a good average living now.

"We could then, after our 'mungare' and 'buvare' (that's what we call eat and drink, and I think it's broken Italian), carry home our 5s. or 6s. each easy. We made long days, and did no night-work. Besides, we was always very indifferent at our business, indeed. I'd be blowed if I'd trust myself out singing as I did then: we should get murdered. It was a new thing, and people thought our blunders was intended. We used to use blacking then to do our faces—we got Messrs. Day and Martin to do our complexion then. Burnt cork and beer wasn't so popular then.

"I continued at the nigger business ever since. I and my mate have been out together, and we've gone out two, and three, and four, up to eleven in a school, and we've shared better when eleven than when we was two. The highest we've got in a day has been £1 6s. each, at the Portsmouth review, when Napier went out with the fleet, above two years ago. We walked down to Portsmouth a-purpose. We got 14s. 6d. each—and there was five of us—at the launch of the 'Albert.'

"The general dress of the nigger is a old white hat and a long-tailed coat; or sometimes, when we first come out, in white waist-coats and coats; or even in striped shirts and wigs, and no hats at all. It's according to fancy and fashion, and what takes.

"When we go to a cheap concert-room, such as the Albion, Ratcliffe-highway, or the Ship and Canal, Bermondsey, our usual business is to open with a chorus, such as 'Happy are we,' though, perhaps, we haven't had a bit of grub all day, and been as wretched as possible; and then we do a song or two, and then 'crack a wid, as we say, that is, tell an anecdote such as this:—

"Three old niggers went to sea on a paving-stone. The first never had any legs, the next never had any arms, and the other was strip stark naked. So the one without any legs said, 'I see de bird; so the one without any arms took up a gun and shot it, and the one without any legs after it, and the one that was strip stark naked put it in his pocket. Now, you tell me what pocket that was?'

"Then another says, 'In his wainscoat pocket.' Then I return, 'How can he if he was naked? Can you give the inflammation of that story? Do you give it up.' Then he says, 'No, won't give it up.' Then I say, 'Would you give it up if you had it.' Then he says, 'Yes!' and I reply, 'The inflammation of that is the biggest lie that ebber was told.'

"Sometimes we do conundrums between the songs. I ask, 'Can you tell me how to spell blind pig in two letters?' and then he, remembering the first story, answers, 'Yes, the biggest lie that ebber was told.' 'No, that's not is.' Then I continue, 'P, g; and if you leave the i out it must be a blind pig, Jim.'

"Then we go on with the concert, and sing perhaps, 'Going ober de Mountain' and 'Mary Blane,' and then I ask such conundrums as these:

" 'Why is mahogany like flannel?' 'Because they are both used to manufacture into drawers;' and then we do this rhyme, 'Because mahogany makes drawers to put your clothes in, and flannel makes drawers to put your toes in.'

"Perhaps we do another conundrum, such as this: — 'Supposing you nigger was dead, what would be the best time to bury you?' One says, 'I shan't suppose.' Another says, 'I don't know.' And then I say, 'Why, the latter end of the summer;' and one asks, 'Why, Jim?' 'Because it's the best time for blackberrying.' Then I cry out, 'Now, you niggers, go on with the consort;' and one of them will add, 'Now, Jim, we'll have that lemoncholy song of Dinah Clare, that poor girl that fell in the water-butt and got burnt to death.'

"Another of our dialogues is this one: — 'Did I ebber tell you about that lemoncholy occurrence, Mary Blane, the young girl that died last night in the house that was burned down this morning, and she's gone to live in a garret?' 'I shall call and see her.' 'You can't.' ' 'Cos why?' ' 'Cos she moved from where she lives now; she's gone to live where she used to come from.' 'Did you ever see her broder Bill?' 'No; he's dead.' 'What! broder Bill dead, too?' 'Yes; I seed him this morning, and axed him how

261

he was.' 'Well, and what did he told you?' 'He told me he was very well, thankye, and he was going to lib along with Dinah; and he'd only been married three weeks. So I asked him how many children he'd got. He said he'd only got one. So I said, "Dere something very dark about that, and I don't think all goes right, if you was to have a son in three weeks." So he said, "Look you here, sir; if the world was made in six days, it's debbilish hard if we can't make a son in three weeks." 'Go on with the consort.'

"Another of our dialogues is this:—'Did I ever tell you, Jim, about my going out a-riding?' 'Neber.' 'Well, then, I'll told you, I had two dollars in my pocket.' 'Had you?' 'And I thought I'd do it gentleman-tell-like.' 'Yes.' 'So I went to the libery dealer.' 'Who?' 'The libery-dealer—the man that keeps the horses' stable.' 'Oh! golly! you mean the stable-man.' 'Yes. Well, I axed him if he could lend me a horse to ride on; so he said, he'd only got one horse.' 'Wall?' 'And that was a grey mare. I thought that would do just as well.' 'Of course.' 'And I axed him what that would cost me? and he said he should charge me two dollars for that—so I paid the two dollars.' 'Wall?' 'And he put me the spurs on my boots, and he puts de bridle on the horse's back.' 'The bridle on the horse's back!—what did he do with the bit?' 'He neber had a bit at all; he put the stirrups in the mouth.' 'Now stop—you mean, he put the saddle on the back, and the bridle in the mouth.' 'I know it was something. Den they put me on the saddle, and my feet on the bridle.' 'You mean he put your foot in the stirrups.' 'So I went out very well. So the mare begun for to gallop, so I caught hold of the turmel of the saddle.' 'The tummel!' 'Yes, Jim, the tummel.' 'No, no; you mean the pummel.' 'Wall, hab it the pummel—you knows—but, but I know, I'm right. So I caught hold of the mane, and I got on berry well till I come to a hill, when the mare began to gallop hard down the hill, because she was shy.' 'What was she shy at?' 'She saw a new-found-out-land dog crossing the wood.' 'A new-found-out-land dog crossing the road!' 'Yes; so I thought I'd try and stop her: so I stuck my knees into her side, and my spur into her, and by golly, she went too fast.' 'And did she now?' 'Till she falled down and broke her kness.' 'Poor thing!' 'Aye, and pitched poor nigger

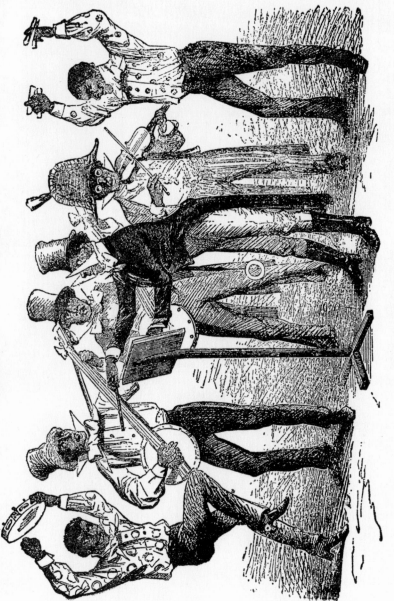

ETHIOPIAN SERENADERS

on his head; so I got up and thought I'd take the debil of a mare back to the stable. So when I got back I told the libery man about it.' 'Yas, the stable-man.' 'And he said I must pay £2 10s.' 'What for?' 'For repairing the mare; so I said I wouldn't; so he said he would take me before the court and I said he might take me down the alley, if he liked; so I thought I had better go and insult a man ob de law about it. So I went to the man ob de law's house and pulled at the servant, and out comed the bell.' 'No; you means you pulled the bell, and out comed the servant. Wall?' 'I said. "Can you conform me is de man ob de law at home?" so she told me he was out, but the man ob de law's wife was at home, so down she come. So I said I wanted to insult the man of de law, and she said, "Insult me; I do just as well." So she says, "Plane yourself." So I said, "Well, den, supposing you was a grey mare, and I hired you for two dollars to ride you, and you was rader rusty, and went too fast for me, and I wanted to stop you, and I stuck my knees in your side, and my spur into you, and you falled down and broke your knees, how could I help it?" So she flung the door in my face and went in. So now go on with the consort.'

"Sometimes when we are engaged for it, we go to concert-rooms and do the nigger-statues, which is the same as the tableaux vivant. We illustrate the adventures of Pompey, or the life of a negro slave. The first position is when he is in the sugar-brake, cutting the sugar cane. Then he is supposed to take it to be weighed, and not being weight, he is ordered to be flogged. My mate is then doing the orator and explaining the story. It's as nice a bit of business as ever was done, and goes out-and-out. You see, it's a new thing from the white ones. The next position is when he is being flogged, and then when he swears revenge upon the overseer, and afterwards when he murders the overseer. Then there's the flight of Pompey, and so on, and I conclude with a variety of sculptures from the statues, such as the Archilles in Hyde-park, and so on. This is really good, and the finest bit of business out, and nobody does it but me; indeed it says in the bill—if you saw it—'for which he stands unrivalled.'

"We sometimes have a greenhorn wants to go out pitching with us—a 'mug,' we calls them; and there's a chap of the name of

'Sparrow-back,' as we called him, because he always wore a bob-tailed coat, and was a rare swell; and he wished to go out with us, and we told him he must have his head shaved first, and Tom held him down while I shaved him, and I took every bit of hair off him. Then he underwent the operation of mugging him up with oil-colour paint, black, and not forgetting the lips, red. Ah, he carried the black marks on him for two months afterwards, and made a real washable nigger. We took him with us to Camberwell fair, and on the way he kept turning round and saying how strong he smelt of turps, and his face was stiff. Ah, he *was* a serenader! How we did scrub it into him with a stiff brush! When we washed at a horse-trough, coming home, he couldn't get a bit of the colour off. It all dried round his nose and eyes.

"When we are out pitching, the finest place for us is where there is anybody sick. If we can see some straw on the ground, or any tan, then we stays. We are sure to play up where the blinds are down. When we have struck up, we rattle away at the banjos, and down will come the servant, saying. 'You're to move on; we don't want you.' Then I'll pretend not to understand what she says, and I'll say, 'Mary Blane did you ask for? O yes, certainly, Miss;' and off we go into full chorus. We don't move for less than a bob, for sixpence ain't enough for a man that's ill. We generally get our two shillings.

"Sometimes gents will come and engage us to go and serenade people, such as at weddings or anything of that sort. Occasionally young gents or students will get us to go to a house late in the morning, to rouse up somebody for a lark, and we have to beat away and chop at the strings till all the windows are thrown up. We had a sovereign given us for doing that.

"The Christmas time is very good for us, for we go out as waits, only we don't black, but only sing; and that I believe – the singing, I mean – is, I believe, the original waits. With what we get for to play and go away, and what we collect on Boxing Day amounts to a tidy sum.

"There's very few schools of niggers going about London now. I don't think there are three schools pitching in the streets. There's the Westminster school – they have kettle-drums and music-stands, and never sings; and there's the New Kent-road gang, or Houghton's mob, and that's the best singing and playing school out; then a St. Giles's lot, but they are dicky—not worth much. The Spitalfields school is broke up. Of course there are other niggers going about, but to the best of my calculation there ain't more than 40 men scattered about.

"Houghton's gang make the tour of the watering-places every year. I've been to Brighton with them, and we did pretty well there in the fine season, making sure of 30s. a-week a man; and it's work that continues all the year round, for when it's fine weather we do pitching, and when it's wet we divide a school into parties of two, and go busking at the public-houses."

THE WHISTLING MAN

IT SOMETIMES happens that a lad or a man, before being thrown
for a living on the streets, has often sung a song to amuse his
companions, or that he has been reckoned "a good whistler," so
he resolves to start out and see if he cannot turn to pecuniary
profits that which until now he had only regarded in the light of
an amusement.

The young man from whom I elicited the annexed statement
was one of this class. His appearance was rather ungainly, and
when he walked across the room he moved in so slovenly a manner
that one leg appeared to drag itself after the other with the
greatest reluctance.

When telling me that he had never been guilty of stealing, nor
imprisoned, all his life, he did so in such a manner, and with such
a tone of voice, as left little doubt on my mind that he had been
kept honest more by the fear of the gaol than by his own moral
principle.

His face was long and thin, and his cheeks so hollowed by long
whistling, that they appeared almost to have had a round piece of
flesh scooped out of the centre of each of them. His large thick
lips were generally kept half-an-inch apart, so that they gave the
man a half-idiotic look; and when he rounded them for whistling,
they reminded me somewhat of a lamb's kidney.

"I am a whistler—that is, I whistle merely with my lips,
without the aid of anything besides. I have been at it about seven
years. I am twenty next birthday. My father was, and is, a coach-
painter. He is, I think, at the present time, working in Great
Queen-street, Lincoln's-inn-fields. I had three sisters and one
brother. I was the youngest but two. When I got to be about
seven years old my mother died, and then I used to get into the
streets and stop out all day playing with other boys, most of them
older than myself; and they often persuaded me to 'hop the wag,'
that is, play truant from school, and spend the money which my
father gave me to take to the master. Sometimes they took me to

Covent Garden or Farringdon Market, where they used to prig a lot of apples and pears, not with the idea of selling them, but to eat. They used to want me to do the same, but I never would nor never did, or else I dare say I should have been better off, for they say 'the biggest rogues get on best.' I was always afraid of being sent to prison, a place I was never in in all my life. At last I was persuaded by two young companions to stop out all night, so we all three went to Mrs. Reding's, Church-lane, and had a fourpenny lodging a-piece. My pals paid for me, because I'd got no money. I left them the next morning, but was afraid to go home; I had got nothing to eat, so I thought I'd see if I could get a few ha'pence by singing a song. I knew two or three, and began with the 'Mariner's Grave,' and then 'Lucy Neal.' I walked about all day, singing nearly the whole of the time, but didn't get a penny till about six o'clock. By nine o'clock I mustered 10*d.*, and then I left off, and went to a lodging-house in Whitechapel, where I got something to eat, and paid my lodging for the night. It's a custom always to pay beforehand. The next morning I felt very down-hearted, and was half a mind to go home, but was afraid I should get a hiding. However, I at last plucked up my spirits, and went out again. I didn't get anything give me till about dinner-time, when a gentleman came up to me and asked me how so young a boy as me came to be in the streets? I told him I couldn't earn my living any other way. He asked my name, and where I lived. I gave him both a false name and address, for I was afraid lest he should go to my father. He said I had better go home with him, so he took me to his house in Grosvenor-square, which was a very fine un—for he was a very rich man, where he gave me plenty to eat, and made me wash myself, and put on a suit of his little boy's left-off clothes. I stayed here three months, being employed to clean knives and boots, and run of errands. He used to send me twice a-week to the Bank of England with a cheque, which he used to write upon and tear out of a book, and I used to bring back the money. They always tied it up safely for me in a bag, and I put it into my pocket, and never took my hand off it till I got safe back again. At the end of three months he called me one day, and told me he was going with his wife and family into the country, where he was sorry to say, there'd be no room for me. He then gave me £3, and told me to go and seek for my friends, and go and live with them if I could.

"I went home to my father, who was greatly pleased at seeing me again; and he asked what I had been doing all the time, and where I had got my clothes and money from. I told him all, and promised I would never run away again, so he forgave me. However, for a long time he would not let me go out. At last, after a good deal of persuasion, he let me out to look after a place, and I soon got one at Mr. Cooper's, Surgeon, in Seven Dials, where I had 4s. a week. I used to be there from seven o'clock in the morning till nine at night, but I went home to my meals. After I'd been at my place four months, I by accident set fire to some naphtha, which I was stirring up in the back-yard, and it burnt off all my eyelashes, and so I 'got the sack.' When he paid me my wages—as I was afraid to tell my father what had happened—I started off to my old quarters in Whitechapel. I stopped there all day on Sunday, and the next three days I wandered about seeking work, but couldn't get none. I then give it up as a bad job, and picked up with a man named Jack Williams, who had no legs. He was an old sailor, who had got frost-bitten in the Arctic regions. I used to lead him about with a big painted board afore him. It was a picture of the place where he was froze in.

"We used to go all about Ratcliffe Highway, and sometimes work up as far as Notting Hill. On the average, we got from 8s. to 10s. a-day. My share was about a third. I was with him for fifteen months, till one night I said something to him when he was a-bed that didn't please him, and he got his knife out and stabbed my leg in two places,—here are the marks. I bled a good deal. The other lodgers didn't like to hit him for it, on account of his having no legs, but they kicked him out of the house, and would not let him back any more. They all wanted me to lock him up, but I wouldn't, as he was an old pal. Two or three silk handkerchiefs was tied round my leg, and the next day I was took to St. Thomas's Hospital, where I remained for about nine days. When I left the head-nurse gave me ten shillings on account of being so destitute—for I was without a ha'penny to call my own.

"As soon as I got out of the hospital I went down to Billingsgate, and bought some bread and pickled whelks at a stall, but when I pulled out my money to pay for 'em some costermongering chaps knocked me down, and robbed me of 5s. I was completely stunned by the blow. The police came up to see what was the matter, and took me to the station-house, where I stopped till the next morning, when the inspector made me tell where my father lived, and I was taken home to him. For about a month my father kept me under lock and key, and after I had been with him about three months more I 'stept it' again, and as I could always whistle very well, I thought I'd try it for a living; so I made a 'pitch' in New-street, Covent Garden, and began by whistling 'Will you love me then as now?' but there wasn't many in the world as loved me. I did very well though that day, for I got about 3s. 6d. or 4s., so I thought I'd practise it and stick to it. I worked all about town till I got well known. I used, sometimes, to go into public-houses and whistle upon a piece of 'baccy pipe, blowing into the bowl, and moving my fingers as if I was playing a flute and nobody could tell the difference if they had not seen me. Sometimes I used to be asked to stand outside hotels, taverns, and even club-houses, and give 'em a tune: I often had sixpences, shillings, and half-crowns thrown me. I only wish I had sich luck now, for the world's topsy-turvy, and I can't get hardly anything. I used then to earn 3s. or 4s. a day, and now it don't amount to more than 1s. 6d.

"After I'd worked London pretty well, I sometimes would start off a few miles out to the towns and villages; but, generally, it wasn't much account. The country chaps like sich tunes as 'The Barley Stack,' or 'The Little House under the Hill.' I often used to whistle to them while they danced. They liked jigs mostly, and always paid me a penny a dance each.

"I recollect once when I was whistling before a gentleman's house down at Hounslow, he sent his servant and called me in. I was taken into a fine large room, full of looking-glasses, and time-pieces, and pictures. I was never in sich a room before, all my life. The gentleman was there with his family — about six on 'em — and he told me if I'd whistle, and learn his birds to sing, he'd give me a sovereign. He had three fine brass-wire cages, with a bird in each, slung all of a row from the ceiling. I set to work 'like a brick,' and the birds begun to sing directly, and I amused 'em very much. I stopped about an hour and a half, and let 'em have all sorts of tunes, and then he gave me a sovereign and told me to call again when I come that way; but before I left he said the servants was to give me something to eat and drink, so I had dinner in the kitchen with the servants, and a jolly good dinner it was.

"From Hounslow I walked to Maidenhead, and took a lodging for the night at the Turk's Head. In the evening some countrymen come into the tap-room and kicked up a row with the missus because she couldn't lodge'em. She run in to turn them away, when three of 'em pitched into her right and left; and if it hadn't been for me and another chap she'd have got killed. When they got her down I jumped upon the table and snatched up the only weapon I could find, a brass candlestick, and knocked one of 'em down senseless, and the other fellow got hold of a broomstick and give it 'em as hard as he could, till we beat 'em right out of the place. There happened to be some police outside, drilling, who came over and took three of them to the stocks, where they was locked in for twenty-four hours. The next day the magistrate sentenced 'em to three months' imprisonment each, and I started for London and never whistled a tune till I reached it, which was three days afterwards. I kept on at the old game, earning about 2s. 6d. a-day, till the militia was being called out, and then I joined them, for I thought it would be the best thing I could do. I was sworn in by Colonel Scrivens at Eton Mews. We was taken into a stable, where there was three horses. Four of us laid hold of a book all together; and then, after asking us if we had any complaints, or were lame, or any way unfit for service, or was married, or had any children; and when we had said No, he asked us if we was free, able, and willing to serve in her Majesty's militia, in either England, Ireland, Scotland, or Wales, for the term of five years, if so long her Majesty required our services; and when we said we was, we took the oath and kissed the book.

"The same day, which was the 11th of June, 1854, we was packed off from the Waterloo Station for Portsmouth. After being drilled for three weeks I was returned for duty, and went on guard. The first guard I mounted was at Detached Dock at Portsmouth—it's where the convicts are. I didn't do any whistling there, I can tell yer; I'd different sorts of work, for part of our duty was to bury the poor fellows that died after coming home invalided from the Crimea. The people through that used to call us the 'garrison undertakers.' I was there thirteen months, and never, the whole time, had more than two nights' bed a-week; and some part of the time the weather was very frosty, and we was often over our ankles in snow. I belonged to the 4th Middlesex and no corps ever did so much duty, or went through so much hardship, as ours. From Portsmouth I was ordered, with my regiment, 950 strong, to Buttervant, county Cork, Ireland.

"When we reached the Irish Channel a storm arose, and we was all fastened under hatches, and not suffered to come upon deck for four days, by which time we reached the Cove of Cork; the Colonel's horse had to be thrown overboard, and they, more than once, had serious thoughts of throwing all the luggage into the sea as well. I was ten months in Ireland. I didn't do any whistling there; and then the regiment was ordered home again on account of the peace. But before we left we had a day's sport, consisting of greasy-pole climbing, jumping in sacks, racing after a pig with a greasy tail, and all them sort of things; and at night the officers had a grand ball. We landed at Portsmouth on a Monday morning at four o'clock, and marched through to the station, and reached Hounslow about four o'clock the same afternoon. A month after we were disembodied, and I came at once to London. I had about £1 5s. in my pocket, and I resolved in my own mind never to go whistling any more. I went to my father, but he refused to help me in any way. I tried for work, but couldn't get any, for the people said, they didn't like a militia man; so, after having spent all my money, I found that I must either starve or whistle, and so, you see, I'm once more on the streets.

"While I was in Ireland I absented myself from the barracks for twenty-one days, but fearing that a picket would get hold of me, I walked in one morning at six o'clock. I was instantly placed under arrest in the guard-room, where I remained four days, when I was taken before the Colonel, and to my great surprise I saw, sitting aside of him, the very gentleman who had given me the pound to whistle to his birds; his name was Colonel Bagot, as I found out afterwards, and he was deputy-magistrate for Middlesex. He asked me if I was not the chap as had been to his house; I told him I was, so he got me off with a good reprimand, and saved me being tried by a court-martial. When I first took to sleeping at lodging-houses they was very different to what they are now. I've seen as many as eighteen people in one cellar sleeping upon loose straw, covered with sheets or blankets, and as many as three in one bed; but now they won't take in any little boys like as I was, unless they are with their parents; and there's very few beds in a room, and never more than one in a bed. Married people have a place always parted off for themselves. The inspector comes in all times — often in the middle of the night — to see that the regulations ain't broken.

"I used, one time, to meet another man whistling, but like old Dick, who was the first at the profession, he's gone dead, and so I'm the only one at it now anywhere. It's very tiring work, and makes you precious hungry when you keep at it for two or three hours; and I only wish I could get something else to do, and you'd see how soon I'd drop it.

"The tunes that are liked best in the streets is sich as 'Ben Bolt' and 'Will you love me then as now?' but a year or two ago, nithin' went down like the 'Low-back Car'. I was always being asked for it. I soon gets hold of the new tunes that comes up. I don't think whistling hurts me, because I don't blow so hard as 'old Dick' used. A gentleman come up to me once in the street that was a doctor, and asked me whether I drunk much, and whether I drawed my breath in or blowed it out. I told him I couldn't get much to drink, and he said I ought at least to have three half-pints of beer a-day, or else I should go into a consumption; and when I said I mostly blowed out when I whistled, he said that was the best, because it didn't strain the lungs so much."

THE WHISTLING AND DANCING BOY

AT THE present time there is only one English boy going about the streets of London dancing, and at the same time playing his own musical accompaniment on a tin whistle. There are two or three Italian boys who dance whilst they perform on either the flute or the hurdy-gurdy, but the lad who gave me the following statement assured me that he was the only Englishman who had made street whistling and dancing "his profession."

He was a red-headed lad, of that peculiar white complexion which accompanies hair of that colour. His forehead was covered with freckles, so thick, that they looked as if a quantity of cayenne pepper had been sprinkled over it; and when he frowned, his hair moved backwards and forwards like the twitching of a horse shaking off flies.

"I've put some ile on my hair, to make me look tidy," he said. The grease had turned his locks to a fiery crimson colour, and as he passed his hands through it, and tossed it backwards, it positively glittered with the fat upon it.

The lad soon grew communicative enough, and proceeded to show me a blue jacket which he had bought that morning for a shilling, and explained to me at the same time how artful he had been over the bargain, for the boy had asked eighteenpence.

I remarked that his shoes seemed in a bad state, for they were really as white as a baker's slippers from want of blacking, and the toe of one gaped like the opening to a tortoise-shell. He explained to me that he wore all his boots out dancing, doing the double shuffle.

"Now these 'ere shoes," he said, "cost me a shilling in Petticoat-lane not a week since, and looked as good as new then, and even now, with a little mending, they'll make a tidy pair of crab-shells again."

To give force to this remark, he lifted his leg up, but, despite his explanation, I could not see how the leather could possibly be repaired.

He went through his dances for me, at the same time accompanying himself on his penny whistle. He took his shoes off and did a hornpipe, thumping his feet upon the floor the while, like palms on a panel, so that I felt nervous lest there should be a pin in the carpet and he be lamed by it.

The boy seemed to have no notion of his age, for although he accounted for twenty-two years of existence, yet he insisted he was only seventeen "come two months." I was sorry to find, moreover, that he was in the habit of drinking, seldom going home after his night's work without being intoxicated; and, indeed, his thin body and pinched face bore evidence of his excess in this respect, though, but for his assertion that "he was never hungry, and food was no good to him," I should have imagined, at the first glance, that he was pining with want.

He seems to be among the more fortunate of those who earn their living in the streets, for although I questioned and cross-questioned him in every possible way, he still clung to his assertion that he made £2 per week. His clothes, however, bore no evidence of his prosperity, for his outer garment was a washed-out linen blouse, such as glaziers wear, whilst his trousers were of coarse canvas, and as black on the thighs as the centre of a drum-head.

He brought with him a penny whistle to show me his musical talents, and certainly, his execution of the tin instrument was rapid and certain.

The following is the statement he gave me:—

"WHISTLING BILLY.

That's my name, and I'm known all round about in the Borough as 'Whistling Billy,' though some, to be sure, calls me 'Whistling Bill', but in general I'm 'Billy.' I'm not looking very respectable now, but you should see me when I'm going to the play; I looks so uncommon respectable, nobody knows me again. I shall go to the theatre next week, and I should just like you to see me. It's surprising.

"I ain't a very fat chap, am I—but I'm just meaty enough for my perfession, which is whistling and dancing in public-houses, where I gives 'em the hornpipe and the bandy jig, that's dancing with my toes turned in.

"My father was a barber. He only charged a penny for shaving, but he wouldn't cut your hair under twopence, and he used to do well — very well sometimes; I don't know whether he's alive now, for I ain't seen him these ten years, nor asked him for a halfpenny. Mother was alive when I left, and so was my two brothers. I don't know whether they're alive now. No, I don't want to go and see him, for I can get my own living. He used to keep a shop near Fitzroy-square.

"I was always fond of dancing, and I runned away from home for to follow it. I don't know my own age exactly: I was as tall then as I am now. I was twelve when I left home, and it must be ten years ago, but I ain't twenty-two: oh, dear no! Why, I ain't got no whiskers nor things. I drink such a lot of beer and stuff, that I can't grow no taller; gentlemen at the public-houses gives it me. Why, this morning I was near tipsy, dancing to some coal-heavers, who gave me drink.

"I used, when I was at father's, to go to a ball, and that's where I learned to dance. It was a shilling ball in the New-road, where there was ladies, regular nice ones, beautifully dressed. They used to see me dancing, and say, when I growed up I should make a beautiful dancer; and so I do, for I'd dance against anybody, and play the whistle all the time. The ladies at these balls would give me money then for dancing before them. Ah! I'd get my entrance shilling back, and four or five into the bargain. I'd generally take it home to mother, after buying a little sweet-stuff, or such-like, and I think that's why mother would let me go, 'cos I picked up a good bit of money.

"It was another boy that put me up to running away from home. He axed me to along with him, and I went. I dare say it troubled father a bit when he found I'd gone. I ain't troubled him for ten years now. If I was to go back to him, he'd only send me to work, and I make a better living by myself. I don't like work, and, to tell you the truth, I never did work, for it's like amusement to me to dance; and it must be an amusement, 'cos it amuses the people, and that's why I gets on so well.

"When I hooked it with that chap, we went to Croydon, in Surrey. We went to a lodging-house where there was men and women, and boys and chaps, and all like that; we all slept in one room. I had no money with me, only my clothes; there was a very nice velvet cap; and I looked very different then to what I do now. This young chap had some tin, and he kept me. I don't know how he earned his tin, for he'd only go out at night time, and then he'd come home and bring in money, and meat and bread, and such-like. He said to me, before I went pals with him, that he'd keep me, and that he'd make plenty of money. He told me he wanted a chum to mate with, so I went with him right off. I can't say what he was. He was about thirteen or fourteen, and I never seed him do no work. He might have been a prig for all I knows.

"After I'd been in the lodging-house, this chap bought a stock of combs and cheap jewels, and then we went out together, and he'd knock at the houses and offer the things for sale, and I'd stand by. There's a lot of gentlemen's houses, if you recollect, sir, round Croydon, on the London road. Sometimes the servants would give us grub instead of money. We had plenty to eat. Now you comes to speak of it, I do remember he used to bring back some old silver with him, such as old table-spoons or ladles, broke up into bits, and he'd make a deal selling them. I think he must have been a prig. At night we used to go to the public-houses and dance. He never danced, but sit down and looked on. He said he was my relation, and I always shared my drink with him, and the people would say, 'Feed me, feed my dog,' seeing me going halves with him.

"I kept along with him for three years, he working in the day, and I at night, dancing. We parted at Plymouth, and I took up with another mate, and worked on to Exeter. I think my new mate was a regular prig, for it was through his putting me up to prigging that I got into trouble there. This chap put me on to taking a brass cock from a foundry. It was in a big wooden butt, with 150 gallons of water in it. I got over a gate and pulled it out, and set all the foundry afloat. We cut away, but hours afterwards the policeman come to the lodging-house, and though there was a lot of boys and girls, he picked me out, and I had two months for it, and all my hair was cut off, and I only had dry bread and gruel every day, and soup twice a-week. I was jolly sorry for that cock business when I was caught, and I made up my mind never to take nothing more. It's going to the lodging-houses puts fellows up to prigging. The chaps brings in legs of beef, and puddens, and clothes, and then they sells 'em cheap. You can sometimes buy a pair of breeches worth ten shillings, for two bob, for the chaps don't like to take 'em to sell at the shops, and would sooner sell 'em for a'most nothing rather than be found out.

"When I came out of quod I had a shilling give me, and I went and bought a penny whistle. I was always fond of music and dancing, and I know'd a little of playing the whistle. Mother and father was both uncommon fond of dancing and music, and used to go out dancing and to concerts, near every night pretty well, after they'd locked the shop up. I made about eleven bob the first week I was out, for I was doing very well of a night, though I had no hair on my head. I didn't do no dancing, but I knew about six tunes, such as 'Rory O'More,' and 'The Girl I left behind me,' two hornpipes, (the fishers' and the sailors') 'St. Patrick's Day,' and 'The Shells of the Ocean,' a new song as had just come up. I can play fifty tunes now. Whistles weren't so common then, they weren't out a quarter so much as now. Swinden had the making of them then, but he weren't the first maker of them. Clarke is the largest manufactury of them now, and he followed Swinden.

"People was astonished at seeing a tune played on a tin whistle, and gave pretty liberal. I believe I was the first as ever got a living on a tin whistle. Now there's more. It was at that time as I took to selling whistles. I carried 'em on a tin tray before me, and a lid used to shut on it, fixed. I'd pitch before a hotel amongst the gentlemen, and I'd get 2d. a-piece for the whistles, and some would give me sixpence or a shilling, just according. The young gents was them as bought most, and then they'd begin playing on them, and afterwards give them to the young ladies passing. They was very pleased with me, for I was so little, and I done well. The first two months I made about 17s. or 18s. a-week, but after that they got rather dull, so I gived up selling of them and took to dancing. It didn't pay me so well as the whistles, for it was pretty near all profit on them—they only cost me 3d. a-dozen. I travelled all round Devonshire, and down to Land's End, in

Cornwall — 320 miles from London, and kept on playing the whistle on the road. I knew all about them parts. I generally pitched before the hotels and the spirit-shops, and began whistling and dancing; but sometimes I'd give the cottagers a turn, and they'd generally hand over a ha'penny a-piece and some bread.

"I stopped travelling about the south of England, and playing and dancing, for a little better than four years and a half. I didn't do so well in winter as in summer. Harvest time was my best time. I'd go to the fields where they was working, and play and dance. Sometimes the master would hollar out, 'Here, you get out of this!' but the men would speak up for me and say, 'Let him stop, master.' Many a chap's got the sack through me, by leaving off his work and beginning to dance. Sometimes, when the last load of hay was going home (you see, that's always considered the jolliest part of the work), they'd make me get up to the top of the load, and then whistle to them. They was all merry — as merry as could be, and would follow after dancing about, men women and boys. I generally played at the harvest suppers, and the farmer himself would give me 4s. 6d. or 5s. the night, besides my quart of ale. Then I'd pick up my 6s. or 7s. in ha'pence among the men. I've had as many as two harvest suppers a week for three weeks or a month following, for I used to ax the people round what time they was going to have a supper, and where, and set off, walking nine or ten miles to reach the farm, and after that we find another spot.

"Its very jolly among farm people. They give you plenty of cider and ale. I've drunk the cider hot, whilst they was brewing it — new cider, you know. You never want food neither, for there's more than you can eat, generally bread and cheese, or maybe a little cold biled pork. At night, the men and women used to sleep in a kind of barn among the clean straw; and after the beer-shops had closed — they are all little beer-shops, 3d. a quart in your own jugs, and like that — they'd say to me, 'Come up to the doss and give us a tune,' and they'd come outside and dance in the open air, for they wouldn't let them have no candles nor matches. Then they'd make theirselves happy, and I'd play to 'em, and they'd club up and give me money, sometimes as much as 7s., but I've never had no higher than that, but never no less than 3s. One man used to take all the money for me, and I'd give him a pot o' ale in the morning. It was a penny a dance for each of 'em as danced, and each stand-up took a quarter of a hour, and there was generally two hours of it; that makes about seven dances, allowing for resting. I've had as many as forty dancing at a time, and sometimes there was only nine of 'em. I've seen all the men get up together and dance a hornpipe, and the women look on. They always did a hornpipe or a country dance. You see, some of 'em would sit down and drink during the dance, but it amounted to almost three dances each person, and generally there was about fifty present. Usually the men would pay for the women, but if they was hard up and been free with their money, the girls would pay for them. They was mostly Irish, and I had to do jigs for them, instead of a hornpipe. My country dance was to the tune 'Oh don't you tease me, pretty little dear.' Any fiddler knows that air. It's always played in the country for country dances. First they dances to each other, and then it's hands across, and then down the middle, and then it's back again and turn. That's the country dance, sir. I used to be regular tired after two hours. They'd stick me up on a box, or a tub, or else they'd make a pile of straw, and stick me a-top of it; or if there was any carts standing by loaded with hay, and the horses out, I was told to mount that. There was very little drinking all this time, because the beer-shops was shut up. Perhaps there might be such a thing as a pint of beer between a man and his partner, which he'd brought in a can along with him. They only danced when it was moonlight. It never cost me nothing for lodgings all the harvest times, for they would make me stop in the barn along with them; and they was very good company, and took especial care of me. You mustn't think this dancing took place every night, but only three or four nights a-week. I find 'em out travelling along the road. Sometimes they've sent a man from one farm-house to bespeak me whilst I was playing at another. There was a man as played on the clarionet as used to be a favourite among haymakers, but they prefer the penny tin whistle, because it makes more noise, and is shriller, and is easier heard; besides, I'm very rapid with my fingers, and makes 'em keep on dancing till they are tired out. Please God, I'll be down among them again this summer. I goes down regular. Last year and the year before, and ever since I can recollect.

"When I'm in London I make a good living at dancing and playing, for I'm the only one that plays the whistle and dances at the same time. I'm reckoned the best hand at it of any man in town or country. I've often been backed by the company to dance and play against another man, and I generally win. I've been in hotels, and danced to gentlemen, and made plenty of money at it. I do all manner of tricks just to make 'em laugh — capering, or 'hanky-panky,' as I term it. I once had half-a-sovereign given to me, but I think it was a mistake, for he says, 'Take that, and go on.' I went home to clean myself, and had my trousers washed, and my shoes blacked, and went half-price to the theatre — the 'Wic,' I think it was — and paid my shilling, and went in as tidy as a gentlemen.

"When I first go into a public-house I go into the tap-room, and say, 'Would you like to hear a tune, gentlemen, or see a dance, or little bit of amusement?' If they say 'No,' I stand still, and begin a-talking, to make 'em laugh. I'm not to be choked off easy. I say, 'Come, gentlemen, can't you help a poor fellow as is the best dancer in England? I must have some pudden for breakfast, because I ain't had nothing for three weeks.' Then some say, 'Well, I will see the best dancer in England; I've got a mag.' Then after dancing I go to the gentleman who has given me most, and ask him six or seven times 'to give me a copper,' declaring he's the only one as has given me nothing, and that makes the others laugh. I also ask the landlord to give a half-pint of beer to grease my feet, and that makes 'em merry. I generally gets good nobbings (that's a collection, you know). They likes the dancing better than the music; but it's doing them together that takes. I ax them if they'll have the hornpipe or the Irish jig, and if they says the jig I do it with my toes turned in, like as if I was bandy; and that's very popular. I have been to as many as forty public-houses in a evening, and dance inside; or if they won't let me come in, they'll say, 'Dance outside as much as you like,' and that's very near as good for me. If I gets inside, I'll mop up 1s. if it's good company, or perhaps 3d. or 4d., and

always plenty to drink—more than I can take, for I'm generally
drunk before I can get home. They never gives me nothing to eat,
but it don't matter, for I'm seldom hungry; but 'I like a drop of
good beer,' as the song says.

"I've been engaged at concert-rooms to dance. I have pumps
put on, and light trousers, and a Guernsey, dressed up as a sailor.
That was in the country, at Canterbury, and I had 7s. and
plenty to eat and drink. I've never appeared at a London concert-
room, though I've been axed to come in and amuse the company;
but I wasn't tidy enough, and didn't like.

"When I dance in a public-house I take my shoes off and say,
'Now, gentlemen, watch my steps.' For the hornpipe I begin
with walking round, or 'twisting' as the term is; then I stands
up, and does a double-shuffle—or the 'straight fives' as we
calls it; then I walk round again before doing the back-snatches,
another kind of double-shuffle. Then I does the rocks of Scilly,
that's when you twists your feet|and bends sideways; next
comes the double steps and rattles, that is, when the heels makes
a rattle coming down; and I finishes with the square step. My
next steps is to walk round and collect the money. The Irish like
to see me do the jig better than the hornpipe. Them two are the
only dances I know.

"I make regular £2 a-week. Yesterday I made 7s. 3d., and it
was rainy, so I couldn't get out till late. At Brighton Regatta
I and my mate made £5 10s. between us, and at Dover Regatta
we made £8 between us. We squandered £2 10s. at the lodging-
house in one night, betting and tossing, and playing at cards.
We always follows up the regatta. We made only £2 10s. at
Hastings Regatta. You see we pick up on a Saturday night our
11s. a-piece, and on other days perhaps 5s. or 8s., according to
they day.

"I used to go about with a mate who had a wooden leg. He was
a beautiful dancer, for he made 'em all laugh. He's a little chap,
and only does the hornpipe, and he's uncommon active, and
knocks his leg against the railings, and makes the people grin.
He was very successful at Brighton, because he was pitied.

"I've also been about with a school of tumblers. I used to do the
dancing between the posturing and likes of that. I've learnt tum-

bling, and I was cricked for the purpose, to teach me. I couldn't walk for three days. They put my legs round my neck, and then couldn't get 'em back again. I was in that state, regular doubled up, for two hours, and thought I was done for. Some of my mates said, 'There, you've been and spoiled that chap.' It's dreadful painful learning tumbling. When I was out with the posturers I used to play the drum and mouth-pipes; I had a old hat and coat on. Then when my turn come, I'd appear in my professional costume, and a young chap who was a fluter — not a whistler, like me, — would give a tune, and I'd go on the carpet and give the Irish jig or the hornpipe.

"There was four of us in the school, and we'd share a pound a-week each. We were down at Dover there, and put up at the Jolly Sailors. I left them there, and went alone on to the camp where the German Legion was — at Shorncliffe, that's the place. I stopped there for three weeks, and did very well, taking my 7s. or 8s. a-day.

"After that I got tired of dancing, and thought I'd like a change, so I went out on a fishing-boat. They didn't give me nothing a-week, only 4s. when we come home after two months, and your clothes and victuals a-board. We first went fishing for plaice, and soles, and turbots, and we'd land them at Yarmouth and they'd send them on to Lowestoft, and from there on to London. Then we went codding off the coast of Holland for cod and haddock. It was just drawing on winter, and very cold. They set me with a line and I had to keep sawing it backwards and forwards till I felt a fish bite, then to hawl it up. One night I was near froze, and suddenly I had two cods bite at once, and they nearly pulled me over, for they dart about like mad, and tug awful; so I said to the master, 'I don't like this work,' but he answers, 'You must like it the time you stops here.' So I made up my mind to bolt the first time I got to shore. I only did it as a change, to see if I liked it. You're right there, there ain't no drinking on board.

"When you hawl up a cod they bound about the deck, and they're as strong as a Scotch terrier dog. When we hold 'em down, we prick them under the fin, to let the wind out of them. It would choke them if we didn't let it out, for it hisses as it comes off. It's from dragging them up so quick out of fifteen-fathom water that gives 'em the wind. When they were pricked, we chucked them into the well in the hold and let them swim about. We killed them when we got to Gravesend by hitting them on the head with tomboys—the sticks we hauls the line though. After three or four blows they're stunned, and the blood comes, and they're killed.

"When I goes into the public-houses, part of my performance is to play the whistle up my nose. I don't do it in the streets, because if I did there'd be thousands looking at me, and then the police would make a row. Last night I did it. I only pitched at one place, and did my night's work right off. I took 4s. 3$^1/_2$d. and lots of beer in an hour, from the cabbies and the people and all. At last the police told me to move on. When I plays the whistle up my nose, I puts the end on it in my nostril, and blows down it. I can do that just as easy as with my mouth, only not as loud. I do it as a variety, first in my mouth, then in my nose, and then back again in my mouth. It makes the people laugh. I've got a cold now, so I can't do it so well as at times, but I'll let you see what it is like."

He then inserted the wooden tongue of the whistle into his nostril, and blowing down it, began a hornpipe, which, although not so shrill as when he played it with the mouth, was still loud enough to be heard all over the house.

A PHOTOGRAPHIC MAN

"I've BEEN on and off at photographic-portrait taking since its commencement—that is to say, since they were taken cheap—two years this summer. I lodged in a room in Lambeth, and I used to take them in the back-yard—a kind of garden; I used to take a blanket off the bed, and used to tack it on a clothes-horse, and my mate used to hold it, if the wind was high, whilst I took the portrait.

"The reason why I took to photographing was, that I thought I should like it better than what I was at. I was out busking and drag-pitching with a banjo then. Busking is going into public-houses and playing, and singing, and dancing; and drag-pitching is going out in the day down the little courts—tidy places, little terraces, no thoroughfares, we call drags. I'm a very determined chap, and when I take a hidea into my head I always do it somehow or other. I didn't know anything about photographs then, not a mite, but I saved up my money; sometimes a 1s.; if I had a good day, 1s. 6d.; and my wife she went to work at day boot-binding, and at night dancing at a exhibition, or such-like (she's a tolerable good dancer—a penny exhibition or a parade dancer at fairs; that is, outside a show); sometimes she is Mademoiselle, or Madame, or what it may be. I got a loan of £3 (and had to pay £4 3s. for it), and with what I'd saved, I managed to get together £5 5s., and I went to Gilbert Flemming's in Oxford-street, and bought a complete apparatus for taking pictures; 6¹/₂ by 4³/₄, for £5 5s. Then I took it home, and opened the next day to take portraits for what we could get—1s. and over.

"I never knew anything about taking portraits then, though they showed me when I bought the apparatus (but that was as good as nothing, for it takes months to learn). But I had cards ready printed to put in the window before I bought the apparatus. The very next day I had the camera, I had a customer before I had even tried it, so I tried it on him, and gave him a black picture (for I didn't know how to make the portrait, and it was all black when I took the glass out), and told him that it would come out bright as it dried, and he went away quite delighted. I took the first Sunday after we had opened £1 5s. 6d., and everybody was quite pleased with their spotted and black pictures, for we still told them they would come out as they dried. But the next week they brought them back to be changed, and I could do them better, and they had middling pictures — for I had picked it up very quick.

'I had one fellow for a half-guinea portrait, and he was from Woolwich, and I made him come three times, like a lamb, and he stood pipes and 'bacca, and it was a thundering bad one after all. He was delighted, and he swears now it's the best he ever had took, for it don't fade, but will stop black to the end of the world; though he remarks that I deceived him in one thing, for it don't come out bright.

"You see, when first photography come up I had my eye on it, for I could see it would turn me in something some time. I went and worked as a regular labourer, carrying pails and so on, so as to try and learn something about chemistry; for I always had a hankling after science. Me and Jim was out at Stratford, pitching with the banjo, and I saw some men coming out of a chemical works, and we went to 'nob' them (that's get some halfpence out of them). Jim was tambo beating, and we was both black, and they called us lazy beggars, and said we ought to work as they did. So we told them we couldn't get work, we had no characters. As we went home I and Jim got talking, and he says, 'What a fine thing if we could get into the berth, for you'd soon learn about them portraits if you get among the chemicals;' so I agreed to go and try for the situation, and told him that if I got the berth I'd 'nanti panka his nabs snide;' that means, I wouldn't turn him up, or act nasty to him, but would share money the same as if we were pitching again. That slang is mummers' slang, used by strolling professionals.

"I stopped there for near twelve months, on and off. I had 10s. at first, but I got up to 16s.; and if I'd stopped I've no doubt I should have been foreman of one of the departments, for I got at last to almost the management of the oxalic acid. They used to make sulphate of iron — ferri sulp is the word for it — and carbonate of iron, too, and I used to be like the red man of Agar then, all over red, and a' most thought of cutting that to go for a soldier, for I shouldn't have wanted a uniform. Then I got to charging the retorts to make carbonate of ammonia, and from that I went to oxalic acid.

"At night me and Jim used to go out with the banjo and tamborine, and we could manage to make up our shares to from 18s. to a guinea a-week each; that is, sharing my wages and all; for when we chum together we always panka each other bona (that is, share). We always made our ponta (that is, a pound) a-week, for we could average our duey bionk peroon a darkey, or two shillings each, in the night.

"That's how I got an idea of chemicals, and when I went to photography many of the very things I used to manufacture was the very same as we used to take portraits, such as the hyposulphate of soda, and the nitrate of silver and the sulphate of iron.

"One of the reasons why I couldn't take portraits was, that when I bought my camera at Flemming's he took a portrait of me with it to show me how to use it, and as it was a dull afternoon he took 90 seconds to produce the picture. So, you see, when I went to work I thought I ought to let my pictures go the same time; and hand me if I didn't, whether the sun was shining or not. I let my plate stop 90 seconds, and of course they used to come out overdone and quite white, and as the evening grew darker they came better. When I got a good one I was surprised, and that picture went miles to be shown about. Then I formed an idea that I had made a miscalculation as to my time, and by referring to the sixpenny book of instructions I saw my mistake, and by the Sunday — that was five days after — I was very much improved, and by a month I could take a very tidy picture.

"I was getting on so well I got some of my portraits, when they was good ones, put in a chandler's shop; and to be sure I got first-rate specimens. I used to go to the different shilling portrait galleries and have a likeness of myself or friends done, to exhibit in my own window. That's the way I got my samples to begin with and I believe it's done all over London.

"I kept at this all the winter, and all the time I suppose I earned

30s. a-week. When summer come again I took a place with a
garden in the Old Kent-road, and there I done middling, but I lost
the majority of my business by not opening on a Sunday, for it
was a religious neighbourhood, and I could have earned my £5
a-week comfortable, for as it was I cleared my £2 regular. Then I
had a regular tent built up out of clothes-horses. I stopped there
till I had an offer of a good situation, and I accepted of it, at
£2 a-week.

"My new place was in Whitechapel, and we lowered the price
from a shilling to sixpence. We did well there, that is the governor
did, you know, for I've taken on the average from 60 to 100 a-day,
varying in price from sixpence to half-a-guinea, and the majority
was shilling ones. The greatest quantity I ever took was 146 in
one day, and 124 was taken away as they was done. The governor
used to take £20 a-week, and of that £8 clear profit, after
paying me £2, the men at the door 24s., a man and woman
29s., and rent £2. My governor had, to my knowledge, 11 other
shops, and I don't know all of his establishments; I managed
my concern for him, and he never come near us sometimes for
a month.

"I left on my own accord after four months, and I joined two
others on equal shares, and opened a place of my own in Southwark. Unfortunately, I begun too late in the season, or I should
have done well there; but at first we realised about £2 a-week
each, and up to last week we have shared our 25s. a-head.

"Sunday is the best day for shilling portraits; in fact, the majority is shilling ones, because then, you see, people have got
their wages, and don't mind spending. Nobody knows about
men's ways better than we do. Sunday and Monday is the Derby-
day like, and then after that they are about cracked up and
done. The largest amount I've taken at Southwark on a Sunday
is 80 — over £4 worth, but then in the week-days it's different;
Sunday's 15s. we think that very tidy, some days only 3s. or 4s.

"You see we are obliged to resort to all sort of dodges to make
sixpenny portaits pay. It's a very neat little picture our sixpenny
ones is; with a little brass rim round them, and a neat metal
inside, and a front glass; so how can that pay if you do the legiti-
mate business? The glass will cost you 2d. a-dozen — this small

size—and you give two with every picture; then the chemicals will cost quite a halfpenny, and varnish, and frame, and fittings about 2d. We reckon 3d. out of each portrait. And then you see there's house-rent and a man at the door, and boy at the table, and the operator, all to pay their wages out of this 6d.; so you may guess where the profit is.

"One of our dodges is what we term 'An American Air-Preserver;' which is nothing more than a card,—old benefit tickets, or, if we are hard up, even brown paper, or anything,——soap wrappings, just varnished on one side. Between our private residence and our shop, no piece of card or old paper escapes us. Supposing a party come in, and says 'I should like a portrait;' then I inquire which they'll have, a shilling or sixpenny one. If they prefer a sixpenny one, I then make them one up, and I show them one of the air-preservers,—which we keep ready made up,—and I tell them that they are all chemicalized, and come from America, and that without them their picture will fade. I also tell them that I make nothing out of them, for that they are only 2d. and cost all the money; and that makes 'em buy one directly. They always bite at them; and we've actually had people come to us to have our preservers put upon other persons portraits, saying they've been everywhere for them and can't get them. I charge 3d. if it's not one of our pictures. I'm the original inventor of the 'Patent American Air-Preserver.' We first called them the 'London Air-Preservers;' but they didn't go so well as since they've been the Americans.

"Another dodge is, I always take the portrait on a shilling size; and after they are done, I show them what they can have for a shilling,—the full size, with the knees; and table and a vase on it,—and let them understand that for sixpence they have all the background and legs cut off; so as many take the shilling portraits as sixpenny ones.

"Talking of them preservers, it is astonishing how they go. We've actually had photographers themselves come to us to buy our 'American Air-Preservers.' We tells them it's a secret, and we manufacture them ourselves. People won't use their eyes. Why, I've actually cut up an old band-box afore the people's eyes, and varnished it and dried it on the hob before their eyes, and yet they still fancy they come from America! Why, we picks up the old paper from the shop-sweeping, and they make first-rate 'Patent American Air-Preservers.' Actually, when we've been short, I've torn off a bit of old sugar-paper, and stuck it on without any varnish at all, and the party has gone away quite happy and contented. But you must remember it is really a useful thing, for it does do good and do preserve the picture.

"Another of our dodges, – and it is a splendid dodge, though it wants a nerve to do it, – is the brightening solution, which is nothing more than aqua distilled, or pure water. When we take a portrait, Jim, my mate, who stops in the room, hollows to me, 'Is it bona?' That is, – Is it good? If it is, I say, 'Say'. That is, – Yes. If not, I say 'Nanti.' If it is a good one he takes care to publicly expose that one, that all may see it, as a recommendation to others. If I say 'Nanti', then Jim takes it and finishes it up, drying it and putting it up in its frame. Then he wraps it up in a large piece of paper, so that it will take sometime to unroll it, at the same time crying out, 'Take sixpence from this lady, if you please.' Sometimes she says, 'Oh let me see it first;' but he always answers, 'Money first, if you please ma'am; pay for it first, and then you can do what you like with it. Here, take sixpence from this lady.' When she sees it, if it is a black one, she'll say, 'Why this ain't like me; there's no picture at all.' Then Jim says, 'It will become better as it dries, and come to your natural complexion.' If she still grumbles, he tells her that if she likes to have it passed through the brightening solution, it will come out lighter in an hour or two. They in general have it brightened; and then, before their face, we dip it into some water. We then dry it off and replace it in the frame, wrap it up carefully, and tell them not to expose it to the air, but put it in their bosom, and in an hour or two it will be all right. This is only done when the portrait come out black, as it doesn't pay to take two for sixpence. Sometimes they brings them back the next day, and says, 'It's not dried out as you told us;' and then we take another portrait, and charge them 3*d*. more.

"We also do what we call the 'bathing', – another dodge. Now to-day a party came in during a shower of rain, when it was so dark it was impossible to take a portrait; or they will come in, sometimes, just as we are shutting up, and when the gas is lighted, to have their portraits taken; then we do this. We never turn business away, and yet it's impossible to take a portrait; so we ask them to sit down, and then we go through the whole process of taking a portrait, only we don't put any plate in the camera. We always make 'em sit a long time, to make 'em think it's all right, — I've had them for two-and-a-half minutes, till their eyes run down with water. We then tell them that we've taken the portrait, but that we shall have to keep it all night in the chemical bath to bring it out, because the weather's so bad. We always take the money as a deposit, and give them a written paper as an order for the picture. If in the morning they come themselves we get them to sit again, and then we do really take a portrait of them; but if they send anybody, we either say that the bath was too strong and eat the picture out, or that it was too weak and didn't bring it out; or else I blow up Jim, and pretend he had upset the bath and broke the picture. We have had as many as ten pictures to bathe in one afternoon.

"If the eyes in a portrait are not seen, and they complain, we take a pin and dot them; and that brings the eye out, and they like it. If the hair, too, is not visible we takes the pin again, and soon puts in a beautiful head of hair. It requires a deal of nerve to do it; but if they still grumble I say, 'It's a beautiful picture, and worth half-a-crown, at the least;' and in the end they generally go off contented and happy.

"When we are not busy, we always fill up the time taking specimens for the window. Anybody who'll sit we take him; or we do one another, and the young woman in the shop who colours. Specimens are very useful things to us, for this reason, — if anybody comes in a hurry, and won't give us time to do the picture, then, as we can't afford to let her go, we sit her and through all the business, and I says to Jim, 'Get one from window,' and then he takes the first specimen that comes to hand. Then we fold it up in paper, and don't allow her to see it until she pays for it, and tell her not to expose it to the air for three days, and that if then she doesn't approve of it and will call again we will take her another. Of course they in general comes back. We have made some queer mistakes doing this. One day a young lady

293

came in, and wouldn't wait, so Jim takes a specimen from the window, and, as luck would have it, it was the portrait of a widow in her cap. She insisted upon opening, and then she said. 'This isn't me, it's got a widow's cap, and I was never married in all my life!' Jim answers, 'Oh, miss! why it's a beautiful picture and a correct likeness.'—and so it was, and no lies, but it wasn't of her.—Jim talked to her, and says he, 'Why, this ain't a cap, it's the shadow of the hair,'—for she had ringlets,—and she positively took it away believing that such was the case; and even promised to send us customers, which she did.

"There was another lady that came in a hurry, and would stop if we were not more than a minute; so Jim ups with a specimen, without looking at it, and it was the picture of a woman and her child. We went throught the business of focussing the camera, and then gave her the portrait and took the 6d. When she saw it she cries out, 'Bless me! there's a child: I haven't ne'er a child!' Jim looked at her, and then at the picture, as if comparing, and says he, 'It is certainly a wonderful likeness, miss, and one of the best we ever took. It's the way you sat; and what has occasioned it was a child passing through the yard.' She said she supposed it must be so, and took the portrait away highly delighted.

"Once a sailor came in, and as he was in haste, I shoved on to him the picture of a carpenter, who was to call in the afternoon for his portrait. The jacket was dark, but there was a white waistcoat; still I persuaded him that it was his blue Guernsey which had come up very light, and he was so pleased, that he gave us 9d. instead of 6d. The fact is, people don't know their own faces. Half of 'em have never looked in a glass half a dozen times in their life, and directly they see a pair of eyes and a nose, they fancy they are their own.

"The only time we were done was with an old woman. We had only one specimen left, and that was a sailor man, very dark—one of our black pictures. But she put on her spectacles, and she looked at it up and down, and says, 'Eh?' I said, 'Did you speak' ma'am?' and she cries, 'Why, this is a man! here's the whiskers' I left, and Jim tried to humbug her, for I was bursting with laughing. Jim said, 'It's you, ma'am; and a very excellent likeness, I can assure you.' But she kept on saying, 'Nonsense, I ain't a man,' and wouldn't have it. Jim wanted her to leave a deposit, and come next day, but she never called. It was a little too strong.

"There was an old woman come in once and wanted to be taken with a favourite hen in her lap. It was a very bad picture, and so black there was nothing but the outline of her face and a white speck for the beak of the bird. When she saw it, she asked where the bird was. So Jim took a pin and scratched in an eye, and said, 'These it is, ma'am — that's her eye, it's coming out,' and then he made a line for the comb on the head, and she kept saying, 'Wonderful!' and was quite delighted.

"The only bad money we have taken was from a Methodist clergyman, who came in for a 1s. 6d. portrait. He gave us a bad sixpence.

"For colouring we charge 3d. more. If the portraits are bad or dark we tell them, that if they have them coloured the likeness will be perfect. We flesh the face, scratch the eye in, and blue the coat and colour the tablecloth. Sometimes the girl who does it puts in such a lot of flesh paint, that you can scarcely distinguish a feature of the person. If they grumble, we tell them in will be all right, when the picture's dry. If it's a good picture, the colour looks very nice, but in the black ones we are obliged to stick it on at a tremendous rate, to make it show.

"Jim stands at the door, and he keeps on saying, 'A correct portrait, framed and glazed, for sixpence, beautifully enamelled.' Then, when they are listening, he shows the specimen in his hands, and adds, 'If not approved of, no charge made.'

"One morning, when we had been doing 'quisby,' that is, stopping idle, we hit upon another dodge. Some friends dropped in to see me, and as I left to accompany them to a tavern close by, I cried to Jim, 'Take that public-house oposite.' He brought the camera and stand to the door, and a mob soon collected. He kept saying, 'Stand back, gentlemen, stand back! I am about to take the public-house in front by this wonderful process.' Then he went over to the house, and asked the landlord, and asked some gentlemen drinking there to step into the road whilst he took the house with them facing it. Then he went to a policeman and asked him to stop the carts from passing, and he actually did. By this way he got up a tremendous mob. He then put in the slide, pulled off the cap of the camera, and focussed the house, and pretended to take the picture, though he had no prepared glass, nor nothing. When he had done, he called out, 'Portraits taken in one minute. We are now taking portraits for 6*d*. only. Time of sitting, two seconds only. Step inside and have your'n taken immediately.' There was a regular rush, and I had to be fetched, and we took 6*s*, worth right off.

"People seem to think the camera will do anything. We actually persuade them that it will mesmerise them. After their portrait is taken, we ask them if they would like to be mesmerised by the camera, and the charge is only 2*d*. We then focus the camera, and tell them to look firm at the tube; and they stop there for two or three minutes staring, till their eyes begin to water, and then they complain of a dizziness in the head, and give it up, saying they 'can't stand it'. I always tell them the operation was beginning, and they were just going off, only they didn't stay long enough. They always remark. 'Well, it certainly is a wonderful machine, and a most curious invention.' Once a coalheaver came in to be mesmerised, but he got into a rage after five or six minutes, and said, 'Strike me dead, ain't you keeping me a while!' He wouldn't stop still, so Jim told him his sensitive nerves was too powerful, and sent him off cursing and swearing because he couldn't be mesmerised. We don't have many of these mesmerism customers, not more than four in these five months; but it's a curious circumstance, proving what fools people is. Jim says he only introduces these games when business is dull, to keep my spirits up — and they certainly are most laughable.

"I also profess to remove warts, which I do by touching them with nitric acid. My price is a penny a wart, or a shilling for the job; for some of the hands is pretty well smothered with them. You see, we never turn money away, for it's hard work to make a living at sixpenny portraits. My wart patients seldom come twice, for they screams out ten thousand blue murders when the acid bites them.

"Another of my callings is to dye the hair. You see I have a good many refuse baths, which is mostly nitrate of silver, the same as all hair-dyes is composed of. I dyes the whiskers and moustaches for 1*s*. The worst of it is, that nitrate of silver also blacks the skin wherever it touches. One fellow with carroty hair came in one day to have his whiskers dyed, and I went clumsily to work and let the stuff trickle down his chin and on his cheeks, as well as making the flesh at the roots as black as a hat. He came the next day to have it taken off, and I made him pay 3*d.* more, and then removed it with cyanide, which certainly did clean him, but made him smart awfully.

"I have been told that there are near upon 250 houses in London now getting a livelihood taking sixpenny portraits. There's ninety of 'em I'm personally acquainted with, and one man I know has ten different shops of his own. There's eight in the Whitehapel-road alone, from Butcher-row to the Mile-end turnpike. Bless you, yes! they all make a good living at it. Why, I could go tomorrow, and they would be glad to employ me at £2 a-week — indeed they have told me so.

"If we had begun earlier this summer, we could, only with our little affair, have made from £8 to £10 a-week, and about one-third of that is expenses. You see, I operate myself, and that cuts out £2 a-week."

THE HAPPY FAMILY EXHIBITOR

"HAPPY FAMILIES," or assemblages of animals of diverse habits and propensities living amicably, or at least quietly, in one cage, are so well known as to need no further description here. Concerning them I received the following account: —

"I have been three years connected with happy families, living by such connexion. These exhibitions were first started at Coventry, sixteen years ago, by a man who was my teacher. He was a stocking-weaver, and a fancier of animals and birds, having a good many in his place — hawks, owls, pigeons, starlings, cats, dogs, rats, mice, guinea-pigs, jackdaws, fowls, ravens, and monkeys. He used to keep them separate and for his own amusement, or would train them for sale, teaching the dogs tricks, and suchlike. He found his animals agree so well together, that he had a notion — and a snake-charmer, an old Indian, used to advise him on the subject — that he could show in public animals and birds, supposed to be one another's enemies and victims, living in quiet together. He did show them in public, beginning with cats, rats, and pigeons, in one cage; and then kept adding by degrees all the other creatures I have mentioned. He did very well at Coventry, but I don't know what he took. His way of training the animals is a secret, which he has taught to me. It's principally done, however, I may tell you, by continued kindness and petting, and studying the nature of the creatures.

"Hundreds have tried their hands at happy families, and have failed. The cat has killed the mice, and the hawks have killed the birds, the dogs the rats, and even the cats, the rats, the birds, and even one another; indeed, it was anything but a happy family. By our system we never have a mishap; and have had animals eight or nine years in the cage — until they've died of age, indeed. In our present cage we have 54 birds and animals, and of 17 different kinds; 3 cats, 2 dogs (a terrier and a spaniel), 2 monkeys, 2 magpies, 2 jackdaws, 2 jays, 10 starlings (some of them talk), 6 pigeons, 2 hawks, 2 barn fowls, 1 screech owl, 5 common sewer-rats, 5 white rats (a novelty), 8 guinea-pigs, 2 rabbits (1 wild and 1 tame), 1 hedgehog, and 1 tortoise. Of all these, the rat is the most difficult to make a member of a happy family: among birds, the hawks. The easiest trained animal is a monkey, and the easiest trained bird a pigeon. They lived together in their cages all night, and sleep in a stable, unattended by any one. They were once thirty-six hours, as a trial, without food—that was in Cambridge; and no creature was injured; but they were very peckish, especially the birds of prey. I wouldn't allow it to be tried (it was for a scientific gentleman) any longer, and I fed them well to begin upon.

"There are now in London five happy families, all belonging to two families of men. Mine, that is the one I have the care of, is the strongest—fifty-four creatures: the others will average forty each, or 214 birds and beasts in happy families. Our only regular places now are Waterloo-bridge and the National Gallery. The expense of keeping my fifty-four is 12s. a-week; and in a good week—indeed, the best week—we take 30s.; and in a bad week sometimes not 8s. It's only a poor trade, though there are more good weeks than bad: but the weather has so much to do with it. The middle class of society are our best supporters. When the happy family—only one—was first in London, fourteen years ago, the proprietor took £1 a-day on Waterloo-bridge; and only showed in the summer. The second happy family was started eight years ago, and did as well for a short time as the first. Now there are too many happy families. There are none in the country.

"The first who ever took out a happy family to exhibit in the streets was a man of the name of John Austin, who lived in Nottingham. It was entirely his own idea, and he never copied it from any one. He was a very ingenious man indeed, and fond of all kinds of animals, and a fancier of all kinds of small birds. From what I have heard him say, he had a lot of cats he was very fond of, and also some white-mice, and the notion struck him that it would be very extraordinary if he could make his pets live together, and teach creatures of opposite natures to dwell in the same cage. In the commencement of his experiments he took the young, and learnt them to live happily together. He found it succeed very well indeed; and when he gets this to his liking he goes from Nottingham to Manchester, and exhibits them, for he

was told people would like to see the curious sight. He then
had cats, mice, and all sorts of little birds. He was a weaver by
trade, was Austin—a stocking-weaver. He didn't exhibit for
money in Manchester. It was his hobby and amusement, and he
only showed it for a curiosity to his friends. Then he was persuaded
to come to London to exhibit. When he first came to London he
turned to carpentering and cabinet-making work, for which he
had a natural gift, and he laid the happy family aside. He didn't
know London, and couldn't make his mind up to exhibiting in
a strange place. At last he began to miss his pets; and then he
gathered them together again, one here and one there, as he could
get them into training. When he had a little stock round him he
was advised by people to build a cage, and take them out to
exhibit them.

"There was no bridge to the Waterloo-road in those days, but
he took up his pitch in Waterloo-road, close to the Feathers public
house, where the foot of Waterloo-bridge is now. He had a
tremendous success. Everybody who passed gave him money.
Noblemen and gentlepeople came far and near to see the sight.
When first he went there he could go out at four o'clock in the
afternoon, on any fine day as he thought proper to leave his work
to go out, and he could take from his 14s. to £1. He stopped on
this same spot opposite the Feathers public-house, from his first
coming to the day he left it a short space before he died, for
36 years all but 5 months. He's been dead for four years the 17th
of last February, 1856, and then he wasn't getting 2s. 6d. a -day.
Many had imitated him, and there was four happy family cages
in London. When the old man saw people could do as much as he
did himself, and rather got before him in their collections, it
caused him to fret. He was too old to return to carpentering, and
he had never been a prudent man, so he never saved anything.
He was too generous to his friends when they were distressed,
and a better man to his fellowmen never walked in two shoes. If
he made £5 in a week, there was money and food for them who
wanted. He found that people were not so generous to him as he
was to them; that he proved to his sorrow. He was a good man.

"In the year 1833 he had the honour of exhibiting before Her
Majesty the Queen. She sent for him expressly, and he went to

Buckingham Palace. He never would tell anybody what she gave him; but everybody considered that he had been handsomely rewarded. A few days after this there was a gentleman came to him at Waterloo-bridge (he was there all the time the bridge was building), and this party engaged him and his happy family, and took him down to exhibit at the Mechanics' Institution, down at Hull. I don't know what he got for the journey. After that he was engaged to go to the Mechanics' Institution in Liverpool. He travelled in this way all about the country, engaged at the different Institutions.

"I was with him as assistant for eight years before he died, and a better master there could not be living in the world. I had been travelling with him through Kent, showing the happy family, and business run bad and did not meet his approbation, so he at last said he would return to his station on Waterloo-bridge. Then I was left in the country, so I started a collection of animals for myself. It was a small collection of two monkeys, white rats and piebald ones, cats, dogs, hawks, owls, magpies, ferrets, and a cotamundi, a long-nosed animal from the Brazils.

"I came to London after working in the country. He was perfectly agreeable to my exhibiting in the streets. He was a good old man, and I wish I knew to be as good, for I can't know how to be as good. I took the West-end, and he kept to the bridge. For a time I did pretty well. I'd take about 6s. a-day, but then it cost me 1s. a-day for feeding the collection; and then I had a quantity of things given to me, such as bits of meat at the butchers', and so on. In 1851 my stand was in Regent-street, by the corner of Castle-street. I did there very well when the Exhibition was open, and as soon as it was done I fell from taking about 8s. a-day down to 1s., and that's speaking the truth. Then I shifted my post, and went and pitched upon Tower-hill.

"I done pretty well for the first 18 months as I was there. The sailors was the most generous people to me, and those I had most to depend upon whilst I was on Tower-hill. I've taken 8s. in one day on Tower-hill, and I've also been there, and stood there eight hours on Tower-hill and only taken $1\frac{1}{2}d$. It was all casual as could be. I can say I took on the average 3s. a-day then, and then I had to feed the collection. I stayed at Tower-hill till I found that there wasn't positively a living to be made any longer there and then I shifted from place to place pitching at the corners of streets, and doing worse and worse, until I actually hadn't hardly strength to drag my cage about—for it's a tidy load. Then I returns to the old man's original spot, on Waterloo-bridge, to try that; for the old man was dead. The first five or six weeks as I was there, during the summer, I got a tolerable good living, and I continued there till I wasn't able to get a crust for myself. I was obliged to leave if off, and I got a situation to go to work for a firework-maker in the Westminster-road. Now I only take to the streets when I have no other employment. It isn't barely a living. I keep my collection always by me, as a resource when no other work is in hand, but if I could get constant employment I'd never go out in the streets no more.

"The animal that takes the longest to train is the ferret. I was the first that ever introduced one into a cage, and that was at Greenwich. It's a very savage little animal, and will attack almost anything. People have a notion that we use drugs to train a happy family; they have said to me, 'It's done with opium;' but, sir, believe me, there is no drugs used at all: it's only patience, and kindness, and petting them that is used, and nothing else of any sort. The first ferret as I had, it killed me about £2 worth of things before I could get him in any way to get into the happy family. He destroyed birds, and rabbits, and guinea-pigs; and he'd seize them at any time, whether he was hungry or not. I watched that ferret till I could see that there was a better method to be used with a ferret, and then I sold my one to a rat-catcher, and then I bought two others. I tried my new system, and it succeeded. It's a secret which I used, so I can't mention it, but it's the simplest thing in the world. It's not drawing their teeth out, or operating on them; it's only kindness and such-like, and patience. I put my new ferrets into the cage, and there they have been ever since, as may have been seen on Tower-hill and such places as I've pitched on. My ferrets would play with the rats and sleep at night with them, while I've put them in the rat-box along with the rats, to carry them home together at night. My ferrets would come and eat out of my mouth and play with children, or anything. Now, I'll tell you this anecdote as a proof of their docility. They caught a rat one night at the Coopers' Arms public-house, Tower-hill, and they gave it to me, and I put it into the cage. The landlord and gentlemen in the parlour came out to see it, and they saw my ferrets hunt out the newcomer and kill him. They tossed over the white and brown and black rats that belonged to me, and seized the public house rat and killed him. I always took the dead bodies away when they were killed, and didn't let the ferrets suck their blood, or anything of that. I've trained my animals to that state, that if I wasn't to feed them they'd sit down and starve by each other's side without eating one another.

"The monkey is almost as bad as a ferret for training for a happy family, for this reason – when they are playing they use their teeth. They are the best playfellows in the world, and never fall out or cry when they bite. They are the life and amusement of the company.

"Now, this is a curious thing with the ferret's nature. If he's ever so well trained for a happy family, he will always be avenged if he's crossed. For instance, if my ferret has a bit of meat, and the hawk comes near him and claws him, he'll, if it's months afterwards, kill that hawk. He'll wait a long time, but he's sure to kill the hawk, he's that spiteful. So that when he's crossed he never forgives. When the monkey and the ferret play, they always use their teeth, not to bite, but it's their nature in their play. Mr. Monkey, when he has played with Mr. Ferret till he has made him in a rage, will mount the perches and take Mr. Ferret by the tail and swing him backward and forwards. The ferret gets into an awful rage, and he'll try all he knows to get hold of Mr. Monkey, but Mr. Monkey will pat him on the head, and knock him back as he tries to turn round and bite him. The ferret is the kindest of animals when at play. He don't bear no rancour to Mr. Monkey for this. He never cares for a bit of fun, but if it's an insult as is offered him, such as taking his food, he won't rest till he's revenged.

"The danger with a monkey is this. Now I've got a puppy as was given me by a friend of mine, and I both respects the gentleman as give it me and the mother of the little dog, and I've taken all the pains in the world to train this pup to the happy family, but he's a yelping, noising animal. Now, my monkey is the most pleasant and best-tempered one in the world, and the amusement

and delight of all who see him, as many on Waterloo-bridge can
testify. Whenever this monkey goes near the dog, it howls at him.
So the monkey plays with him, pulling his tail and nibbling his
ears and hair, and biting his toe, and so on. Anything that'll play
with the monkey, it's all right, and they are the best friends in the
world; but if they show any fear, then it's war, for the monkey
won't be put upon. Now, there's another pup in the same cage
which the monkey is just as fond of. They play open-mouthed
together, and I've seen Mr. Monkey put his arms round the pup's
neck and pull it down, and then they go to sleep together. I've
actually seen when a lady has given the monkey a bit of biscuit,
or what not, he's gone and crumbled some bits before the pup
to give it its share. This is truth. My monkey is a lady monkey.

"The monkeys are very fond of cuddling the rats in their arms,
like children. They also pull their tails and swing them. The rats
are afraid, and then Mr. Monkey keeps on teasing them. If ever
Mr. Rat do turn round and bite Mr. Monkey, he's sure to feel it
by and by, for he'll get a swing by his tail, and he'll catch the
tail whilst he's trying to run away, and bite the tip, and worry
him near out of his life. A monkey is the peace-maker and peace-
breaker of a collection. He breaks peace first and then he'll go and
caress afterwards, as much as to say, 'Never mind, it's only
a lark.' He's very fond of the cat—for warmth, I think. He'll go
and cuddle her for an hour at a time; but if Miss Puss won't lay
still to suit his comfort, he takes her round the neck, and tries to
pull her down, and if then she turns rusty, he's good to go behind
her, for he's afraid to face her, and then he'll lay hold of the tip
of her tail and give her a nip with his teeth. The cat and monkey
are the best of friends, so long as Miss Puss will lie still to be
cuddled and suit his convenience, for he will be Mr. Master, and
have everything to suit his ways. For that reason I never would
allow either of my cats to kitten in the cage, because Mr. Monkey
would be sure to want to know all about it, and then it would be
all war; for if he went to touch Miss Puss or her babies, there
would be a fight. Now a monkey is always fond of anything young,
such as a kitten, and puss and he'd want to nurse the children.
A monkey is kind to everything so long as it ain't afraid of him;
but if so be as it is, then the bullying and teasing begins. My

monkey always likes to get hold of a kitten, and hold it up in his arms, just the same as a baby.

"There's often very good amusement between the owl and the monkey in this way. The monkey will go and stare Mr. Owl in the face, and directly he does so Mr. Owl will begin swaying from side to side; and then Mr. Monkey will pat him in the face or the nose. After he's bullied the owl till it's in an awful rage, the owl will take and dive at Mr. Monkey with his open claws, and perhaps get in his back. Then Mr. Monkey will go climbing all over the cage, chattering at the owl, and frightening him, and making him flutter all about. My owls can see well enough in the day-time, for they are used to be in the open air, and they get used to it.

"I compare my monkey to the clown of the cage, for he's mis-chievous, and clever, and good-natured. He'll never bully any of them very long after he sees they are in a regular passion, but leave them and go to some other bird or beast. One of my pups is my monkeys' best friend, for neither of them are ever tired of playing.

"The cats and the birds are very good friends indeed; they'll perch on her back, and I've even seen them come on her head and pick up the bits of dirt as you'll generally find in a cat's head. I've tried a very curious experiment with cats and birds. I've intro-duced a strange cat into my cage, and instantly she gets into the cage she gets frightened, and looks round for a moment, and then she'll make a dart upon almost the first thing that is facing her. If it's the owl, monkey, small birds, or any thing, she'll fly at it. It's in general then that the monkey is the greatest enemy to the strange cat of anything in the cage. He'll go and bite her tail, but he won't face her. Then the other cats will be all with their hairs up and their tails swelled up to fly at the stranger, but then I gen-erally takes her out, or else there would be a fight. All the rats will be on the look-out and run away from the strange cat, and the little birds fly to the top of the cage, fluttering chirriping with fear.

"The hawk I had a good deal of difficulty with to make him live happily with the small birds. When training a hawk, I always put him in with the large things first, and after he's accustomed to them, then I introduce smaller birds. He's always excited when he first comes amongst the smaller birds. I find Mr. Monkey is always the guard, as he doesn't hurt them. When he sees the hawk fluttering and driving about after the small birds, Mr. Monkey will go and pat him, as much as to say, 'You mustn't hurt them,' and also to take his attention off. After Mr. Hawk has been in the cage four, five, or six different times in training, the starlings gets accustomed to him, and will perch alongside of him; and it's as common as possible to see the starlings, when the hawk was feeding, go and eat off the same raw meat, and actually perch on his back and pick the bits off his bill as he is eating them.

"A magpie in a cage has as much as he can do to look after himself to keep his tail all right. It's a bird that is very scared, and here and there and everywhere, always flying about the cage. His time is taken up keeping out of Mr. Monkey's way. It's very rarely you see Mr. Monkey interfere with him. A magpie will pitch upon something smaller than himself, such as pigeons, which is inoffensive, or starlings, as is weaker; but he never attempts to tackle anything as is likely to be stronger than himself. He fights shy of the big animals.

"A good jackdaw, well trained to a happy family, is the life of the cage next to the monkey. He's at all the roguishness and mischief that it is possible for a man to be at. If he sees a cat or a dog, or anything asleep and quiet, he'll perch on its head, and peck away to rouse it. He's very fond of pitching on the top of the cat and turning the fur over, or pecking at the ears, till the cat turns round, and then he's off. If there's a rat in his way, he'll peck at its nose till it turns round, and then peck at its tail. If Mr. Rat gets spiteful he'll fly to the preches for it, and then hollow out Jack Daws, as much as to say, 'I had the best of you.' The people are very fond of the jackdaw, too, and they like putting their fingers to the wires, and Jack'll peck them. He's very fond of stealing things and hiding them. He'll take the halfpence and conceal them. He looks round, as if seeing whether he was watched, and go off to some sly corner where there is nothing near him. If he can get hold of any of the others' food, that pleases him better than anything. My monkey and the jackdaw ain't very good company. When Mr. Jack begins his fun, it is generally when Mr. Monkey is lying still, cuddling his best friend, and that's

one of the little dogs. If Mr. Monkey is lying down with his tail
out, he'll go and peck him hard on it, and he'll hollow out 'Jackdaw,' and off he is to the perches. But Mr. Monkey will be after
him, climbing after him, and he's sure to catch hold of him at last,
and then Mr. Jack is as good as his master, for he'll hollow out to
attract me, and I have to rattle my cane along the wires, to tell
them to give over. Then, as sure as ever the monkey was gone, the
jack would begin to crow.

"I had a heron once, and it died; I had it about fourteen months.
The way as he met with his death was – he was all well in the
cage, and standing about, when he took a false step, and fell, and
lamed himself. I was obliged to leave him at home, and then he
pined and died. He was the only bird I ever had, or the only
creature that ever was in a happy-family cage, that could keep
Mr. Monkey at bay. Mr. Monkey was afraid of him, for he would
give such nips with his long bill that would snip a piece out of Mr.
Monkey, and he soon finds out when he would get the worst of
it. I fed my heron on flesh, though he likes fish best. It's the most
daintiest bird that is in its eating.

"The cotamundi was an animal as was civil and quiet with
everything in the cage. But his propensity and habits for anything
that was in a cage was a cat. It was always his bed-fellow; he'd
fight for a cat; he'd bully the monkey for a cat. He and the cat
were the best of friends, and they made common cause against Mr.
Monkey. He was very fond of routing about the cage. He had very
good teeth and rare claws, and a monkey will never stand against
any thing as punishes him. Anything as is afraid of him he'll bully.

"I had an old crow once, who was a great favourite of mine and
when he died I could almost have cried. To tell you what he could
do is almost too much for me to say, for it was everything he was
capable of. He would never stand to fight; always run away and
hollow. He and the jackdaw was two birds as always kept apart
from each other: they was both of a trade, and couldn't agree. He
was very fond of getting on a perch next to any other bird – an
owl, for instance – and then he'd pretend to be looking at nothing,
and then suddenly peck at the feet of his neighbour on the sly, and
then try and look innocent. After a time the other bird would turn
round on him, and then he was off, screaming 'Caw' at the top of

his beak, as I may say. He was a general favourite with everybody. It's a curious thing, but I never know a crow, or a jackdaw
either, to be hungry, but what they'd come and ask for food by
hollowing out the same as in their wild state. Mine was a carrion
crow, and eat flesh. At feeding-time he'd always pick out the
biggest pieces he could, or three or four of them, if he could lay
hold of them in his beak, and than he'd be off to a corner and eat
what he could and then, hide the remainder, and go and fetch it
out as he felt hungry again. He knew me perfectly well, and would
come and perch on my shoulder, and peck me over the finger, and
look at me and make his noise. As soon as he see me going to fetch
the food he would, if he was loose in the court where I lived in,
run to me directly, but not at other times. He was a knowing
fellow. I had him about one year and nine months. I used to call
him the pantaloon to Mr. Monkey's clown, and they was always
at their pantomime tricks. Once an old woman came down our
court when he was loose, and he cut after her and pecked at her
naked feet, and she was so frightened she fell down. Then off he
went, 'caw, caw', as pleased as he could be. He always followed
the children, picking at their heels. Nothing delighted him so
much as all the roguishness and mischief as he could get into.

"For finding a happy family in good order, with 2 monkeys,
3 cats, 2 dogs, 16 rats, 6 starlings, 2 hawks, jacks, jackdaw, 3 owls,
magpie, 2 guinea-pigs, one rabbit, will take about 1s. 4d. a-day.
I buy leg of beef for the birds, about 1½lb., and the dogs have
two pen'orth of proper dogs' meat; and there are apples and nuts
for the monkey, about one pen'orth, and then there's corn of
different kinds, and seeds and sopped bread for the rats, and hay
and sand-dust for the birds. It all tells up, and comes to about
1s. 4d. a-day.

"There are two happy families in London town, including my
own. I don't know where the other man stands, for he moves
about. Now I like going to one place, where I gets known. It isn't
a living for any man now. I wouldn't stick to it if I could get any
work to do; and yet it's an ingenious exhibition and ought to be
patronized. People will come and stand round for hours, and
never give a penny. Even very respectable people will come up,
and as soon as ever I hand the cup to them, they'll be off about

their business. There are some gentlemen who give me regularly a penny or twopence a-week. I could mention several professional actors who do that to me. I make the most money when the monkey is at his tricks, for then they want to stop and see him at his fun, and I keep asking them for money, and do it so often, that as last they are obliged to give something.

"My cage has wire-work all round, and blinds to pull down when I change my pitch. There are springs under the cage to save the jolting over the stones.

"I forgot to tell you that I've had cats, whose kittens have been taken from them, suckle rats which been put in their places when they are still blind, and only eight days old. She'll take to the rats instead of her kittens. I've not put them in the cage at this small age, but waited until they were old enough to run about. They'll keep on suckling at the cat till they get to a tidy size, till she gets annoyed with them and beats them off; but she'll caress them at other times, and allow them to come and lay under her belly, and protect them from Mr. Monkey. Many a time has a cat been seen suckling rats in my cage, but then they've been pretty old rats — of about eight or ten weeks old; and a cat will suckle then, and they'll follow her about and go and lie under her belly, just the same as chickens under a hen — just the same.

"At night I don't let my collection sleep together in the cage, it's four years since I first took to separating of them, for this reason: I had the cleverest monkey in London; there never was a better. I used to wheel the cage into the back-yard, and there let them sleep. One night somebody was so kind as to come and steal my monkey away. I found out my loss the same night. I had only gone into the house to fetch food, and when I came back Mr. Monkey was gone. He didn't run away, for he was too fond of the cage, and wouldn't leave it. I've often put him outside, and let him loose upon Tower-hill, and to run about gardens, and he'd come back again when I called him. I had only to turn his favourite dog out, and as soon as he see'd the dog he'd be on to his back and have a nice ride back to the cage and inside in a moment. Since that loss I've always carried the collection into the house, and let them sleep in the same room where I've slept in. They all know their beds now, and will go to them of their own accord, both the cats, the dogs, and the monkeys. I've a rat-box, too, and at night when I'm going home I just open the door of the cage and that of the rat-box, and the rats run into their sleeping-place as quick as possible, and come out again in the morning of their own accord.

"My family are fed on the best: they have as good as any noble-man's favourite dog. They've often had a deal more, and better, than their master.

"I don't know why happy families don't pay, for they all look at the cage, and seem as pleased as ever; but there's poverty or something in the way, for they don't seem to have any money. When I left off last—only a month ago—I wasn't taking 6d. a-day. It didn't pay for feeding my little stock. I went to firework-making. They are always busy with firework-making, ready for the 5th of November. I'm sick and tired of the other affair, and would do anything to get from it; but people are afraid to employ me, for they seem to fancy that after being in the streets we are no use for anything.

"I'm fond of my little stock, and always was from a child of dumb animals. I'd a deal sooner that anybody hurt me than any of my favourites."

VAGRANTS

THE FIRST vagrant was one who had the thorough look of a "professional." He was literally a mass of rags and filth. He was, indeed, exactly what in the Act of Henry VIII is denominated a "valiant beggar." He stood near upon six feet high, was not more than twenty-five, and had altogether the frame and constitution of a stalwart labouring man. His clothes, which were of fustian and corduroy, tied close to his body with pieces of string, were black and shiny with filth, which looked more like pitch than grease. He had no shirt, as was plain from the fact that, where his clothes were torn, his bare skin was seen. The ragged sleeves of his fustian jacket were tied like the other part of his dress, close to his wrists, with string. This was clearly to keep the bleak air from his body. His cap was an old, brimless "wide-awake," and when on his head gave the man a most unprepossessing appearance. His story was as follows:—

"I am a carpet-weaver by trade. I served my time to it. My father was a clerk in a shoe-thread manufactory at ——. He got 35s. a-week, and his house, coals, and candles found him. He lived very comfortably; indeed, I was very happy. Before I left home, I knew none of the cares of the world and that I have known since I left him. My father and mother are living still. He is still as well off as when I was at home. I know this, because I have heard from him twice, and seen him once. He won't do anything to assist me. I have transgressed so many times, that he won't take me in hand any more. I will tell you the truth, you may depend upon it; yes, indeed, I would, even if it were to injure myself. He has tried me many times, but now he has given me up. At the age of twenty-one he told me to go from home and seek a living for myself. He said he had given me a home ever since I was a child, but now I had come to manhood I was able to provide for myself. He gave me a good education, and I might have been a better scholar at the present time, had I not neglected my studies. He put me to a day-school in the town when I was

eight years old, and I continued there till I was between twelve
and thirteen. I learnt reading, writing, and ciphering. I was
taught the catechism, the history of England, geography, and
drawing.

"My father was a very harsh man when he was put out of his
way. He was a very violent temper when he was vexed, but kind
to us all when he was pleased. I have five brothers and six sisters.
He never beat me more than twice, to my remembrance. The first
time he thrashed me with a cane, and the last with a horsewhip.
I had stopped out late at night. I was then just rising sixteen, and
had left school. I am sure those thrashings did me no good, but
made me rather worse than before. I was a self-willed lad, and
determined, if I couldn't get my will in one way, I would have it
another. After the last thrashing he told me he would give me
some trade, and after that he would set me off and get rid of me.
Then I was bound apprentice as a carpet-weaver for three years.
My master was a very kind one. I runned away once. The cause
of my going off was a quarrel with one of the workmen that was
put over me. He was very harsh, and I scarce could do anything
to please him; so I made up my mind to leave.

"The first place I went when I bolted was to Crewkerne, in
Somersetshire. There I asked for employment at carpet-weaving.
I got some, and remained there three days, when my father found
out where I was, and sent my brother and a special constable after
me. They took me from shop where I was at work, and brought
me back to ——, and would have sent me to prison had I not
promised to behave myself, and serve my time out as I ought.
I went to work again; and when the expiration of my apprenticeship occurred, my father said to me, 'Sam, you have a trade at
your fingers' ends: you are able to provide for yourself.' So then
I left home. I was twenty-one years of age. He gave me money,
£3 10s., to take me into Wales, where I told him I should go.
I was up for going about through the country. I made my father
believe I was going into Wales to get work; but all I wanted was
to go and see the place. After I had runned away once from my
apprenticeship, I found it very hard to stop at home. I couldn't
bring myself to work somehow. While I sat at the work, I thought
I should like to be away in the country: work seemed a burden to

me. I found it very difficult to stick to anything for a long time; so I made up my mind, when my time was out, that I'd be off roving, and see a little of life. I went by the packet from Bristol to Newport. After being there three weeks, I had spent all the money that I had brought from home. I spent it in drinking — most of it, and idling about. After that I was obliged to sell my clothes, &c.

"The first thing I sold was my watch; I got £2 5s. for that. Then I was obliged to part with my suit of clothes. For these I got £1 5s. With this I started from Newport to go farther up over the hills. I liked this kind of life much better than working, while the money lasted. I was in the public-house three parts of my time out of four. I was a great slave to drink. I began to like drink when I was between thirteen and fourteen. At that time my uncle was keeping a public-house, and I used to go there, backwards and forward, more or less every week. Whenever I went to see my uncle he gave me some beer. I very soon got to like it so much, that, while an apprentice, I would spend all I could get in liquor. This was the cause of my quarrels with my father, and when I went away to Newport I did so to be my own master, and drink as much as I pleased, without anybody saying anything to me about it. I got up to Nant-y-glo, and there I sought for work at the iron-foundry, but I could not get it. I stopped at this place three weeks, still drinking. The last day of the three weeks I sold the boots off my feet to get food, for all my money and clothes were now gone. I was sorry then that I had ever left my father's house; but, alas! I found it too late. I didn't write home to tell them how I was off; my stubborn temper would not allow me.

"I then started off barefoot, begging my way from Nant-y-glo to Monmouth. I told the people that I was a carper-weaver by trade, who could not get any employment, and that I was obliged to travel the country against my own wish. I didn't say a word about the drink — that would never have done. I only took $2^1/_2d$. on the road, 19 miles long; and I'm sure I must have asked assistance from more than a hundred people. They said, some of them, that they had, 'nout' for me; and others did give me a bit of 'bara caws,' or 'bara minny' (that is, bread and cheese, or bread and butter). Money is very scarce among the Welsh, and what they have they are very fond of. They don't mind giving food; if you wanted a bagful you might have it there of the working people. I inquired for a night's lodging at the union in Monmouth. That was the first time I ever asked for shelter in a workhouse in my life. I was admitted in to the tramp-room. Oh, I felt then that I would much rather be in prison than in such a place, though I never knew what the inside of a prison was — no, not then. I thought of the kindness of my father and mother. I would have been better, but I knew that, as I had been carrying on, I could never expect shelter under my father's roof any more; I knew he would not have taken me in had I gone back, or I would have returned. Oh, I was off from home, and I didn't much trouble my head about it after a few minutes; I plucked up my spirits and soon forgot where I was. I made no male friends in the union; I was savage that I had so hard a bed to lie upon; it was nothing more than the bare boards, and a rug to cover me. I knew very well it wasn't my bed, but still I thought I ought to have a better. I merely felt annoyed at its being so bad a place, and didn't think much about the rights of it.

"In the morning I was turned out, and after I had left I picked up with a young woman, who had slept in the union over-night. I said I was going on the road across country to Birmingham, and I axed her to go with me. I had never seen her before. She consented, and we went along together, begging our way. We passed as man and wife, and I was a carpet-weaver out of employment. We slept in unions and lodging-houses by the way. In the lodging-houses we lived together as man and wife, and in the unions we were separated. I never stole anything during all this time. After I got to Birmingham I made my way to Wolverhampton. My reason for going to Wolverhampton was, that there was a good many weavers there, and I thought I should make a good bit of money by begging of them. Oh, yes, I have found that I could always get more money out of my own trade than any other people. I did so well at Wolverhampton, begging, that I stopped there three weeks. I never troubled my head whether I was doing right or wrong by asking my brother-weavers for a portion of their hard earnings to keep me in idleness. Many a time I have given part of my wages to others myself. I can't say that I would have given it to them if I had known they wouldn't work like me. I wouldn't have worked sometimes if I could have got it. I can't tell why, but somehow it was painful to me to stick long at anything.

"To tell the truth, I loved a roving, idle life. I would much rather have been on the road than at my home. I drank away all I got, and feared and cared for nothing. When I got drunk overnight, it would have been impossible for me to have gone to work in the morning, even if I could have got it. The drink seemed to take all the work out of me. This oftentimes led me to think of what my father used to tell me, that 'the bird that can sing and won't sing ought to be made to sing.' During my stay at Wolverhampton I lived at a tramper's house, and there I fell in with two men well acquainted with the town, and they asked me to join them in breaking open a shop. No, sir, no, I didn't give a thought whether I was doing right or wrong at it. I didn't think my father would ever know anything at all about it, so I didn't care. I liked my mother best, much the best. She had always been a kind, good soul to me, often kept me from my father's blows, and helped me to things unknown to my father. But when I was away on the road I gave no heed to her. I didn't think of either father or mother till after I was taken into custody for that same job. Well, I agreed to go with the other two; they were old hands at the business—regular housebreakers. We went away between twelve and one at night. It was pitch dark. My two pals broke into the back part of the house, and I stopped outside to keep watch. After watching for about a quarter of an hour, a policeman came up to me and asked what I was stopping there for. I told him I was waiting for a man that was in a public-house at the corner. This led him to suspect me, it being so late at night. He went to the public-house to see whether it was open, and found it shut, and then came back to me. As he was returning he saw my two comrades coming through the back window (that was the way they had got in). He took us all three in custody; some of the passers-by assisted him in seizing us. The other two had six months' imprisonment each, and I, being a stranger, had only fourteen days.

"When I was sent to prison, I thought of my mother. I would have written to her, but couldn't get leave. Being the first time I ever was nailed, I was very downhearted at it. I didn't say I'd give it up. While I was locked up, I thought I'd go to work again, and be a sober man, when I got out. These thoughts used to come over me when I was 'on the stepper,' that is, on the wheel. But I concealed all them thoughts in my breast. I said nothing to no one. My mother was the only one that I ever thought upon. When I got out of prison, all these thoughts went away from me, and I went again at my old tricks. From Wolverhampton I went to Manchester, and from Manchester I came to London, begging and stealing wherever I had a chance. This is not my first year in London. I tell you the truth, because I am known here; and if I tell you a lie, you'll say 'You spoke an untruth in one thing, and you'll do so in another.' The first time I was in London, I was put in prison fourteen days for begging, and after I had a month at Westminster Bridewell, for begging and abusing the policeman.

"Sometimes I'd think I'd rather go anywhere, and do anything, than continue as I was; but then I had no clothes, no friends, no house, no home, no means of doing better. I had made myself what I was. I had made my father and mother turn their backs upon me, and what could I do, but go on? I was as bad off then as I am now, and I couldn't have got work then if I would. I should have spent all I got in drink then, I know. I wrote home twice. I told my mother I was hard up; had neither a shoe to my foot, a coat to my back, nor a roof over my head. I had no answer to my first letter, because it fell into the hands of my brother, and he tore it up, fearing that my mother might see it. To the second letter that I sent home my mother sent me an answer herself. She sent me a sovereign. She told me that my father was the same as when I first left home, and it was no use my coming back. She sent me the money, bidding me get some clothes and seek for work. I didn't do as she bade. I spent the money—most part in drink. I didn't give any heed whether it was wrong or right. Soon got, soon gone; and I know they could have sent me much more than that if they had pleased. It was last June twelvemonth when I first came to London, and I stopped till the 10th of last March. I lost the young woman when I was put in prison in Manchester. She never came to see me in quod. She cared nothing for me. She only kept company with me to have some one on the road along with her; and I didn't care for her, not I.

"One half of my time last winter I stopped at the 'Straw-yards,' that is, in the asylums for the houseless poor here and at Glass-house. When I could get money I had a lodging. After March I started off through Somersetshire. I went to my father's house then. I didn't go in. I saw my father at the door, and he wouldn't let me in. I was a little better dressed than I am now. He said he had enough children at home without me, and gave me 10s. to go. He could not have been kind to me, or else he would not have turned me from his roof. My mother came out to the garden in front of the house, after my father had gone to his work, and spoke to me. She wished me to reform my character. I could not make any rash promises then. I had but very little to say to her. I felt myself at that same time, for the very first time in my life, that I was doing wrong. I thought, if I could hurt my mother so, it must be wrong to go on as I did. I never had such thoughts before. My father's harsh words always drove such thoughts out of my head; but when I saw my mother's tears, it was more than I could stand. I was wanting to get away as fast as I could from the house. After that I stopped knocking about the country, sleeping in unions, up to November. Then I came to London again, and remained up to this time.

"Since I have been in town I have sought for work at the floor-cloth and carpet manufactory in the Borough, and they wouldn't even look at me in my present state. I am heartily tired of my life now altogether, and would like to get out of it if I could. I hope at least I have given up my love of drink, and I am sure, if I could once again lay my hand on some work, I should be quite a reformed character. Well, I am altogether tired of carrying on like this. I haven't made 6d. a-day ever since I have been in London this time. I go tramping it across the country just to pass the time, and see a little of new places. When the summer comes I want to be off. I am sure I have seen enough of this country now, and I should like to have a look at some foreign land. Old England has nothing new in it now for me. I think a beggar's life is the worst kind of life that a man can lead. A beggar is no more thought upon than a dog in the street, and there are too many at the trade. I wasn't brought up to a bad life. You can see that by little things—by my handwriting; and, indeed, I should like to have a chance at something else. I have had the feelings of a vagabond for full ten years. I know, and now I am sure I'm getting a different man. I begin to have thoughts and ideas I never had before. Once I never feared nor cared for anything, and I wouldn't have altered if I could; but now I'm tired out, and if I haven't a chance of going right, why I must go wrong."

The next was a short, thick-set man, with a frequent grin on his countenance, which was rather expressive of humour. He wore a very dirty smock-frock, dirtier trousers, shirt and neckerchief, and broken shoes. He answered readily, and as if he enjoyed his story.

"I never was at school, and was brought up as a farm labourer at Devizes," he said, "where my parents were labourers. I worked that way three or four years, and then ran away. My master wouldn't give me money enough—only 3s. 6d. a-week,—and my parents were very harsh; so I ran away, rather than be licked for ever. I'd heard people say, 'Go to Bath,' and I went there; and I was only about eleven then. I'm now twenty-three. I tried to get work on the railway there, and I did. I next got into prison for stealing three shovels. I was hard-up, having lost my work, and so I stole them. I was ten weeks in prison. I came out worse that I went in, for I mixed with the old hands, and they put me up to a few capers. When I got out I thought I could live as well that way as by hard work; so I took to the country. I began to beg. At first I took 'No' for an answer, when I asked for 'Charity to a poor boy;' but I found that wouldn't do, so I learned to stick to them. I was forced, or I must have starved, and that wouldn't do at all. I did middling; plenty to eat, and sometimes a drop to drink, but not often. I was forced to be merry, because it's no good being down-hearted. I begged for two years,—that is, steal and beg together: I couldn't starve. I did best in country villages in Somersetshire; there's always odds and ends to be picked up there. I got into scrapes now and then.

"Once in Devonshire, me and another slept at a farm-house, and in the morning, we went egg-hunting. I must have stowed three dozen of eggs about me, when a dog barked, and we were alarmed and ran away, and in getting over a gate I fell, and there I lay among the smashed eggs. I can't help laughing at it still: but I got away. I was too sharp for them. I have been twenty or thirty times in prison. I have been in for stealing bread, and a side of bacon, and cheese, and shovels, and other things; generally provisions. I generally learn something new in prison. I shall do no good while I stop in England. It's not possible a man like me can get work, so I'm forced to go on this way. Sometimes I haven't a bit to eat all day. At night I may pick up something. An uncle of mine once told me he would like to see me transported, or come to the gallows. I told him I had no fear about the gallows; I should never come to that end; but if I were transported I should be better off than I am now. I can't starve and I won't; and I can't 'list, I'm too short, I came to London the other day, but could do no good. The London hands are quite a different set to us. We seldom do business together. My way's simple. If I see a thing, and I'm hungry, I take it if I can, in London or anywhere. I once had a turn with two Londoners, and we got two coats and two pair of trousers; but the police got them back again. I was only locked up one night for it.

"The country's the best place to get away with anything because there's not so many policemen. There's lots live as I live, because there's no work. I can do a country policeman, generally. I've had sprees at the country lodging-houses — larking, and drinking, and carrying on, and playing cards and dominoes all night for a farthing a game; sometimes fighting about it. I can play at dominoes, but I don't know the cards. They try to cheat one another. Honour among thieves! why, there's no such thing; they take from one another. Sometimes we danced all night — Christmas time, and such times. Young women dance with us, and sometimes old women. We're all merry; some's lying on the floor drunk; some's jumping about, smoking; some's dancing; and so we enjoy ourselves. That's the best part of the life. We are seldom stopped in our merry-makings in the country. It's no good the policemen coming among us; give them beer, and you may knock the house down. We have good meat sometimes; sometimes very rough. Some are very particular about their cookery, as nice as anybody is. They must have their pickels, and their peppers, and their fish-sauces (I've had them myself), to their dishes. Chops, in the country, has the call; or ham and eggs—that's relished. Some's very particular about their drink, too; won't touch bad beer; same way with the gin. It's chiefly gin (I'm talking about the country), very little rum; no brandy: but sometimes, after a good day's work, a drop of wine. We help one another when we are sick, where we're knowed. Some's very good that way. Some lodging-house keepers get rid of anybody that's sick, by taking them to the relieving-officer at once."

A really fine-looking lad of eighteen gave me the following statement. He wore a sort of frock-coat, very thin, buttoned about him, old cloth trousers, and bad shoes. His shirt was tolerably good and clean, and although he had a tidy look and an air of quickness, but not of cunning:—

"My father," he said, "was a bricklayer in Shoreditch parish, and my mother took in washing. They did pretty well; but they're dead and buried two years and a half ago. I used to work in brick-fields at Ball's-pond, living with my parents, and taking home every farthing I earned. I earned 18s. a-week, working from five in the morning until sunset. They had only me. I can read and write middling; when my parents died, I had to look out for myself. I was off work, attending to my father and mother when they were sick. They died within about three weeks of each other, and I lost my work, and I had to part with my clothes; before that I tried to work in brick-fields, and couldn't get it, and work grew slack. When my parents died I was thirteen; and I sometimes got to sleep in the unions; but that was stopped, and then I took to the lodging-houses, and there I met with lads who were enjoying themselves at push-halfpenny and cards; and they were thieves, and they tempted me to join them, and I did for once—but only once. I then went begging about the streets and thieving, as I knew the others do.

"I used to pick pockets. I worked for myself, because I thought that would be best. I had no fence at all—no pals at first, nor anything. I worked by myself for a time. I sold the handkerchiefs

I got to Jews in the streets, chiefly in Field-lane, for 1s. 6d., but I have got as much as 3s. 6d. for your real fancy ones. One of these buyers wanted to cheat me out of 6d., so I would have no more dealings with him. The others paid me. The 'Kingsmen' they call the best handkerchiefs — those that have the pretty-looking flowers on them. Some are only worth 4d. or 5d., some's not worth taking. Those I gave away to strangers, boys like myself, or wore them myself, round my neck. I only threw one away, but it was all rags, though he looked quite like a gentleman that had it. Lord-mayor's day and such times is the best for us. Last Lord-mayor's day I got four handkerchiefs, and I made 11s. There was 6d. tied up in the corner of one handkerchief; another was pinned to the pocket, but I got it out, and after that another chap had him, and cut his pocket clean away, but there was nothing in it. I generally picked my men — regular swells, or good-humoured looking men. I've often followed them a mile.

"I once got a purse with 3s. 6d. in it from a lady when the Coal Exchange was opened. I made 8s. 6d that day — the purse and handkerchiefs. That's the only lady I ever robbed. I was in the crowd when Manning and his wife were hanged. I wanted to see if they died game, as I heard them talk so much about them at our house. I was there all night. I did four good handkerchiefs and a rotten one not worth picking up. I saw them hung. I was right under the drop. I was a bit startled when they brought him up and put the rope round his neck and the cap on, and they brought her out. All said he was hung innocently; it was she that should have been hung by herself. They both dropped together, and I felt faintified, but I soon felt all right again. The police drove us away as soon as it was over, so that I couldn't do any more business; besides, I was knocked down in the crowd and jumped upon, and I won't go to see another hung in a hurry. He didn't deserve it, but she did, every inch of her. I can't say I thought, while I was seeing the execution, that the life I was leading would ever bring me to the gallows.

"After I'd worked by myself a bit, I got to live in a house where lads like me, big and little, were accommodated. We paid 3d. a-night. It was always full; there was twenty or twenty-one of us. We enjoyed ourselves middling. I was happy enough: we drank

sometimes, chiefly beer, and sometimes a drop of gin. One would
say, 'I've done so much,' and another, 'I've done so much'; and
stand a drop. The best I ever heard done was £2 for two coats
from a tailor's, near Bow-church, Cheapside. That was by one
of my pals. We used to share our money with those who did
nothing for a day, and they shared with us when we rested.
There never was any blabbing. We wouldn't do one another out
of a farthing. Of a night some one would now and then read
hymns, out of books they sold about the streets—I'm sure they
were hymns; or else we'd read stories about Jack Sheppard and
Dick Turpin, and all through that set. They were large thick
books, borrowed from the library. They told how they used to
break open the houses, and get out of Newgate, and how Dick got
away to York. We used to think Jack and them very fine fellows.
I wished I could be like Jack (I did then), about the blankets in
his escape, and that old house in West-street—it is a ruin still.

"We played cards and dominoes sometimes at our house, and
at pushing a halfpenny over the table along five lines. We struck
the halfpenny from the edge of the table, and according to
what line it settled on was the game—like as they play at the
Glasshouse—that's the 'model lodging-house' they calls it. Cribbage was always played at cards. I can only play cribbage. We
have played for a shilling a game, but oftener a penny. It was
always fair play. That was the way we passed the time when we
were not out. We used to keep quiet, or the police would have
been down upon us. They knew of the place. They took one boy
there. I wondered what they wanted. They catched him at the
very door. We lived pretty well; anything we liked to get, when
we'd money; we cooked it ourselves. The master of the house was
always on the look-out to keep out those who had no business
there. No girls were admitted. The master of the house had
nothing to do with what we got. I don't know of any other such
house in London; I don't think there are any. The master would
sometimes drink with us—a larking like. He used us pretty
kindly at times. I have been three times in prison, three months
each time; the Compter, Brixton, and Maidstone. I went down
to Maidstone fair, and was caught by a London policeman down
there. He was dressed as a bricklayer. Prison always made me

worse, and as I had nothing given me when I came out, I had to look out again. I generally got hold of something before I had been an hour out of prison. I'm now heartily sick of this life. I wish I'd been transported with some others from Maidstone, where I was tried."

A cotton-spinner (who had subsequently been a soldier), whose appearance was utterly abject, was the next person questioned. He was tall, and had been florid-looking (judging by his present complexion). His coat—very old and worn, and once black—would not button, and would have hardly held together if buttoned. He was out at elbows, and some parts of the collar were pinned together. His waistcoat was of a match with his coat, and his trousers were rags. He had some shirt, as was evident by his waistcoat, held together by one button. A very dirty handkerchief was tied carelessly round his neck. He was tall and erect, and told his adventures with heartiness.

"I am thirty-eight," he said, "and have been a cotton-spinner, working at Chorlton-upon-Medlock. I can neither read nor write. When I was a young man, twenty years ago, I could earn £2 10s., clear money, every week, after paying two piecers and a scavenger. Each piecer had 7s. 6d. a-week—they are girls; the scavenger—a boy to clean the wheels of the cotton-spinning machine—had 2s. 6d. I was master of them wheels in the factory. This state of things continued until about the year 1837. I lived well and enjoyed myself, being a hearty man, noways a drunkard, working every day from half-past five in the morning till half-past seven at night—long hours, that time, master. I didn't care about money as long as I was decent and despectable. I had a turn for sporting at the wakes down there. In 1837, the 'self-actors' (machines with steam power) had come into common use. One girl can mind three pairs—that used to be three men's work—getting 15s. for the work which gave three men £7 10s. Out of one factory 400 hands were flung in one week, men and women together. We had a meeting of the union, but nothing could be done, and we were told to go and mind the three pairs, as the girls did, for 15s. a-week. We wouldn't do that.

"Some went for soldiers, some to sea, some to Stopport [Stockport], to get work in factories where the 'self-actors' weren't agait. The masters there wouldn't have them—at least, some of them. Manchester was full of them; but one gentleman in Hulme still won't have them, for he says he won't turn the men out of bread. I 'listed for a soldier in the 48th. I liked a soldier's life very well until I got flogged—100 lashes for selling my kit (for a spree), and 150 for striking a corporal, who called me an English robber. He was an Irishman. I was confined five days in the hospital after each punishment. It was terrible. It was like a bunch of razors cutting at your back. Your flesh was dragged off by the cats. Flogging was then very common in the regiment. I was flogged in 1840. To this day I feel a pain in the chest from the triangles. I was discharged from the army about two years ago, when the reduction took place. I was only flogged the time I've told you. I had no pension and no friends. I was discharged in Dublin. I turned to, and looked for work. I couldn't get any, and made my way for Manchester. I stole myself aboard of a steamer, and hid myself till she got out to sea, on her way from Dublin to Liverpool. When the captain found me there, he gave me a kick and some bread, and told me to work, so I worked for my passage twenty-four hours. He put me ashore at Liverpool.

"I slept in the union that night—nothing to eat and nothing to cover me—no fire; it was winter. I walked to Manchester, but could get nothing to do there, though I was twelve months knocking about. It wants a friend and a character to get work. I slept in unions in Manchester, and had oatmeal porridge for breakfast, work at grinding logwood in the mill, from six to twelve, and then turn out. That was the way I lived chiefly; but I got a job sometimes in driving cattle, and 3d for it,—or 2d. for carrying baskets in the vegetable markets; and went to Shoedale Union at night. I would get a pint of coffee and half-a-pound of bread, and half-a-pound of bread in the morning, and no work. I took to travelling up to London, half-hungered on the road—that was last winter—eating turnips out of this field, and carrots out of that, and sleeping under hedges and haystacks. I slept under one haystack, and pulled out the hay to cover me, and the snow lay on it a foot deep in the morning. I slept for all that, but wasn't I froze when I woke? An old farmer came up with his cart and pitchfork to load hay. He said: 'Poor fellow! have you been here all night?' I answered, 'Yes.' He gave me some coffee and bread, and one shilling. That was the only good friend I met with on the road. I got fourteen days of it for asking a gentleman for a penny; that was in Stafford.

"I got to London after that, sleeping in unions sometimes, and begging a bite here and there. Sometimes I had to walk all night. I was once forty-eight hours without a bite, until I got hold at last of a Swede turnip, and so at last I got to London. Here I've tried up and down everywhere for work as a labouring man, or in a foundry. I tried London Docks, and Blackwall, and every place; but no job. At one foundry, the boiler-makers made a collection of 4s. for me. I've walked the streets for three nights together. Here, in this fine London, I was refused a night's lodging in Shoreditch and in Gray's-inn-lane. A policeman, the fourth night, at twelve o'clock procured me a lodging, and gave me 2d. I couldn't drag on any longer. I was taken to a doctor's in the city. I fell in the street from hunger and tiredness. The doctor ordered me brandy and water, 2s, 6d., and a quartern loaf, and some coffee, sugar, and butter. He said, what I ailed was hunger. I made that run out long as I could, but I was then as bad off as ever. It's hard to hunger for nights together.

"I was once in 'Steel' [Coldbath-fields] for begging. I was in Tothill-fields for going into a chandler's shop, asking for a quartern loaf and half a pound of cheese, and walking out with it. I got a month for that. I have been in Brixton for taking a loaf out of a baker's basket, all through hunger. Better a prison than to starve. I was well treated because I behaved well in prison. I have slept in coaches when I had a chance. One night on a dunghill, covering the stable straw about me to keep myself warm. This place is a relief. I shave the poor people and cut their hair, on a Sunday. I was handy at that when I was a soldier. I have shaved in public-houses for halfpennies. Some landlords kicks me out. Now, in the days, I may pick up a penny or two that way, and get here of a night. I met two Manchester men in Hyde Park on Saturday, skating. They asked me what I was. I said, 'A beggar.' They gave me 2s. 6d., and I spent part of it for warm coffee and other things. They knew all about Manchester, and knew I was a Manchester man by my talk."

The statement I then took was that of a female vagrant—a young girl with eyes and hair of a remarkable blackness. Her complexion was of the deepest brunette, her cheeks were full of colour, and her lips very thick. This was accounted for. She told me that her father was a mulatto from Philadelphia. She was short, and dressed in a torn old cotton gown, the pattern of which was hardly discernible from wear. A kind of half-shawl, patched and mended in several places, and of very thin woollen texture, was pinned around her neck; her arms, which, with her hands, were full and large, were bare. She wore very old broken boots and ragged stockings. Her demeanour was modest.

"I am now eighteen," she stated. "My father was a coloured man. He came over here as a sailor, I have heard, but I never saw him; for my mother, who was a white woman, was not married to him, but met him at Oxford; and she married afterwards a box-maker, a white man, and has two other children. They are living, I believe, but I don't know where they are. I have heard my mother say that my father—that's my own father—had become a missionary, and had been sent out to America from England as a missionary, by Mr. ——. I believe that was fifteen years ago. I don't know who Mr. —— was, but he was a gentleman, I've heard my mother say. She told me, too, that my father was a good scholar, and that he could speak seven different languages and was a very religious man. He was sent out to Boston, but I never heard whether he was to stay or not, and I don't know what he was to missionary about. He behaved very well to my mother, I have heard her say, until she took up with the other man (the box-maker), and then he left her, and gave her up, and came to London. It was at Oxford that they all three were then; and when my father got away, or came away to London, my mother followed him (she told me so, but she didn't like to talk about it), as she was then in the family way. She didn't find him; but my father heard of her, and left some money with Mr. —— for her, and she got into Poland-street workhouse through Mr. —— I've heard. While there, she received 1s. 6d. a-week, but my father never came to see her or me.

"At one time, my father used to live by teaching languages. He had been in Spain, and France, and Morocco. I've heard, at

VAGRANTS IN THE CASUAL WARD OF A WORKHOUSE

any rate, that he could speak the Moors' language, but I know nothing more. All this is what I've heard from my mother and my grandmother — that's my mother's mother. My grandfather and grandmother are dead. He was a sawyer. I have a great-grandmother living in Oxford, now ninety-two, supported by her parish. I lived with my grandmother at Oxford, who took me out of pity, as my mother never cared about me, when I was four months old. I remained with her until I was ten, and then my mother came from Reading, where she was living, and took me away with her. I lived with her and my step-father, but they were badly off. He couldn't get much to do at his trade as a box-maker, and he drank a great deal. I was with them about nine months, when I ran away. He beat me so; he never liked me. I couldn't bear it. I went to Pangbourne, but there I was stopped by a man my stepfather had sent — at least I suppose so — and I was forced to walk back to Reading — ten miles, perhaps. My father applied to the overseer for support for me, and the overseer was rather harsh, and my father struck him, and for that he was sent to prison for three months.

"My mother and her children then got into the workhouse, but not until my stepfather had been some time in prison. Before that she had an allowance, which was stopped; I don't know how much. I was in the workhouse twenty-one days. I wasn't badly treated. My mother sweared my parish, and I was removed to St. James's, Poland-street, London. I was there three weeks, and then I was sent to New Brentford — it was called the Juvenile Establishment — and I went to school. There was about 150 boys and girls; the boys were sent to Norwood when they were fifteen. Some of the girls were eighteen, kept there until they could get a place. I don't know whether they all belonged to St. James's, or to different parishes, or how. I stayed there about two years. I was very well treated, sufficient to eat; but we worked hard at scrubbing, cleaning, and making shirts. We made all the boys' clothes as well, jackets and trousers, and all. I was then apprenticed a maid-of-all-work, in Duke-street, Grosvenor-square, for three years. I was there two years and a half, when my master failed in business, and had to part with me. They had no servant but me. My mistress was sometimes kind, pretty well. I had to work very hard. She sometimes beat me if I stopped long on my errands. My master beat me once for bringing things wrong from a grocer's. I made a mistake. Once my mistress knocked me down-stairs for being long on an errand to Pimlico, and I'm sure I couldn't help it, and my eye was cut. It was three weeks before I could see well. [There is a slight mark under the girl's eye still.] They beat me with their fists.

"After I left my master, I tried hard to get a place; I'm sure I did, but I really couldn't; so to live, I got watercresses to sell up and down Oxford-street. I stayed at lodging-houses. I tried that two or three months, but couldn't live. My mother had been through the country, and I knew other people that had, through meeting them at the lodging-houses. I first went to Croydon, begging my way. I slept in the workhouse. After that I went to Brighton, begging my way, but couldn't get much, not enough to pay my lodgings. I was constantly insulted, both in the lodging-houses and in the streets. I sung in the streets at Brighton, and got enough to pay my lodgings, and a little for food. I was there a week, and then I went to the Mendicity, and they gave me a piece of bread (morning and night) and a night's lodging. I then went to Lewes and other places, begging, and got into prison at Tunbridge Wells for fourteen days, for begging. I only used to say I was a poor girl out of a place, could they relieve me? I told no lies. I didn't pick my oakum one day, it was such hard stuff; three and a half pounds of it to do from nine to half-past three: so I was put into solitary for three days and three nights, having half a pound of bread and a pint of cold water morning and night; nothing else, and no bed to sleep on. I'm sure I tell you the truth. Some had irons on their hands if they were obstropolous. That's about two months ago.

"I'm sorry to say that during this time I couldn't be virtuous. I know very well what it means, for I can read and write, but no girl can be so circumstanced as I was. I seldom got money for being wicked; I hated being wicked, but I was tricked and cheated. I am truly sorry for it, but what could a poor girl do? I begged my way from London to Hastings, and got here on Saturday last, and having no money, came here. I heard of this asylum from a girl in Whitechapel, who had been here. I met her in lodging-house, where I called to rest in the daytime. They let us rest sometimes in lodging-houses in the daytime.

"I never was in any prison but Tunbridge Wells, and in Gravesend lock-up for being out after twelve at night, when I had no money to get a lodging. I was there one Saturday night, and got out on Sunday morning, but had nothing given me to eat — I was in by myself. It's a bad place — just straw to sleep on, and very cold. I told you I could read and write. I learnt that partly at Oxford, and finished my learning at the Juvenile Establishment at Brentford. There I was taught reading, writing, sums, marking, sewing, and scrubbing. Once I could say all the multiplication table, but I've forgot most of it. I know how to make lace, too, because I was taught by a cousin in Oxford, another grandchild of my grandmother's. I can make it with knitting-needles. I could make cushion-lace with pins, but I'm afraid I've forgot how now. I should like, if I could to get into service again, here or abroad. I have heard of Australia, where I have a cousin. I am sure I could and would conduct myself well in service, I have suffered so much out of it. I am sure of it. I never stole anything in my life, and have told all I have done wrong."

A RETURNED CONVICT

I SHALL now give the statement of a man who was selected at random from amongst a number such as himself, congregated in one of the most respectable lodging-houses. He proved, on examination, to be a returned convict, and one who had gone through the severest bodily and mental agony. He had lived in the bush, and been tried for his life. He was an elderly-looking man, whose hair was just turning grey, and in whose appearance there was nothing remarkable, except that his cheek-bones were unusually high, and that his face presented that collected and composed expression which is common to men exposed to habitual watchfulness from constant danger. He gave me the following statement. His dress was bad, but differed in nothing from that of a long-distressed mechanic. He said: —

"I am now 43 (he looked much older), and had respectable parents, and a respectable education. I am a native of London. When I was young I was fond of a roving life, but cared nothing about drink. I liked to see 'life,' as it was called, and was fond of the company of women. Money was no object in those days; it was like picking up dirt in the streets. I ran away from home. My parents were very kind to me; indeed, I think I was used too well, I was petted so, when I was between 12 and 13. I got acquainted with some boys at Bartlemy-fair a little before that, and saw them spending lots of money and throwing at cockshies, and such-like: and one of them said, 'Why don't you come out like us?' So afterwards I ran away and joined them. I was not kept shorter of money than other boys like me, but I couldn't settle. I couldn't fix my mind to any regular business but a waterman's, and my friends wouldn't hear of that. There was nine boys of us among the lot that I joined, but we didn't all work together. All of 'em came to be sent to Van Dieman's Land as transports except one, and he was sent to Sydney.

"While we were in London it was a merry life, with change of scene, for we travelled about. We were successful in nearly all our plans for several months. I worked in Fleet-street, and could make £3 a-week at handkerchiefs alone, sometimes falling across a pocketbook. The best handkerchiefs then brought 4s. in Field-lane. Our chief enjoyments were at the 'Free and Easy,' where all the thieves and young women went, and sang and danced. I had a young woman for a partner then; she went out to Van Dieman's Land. She went on the lift in London [shopping and stealing from the counter]. She was clever at it. I carried on in this way for about 15 months, when I was grabbed for an attempt on a gentleman's pocket by St. Paul's Cathedral, on a grand charity procession day. I had two months in the Old Horse [Bridewell].

"I never thought of my parents at this time – I wouldn't. I was two years and a half at this same trade. One week was very like another, – successes and escapes, and free-and-easies, and games of all sorts, made up the life. At the end of the two years and a half I got into the way of forged Bank-of-England notes. A man I knew in the course of business, said, 'I would cut that game of 'smatter-hauling' [stealing handkerchiefs], and do a little soft,' [pass bad notes]. So I did, and was very successful at first. I had a mate. He afterwards went out to Sydney, too, for 14 years. I went stylishly dressed as a gentleman, with a watch in my pocket, to pass my notes. I passed a good many in drapers' shops, also at tailors' shops. I never tried jewellers, the're reckoned too good judges. The notes were all finnies (£5 notes), and a good imitation. I made more money at this game, but lived as before, and had my partner still. I was fond of her; she was a nice girl, and I never found that she wronged me in any way. I thought at four month's end of retiring into the country with gambling-tables, as the risk was becoming considerable. They hung them for it in them days, but that never daunted me the least in life. I saw Cashman hung for that gunsmith's shop on Snow-hill, and I saw Fauntleroy hung and a good many others, but it gave me no uneasiness and no fear. The gallows had no terror for people in my way of life.

"I started into the country with another man and his wife – his lawful wife – for I had a few words with my own young woman, or I shouldn't have left her behind me, or, indeed, have started at all. We carried gambling on in different parts of the country for six months. We made most at the E. O. tables, — not those played with a ball, they weren't in vogue then, but throwing dice for prizes marked on a table. The highest prize was ten guineas but the dice were so made that no prize could be thrown; the numbers were not regular as in good dice, and they were loaded as well. If anybody asked to see them, we had good dice ready to show. All sorts played with us. London men and all were taken in. We made most at the races. My mate and his wife told me that at the last Newmarket meeting we attended £65 was made, but they rowed in the same boat. I know they got a deal more. The £65 was shared in three equal portions, but I had to maintain the horse and cart out of my own share.

"We used to go out into the roads [highway robbery] between races, and if we met an 'old bloke' we 'propped him' [knocked him down], and robbed him. We did good stakes that way, and were never found out. We lived as well as any gentleman in the land. Our E. O. table was in a tilted cart. I stayed with this man and his wife two months. She was good-looking, so as to attract people. I thought they didn't use me altogether right, so at Braintree I gave another man in the same way of business £25 for his kit — horse, harness, tilted-cart, and table. I gave him two good £5 notes and three bad ones, for I worked that way still, not throwing much of a chance away. I came to London for a hawker's stock, braces and such like, to sell on the road, just to take the down off [remove suspicion]. In the meantime, the man that I bought the horse, &c., of, had been nailed passing a bad note, and he stated who he got it from, and I was traced. He was in a terrible rage to find himself done, particularly as he used to do the same to other people himself. He got acquitted for that there note after he had me 'pinched'. I got 'fullied' (fully committed). I was tried at the 'Start' [Old Bailey], and pleaded guilty to the minor offence (that of utterance, not knowing the note to be forged), or I should have been hanged for it then.

"It was a favourable sessions when I was tried. Thirty-six were cast for death, and only one was 'topped' [hanged], the very one that expected to be 'turned up' [acquitted] for highway robbery. I was sentenced to 14 years' transportation. I was ten weeks in the Bellerophon hulk at Sheerness, and was then taken to Hobart

Town, Van Dieman's Land, in the *Sir Godfrey Webster*. At Hobart
Town sixty of us were picked out to go to Launceston. There
at Launceston we lay for four days in an old church, guarded
by constables; and then the settlers came there from all parts,
and picked their men out. I got a very bad master. He put me to
harvest work that I had never even seen done before, and I had
the care of pigs as wild boars. After that I was sent to Launceston
with two letters from my master to the superintendent, and the
other servants thought I had luck to get away from Red Barks
to Launceston, which was 16 miles off. I then worked in a Government potato-field; in the Government charcoal-works for
about 11 months; and then was in the Marine department, going
by water from Launceston to George Town, taking Government
officers down in gigs, provisions in boats, and such-like. There was
a crew of six [convicts] in the gigs, and four in the watering-
boats.

"All the time I consider I was very hardly treated, I hadn't
clothes half the time, being allowed only two slop-suits in a year,
and no bed to lie on when we had to stay out all night with boats
by the river Tamar. With 12 years' service at this my time was up,
but I had incurred several punishments before it was up. The
first was 25 lashes, because a bag of flour had been burst, and I
picked up a capful. The flogging is dreadfully severe, a soldier's is
nothing to it. I once had 50 lashes, for taking a hat in a joke
when I was tipsy; and a soldier had 300 the same morning. I was
flogged as a convict, and he as a soldier; and when we were both
at the same hospital after the flogging, and saw each other's backs,
the other convicts said to me, 'D—it, you've got it this time;' and
the soldier, said, when he saw my back, 'You've got it twice as
bad as I have.' 'No,' said the doctor, 'ten times as bad—he's been
flogged; but you, in comparison, have only had a child's whip-
ping.'

"The cats the convicts were then flogged with were each six
feet long, made out of the log-line of a ship of 500 tons burden;
nine over-end knots were in each tail, and nine tails whipped
at each end with wax-end. With this we had half-minute lashes; a
quick lashing would have been certain death. One convict who
had 75 lashes was taken from the triangles to the watch-house

in Launceston, and ask if he would have some tea, – he was found to be dead. The military surgeon kept on saying in this case, 'Go on, do your duty.' I was mustered there, as was every hand belonging to the Government, and saw it, and heard the doctor.

"When I was first flogged, there was an inquiry among my fellow-convicts, as to 'How did D— (meaning me) stand it – did he sing?' The answer was, 'He was a pebble;' that is, I never once said, 'Oh!' or gave out any expression of the pain I suffered. I took my flogging like a stone. If I had sung, some of the convicts would have given me some lush with a locust in it [laudanum hocusing], and when I was asleep would have given me a crack on the head that would have laid me straight. That first flogging made me ripe. I said to myself, 'I can take it like a bullock.' I could have taken the flogger's life at the time, I felt such revenge. Flogging always gives that feeling; I know it does, from what I've heard others say who had been flogged like myself.

"In all I had 875 lashes at my different punishments. I used to boast of it at last. I would say, 'I don't care, I can take it till they see my backbone.' After a flogging, I've rubbed my back against a wall, just to show my bravery like, and squeezed the congealed blood out of it. Once I would not let them dress my back after a flogging, and I had 25 additional for that. At last I bolted to Hobart Town, 120 miles off. There I was taken before Mr. H——, the magistrate, himself a convict formerly, I believe from the Irish Rebellion; but he was a good man to a prisoner. He ordered me 50, and sent me back to Launceston. At Launceston I was 'fullied' by a bench of magistrates, and had 100. Seven years before my time was up I took to the bush. I could stand it no longer, of course not. In the bush I met men with whom, if I had been seen associating, I should have been hanged in any slight charge, such as Brittan was and his pals."

I am not at liberty to continue this man's statement at present: it would be a breach of the trust reposed in me. Suffice it, he was in after days tried for his life. Altogether it was a most extraordinary statement; and from confirmations I received, was altogether truthful. He declared that he was so sick of the life he was now leading, that he would, as a probation, work on any kind of land anywhere for nothing, just to get out of it. He pronounced the lodging-houses the grand encouragements and concealments of crime, though he might be speaking against himself, he said, as he had always hidden safely there during the hottest search. A policeman once walked through the ward in search of him, and he was in bed. He knew the policeman well, and was as well known to the officer, but he was not recognised. He attributed his escape to the thick, bad atmosphere of the place giving his features a different look, and to his having shaved off his whiskers, and pulled his nightcap over his head. The officer, too, seemed half-sick, he said.

It ought also to be added, that this man stated that the severity of the Government in this penal colony was so extreme, that men thought little of giving others a knock on the head with an axe, to get hanged out of the way. Under the discipline of Captain Macconochie, however, who introduced better order with a kindlier system, there wasn't a man but what would have laid down his life for him.

BOY INMATES OF THE CASUAL WARDS OF THE LONDON WORKHOUSES

AN INTELLIGENT-LOOKING boy, of sixteen years of age, whose dress was a series of ragged coats, three in number—as if one was to obviate the deficiency of another, since one would not button, and another was almost sleeveless—gave me the following statement. He had long and rather fair hair, and spoke quietly. He said:—

"I'm a native of Wisbeach, in Cambridgeshire, and am sixteen. My father was a shoe-maker, and my mother died when I was five years old, and my father married again. I was sent to school, and can read and write well. My father and step-mother were kind enough to me. I was apprenticed to a tailor three years ago, but I wasn't long with him; I runned away. I think it was three months I was with him when I first runned away. It was in August—I got as far as Boston in Lincolnshire, and was away a fortnight. I had 4s. 6d. of my own money when I started, and that lasted two or three days. I stopped in lodging-houses until my money was gone, and then I slept anywhere—under the hedges, or anywhere. I didn't see so much of life then, but I've seen plenty of it since. I had to beg my way back from Boston, but was very awkward at first. I lived on turnips mainly. My reason for running off was because my master ill-used me so; he beat me, and kept me from my meals, and made me sit up working late at nights for a punishment; but it was more to his good than to punish me. I hated to be confined to a tailor's shopboard, but I would rather do that sort of work now than hunger about like this. But you see, sir, God punishes you when you don't think of it.

"When I went back my father was glad to see me, and he wouldn't have me go back again to my master, and my indentures were cancelled. I stayed at home seven months, doing odd jobs, in driving sheep, or any country work, but I always wanted to be off to sea. I liked the thoughts of going to sea far better than tailoring. I determined to go to sea if I could. When a dog's determined to have a bone, it's not easy to hinder him. I didn't read stories about the sea then, not even 'Robinson Crusoe,' — indeed I haven't read that still, but I know very well there is such a book. My father had no books but religious books; they were all of a religious turn, and what people might think dull, but they never made me dull. I read Wesley's and Watts's hymns, and religious magazines of different connexions. I had a natural inclination for the sea, and would like to get to it now. I've read a good deal about it since — Clark's 'Lives of Pirates,' 'Tales of Shipwrecks,' and other things in penny numbers (Clark's I got out of a library though).

"I was what people called a deep boy for a book; and am still. Whenever I had a penny, after I got a bellyful of victuals, it went for a book, but I haven't bought many lately. I did buy one yesterday — the 'Family Herald' — one I often read when I can get it. There's good reading in it; it elevates your mind — anybody that has a mind for studying. It has good tales in it. I never read 'Jack Sheppard,' — that is, I haven't read the big book that's written about him; but I've often heard the boys and men talk about it at the lodging-houses and other places. When they haven't their bellies and money to think about they sometimes talk about books; but for such books as them — that's as 'Jack' — I haven't a partiality. I've read 'Windsor Castle,' and 'The Tower,' — they're by the same man. I liked 'Windsor Castle,' and all about Henry VIII and Herne the hunter. It's a book that's connected with history, and that's a good thing in it. I like adventurous tales. I know very little about theatres, as I was never in one.

"Well, after that seven months — I was kindly treated all the time — I runned away again to get to sea; and hearing so much talk about this big London, I comed to it. I couldn't settle down to anything but the sea. I often watched the ships at Wisbeach. I had no particular motive, but a sort of pleasure in it. I was aboard some ships, too; just looking about, as lads will. I started without a farthing, but I couldn't help it. I felt I must come. I forgot all I suffered before — at least, the impression had died off my mind. I came up by the unions when they would take me in. When I started, I didn't know where to sleep any more than the dead; I learned it from other travellers on the road. It was two winters ago, and very cold weather. Sometimes I slept in barns, and I begged my way as well as I could. I never stole anything then or since, except turnips; but I've been often tempted. At last I got to London, and was by myself. I travelled sometimes with others as I came up, but not as mates — not as friends. I came to London for one purpose just by myself.

"I was a week in London before I knew where I was. I didn't know where to go. I slept on door-steps, or anywhere. I used often to stand on London-bridge, but I didn't know where to go to get to sea, or anything of that kind. I was sadly hungered, regularly starved; and I saw so many policemen, I durstn't beg — and I dare not now, in London. I got crusts, but I can hardly tell how I lived. One night I was sleeping under a railway-arch, somewhere about Bishopsgate-street, and a policeman came and asked me what I was up to? I told him I had no place to go to, so he said I must go along with him. In the morning he took me and four or five others to a house in a big street. I don't know where; and a man — a magistrate, I suppose he was — heard what the policeman had to say, and he said there was always a lot of lads there about the arches, young thieves, that gave him a great deal of trouble, and I was one associated with them. I declare I didn't know any of the other boys, not any boys in London — not a soul; and I was under the arch by myself, and only that night. I never saw the policeman himself before that, as I know of. I got fourteen days of it, and they took me in an omnibus, but I don't know to what prison. I was committed for being a rogue and something else. I didn't very well hear what other things I was, but 'rogue' I know was one. They were very strict in prison, and I wasn't allowed to speak. I was put to oakum some days, and others on a wheel. That's the only time I was ever in prison, and I hope it will always be the only time. Something may turn up — there's nobody knows.

"When I was turned out I hadn't a farthing given to me. And so I was again in the streets, without knowing a creature and without a farthing in my pocket, and nothing to get one with but my tongue. I set off that day for the country. I didn't try to get a ship, because I didn't know where to go to ask, and I had got ragged, and they wouldn't hear me out if I asked any people about the bridges. I took the first road that offered, and got to Green

wich. I couldn't still think of going back home. I would if I had
had clothes, but they were rags, and I had no shoes but a pair
of old slippers. I was sometimes sorry I left home, but then I began
to get used to travelling, and to beg a bit in the villages. I had no
regular mate to travel with, and no sweetheart. I slept in the
unions whenever I could get in — that's in the country. I didn't
never sleep in the London workhouses till afterwards. In some
country places there were as many as forty in the casual wards,
men, women, and children; in some, only two or three. There
used to be part boys, like myself, but far more bigger than I was;
they were generally from eighteen to twenty-three: London
chaps, chiefly, I believe.

"They were a regularly jolly set. They used to sing and dance
a part of the nights and mornings in the wards, and I got to sing
and dance with them. We were all in a mess; there was no better
or no worse among us. We used to sing comic and sentimental
songs, both. I used to sing 'Tom Elliott,' that's a sea song, for
I hankered about the sea, and 'I'm Afloat.' I hardly know any but
sea-songs. Many used to sing indecent songs; they're impudent
blackguards. They used to sell these songs among the others, but
I never sold any of them, and I never had any, though I know
some, from hearing them often. We told stories sometimes;
romantic tales, some; others blackguard kind of tales, about bad
women; and others about thieving and roguery; not so much
about what they'd done themselves, as about some big thief that
was very clever at stealing, and could trick anybody. Not stories
such as Dick Turpin or Jack Sheppard, or things that's in history,
but inventions. I used to say when I was telling a story — for I've
told one story that I invented till I learnt it, —

[I give this story to show what are the objects of admiration
with these vagrants.]

" 'You see, mates, there was once upon a time, and a very good
time it was, a young man, and he runned away, and got along
with a gang of thieves, and he went to a gentleman's house, and
got in, because one of his mates sweethearted the servant, and
got her away, and she left the door open.' ["But don't," he ex-
postulated, "take it all down that way; it's foolishness. I'm
ashamed of it — it's just what we say to amuse ourselves."] 'And

the door being left open, the young man got in and robbed the house of a lot of money, £1000, and he took it to their gang at the cave. Next day there was a reward out to find the robber. Nobody found him. So the gentleman put out two men and a horse in a field, and the men were hidden in the field, and the gentleman put a notice that anybody that could catch the horse should have him for his cleverness, and a reward as well; for he thought the man that got the £1000 was sure to try to catch that there horse, because he was so bold and clever, and then the two men hid would nab him. This here Jack (that's the young man) was watching, and he saw the two men, and he went and caught two live hares. Then he hid himself behind a hedge, and let one hare go, and one man said to the other, "There goes a hare," and they both run after it, not thinking Jack's there. And while they were running he let go the t'other one, and then said, "There's another hare," and they ran different ways, and so Jack went and got the horse, and took it to the man that offered the reward, and got the reward; it was £100; and the gentleman said "D——n it Jack's done me this time." The gentleman then wanted to serve out the parson, and he said to Jack, "I'll give you another £100 if you'll do something to the parson as bad as you've done to me. Jack said, "Well, I will;" and Jack went to the church and lighted up the lamps, and rang the bells, and the parson he got up to see what was up. Jack was standing in one of the pews like an angel, when the parson got to the church. Jack said, "Go and put your plate in a bag; I'm an angel come to take you up to heaven." And the parson did so, and it was as much as he could drag to church from his house in a bag; for he was very rich. And when he got to the church Jack put the parson in one bag, and the money stayed in the other; and he tied them both together, and put them across his horse, and took them up hills and through water to the gentleman's, and then he took the parson out of the bag, and the parson was wringing wet. Jack fetched the gentleman, and the gentleman gave the parson a horsewhipping, and the parson cut away, and Jack got all the parson's money and the second £100, and gave it all to the poor. And the parson brought an action against the gentleman for horsewhipping him, and they both were ruined. That's the end of it.'

"That's the sort of story that's liked best, sir. Sometimes there was fighting in the casual wards. Sometimes I was in it, I was like the rest. We jawed each other often, calling names, and coming to fight at last. At Romsey a lot of young fellows broke all the windows they could get at, because they were too late to be admitted. They broke them from the outside. We couldn't get at them from inside. I've carried on begging, and going from union to union to sleep, until now. Once I got work in Northampton with a drover. I kept working when he'd a job, from August last to the week before Christmas.

"I always tried to get a ship in a seaport, but couldn't. I've been to Portsmouth, Plymouth, Bristol, Southampton, Ipswich, Liverpool, Brighton, Dover, Shoreham, Hastings, and all through Lincolnshire, Nottinghamshire, Cambridgeshire, and Suffolk—not in Norfolk—they won't let you go there. I don't know why. All this time I used to meet boys like myself, but mostly bigger and older; plenty of them could read and write, some were gentlemen's sons, they said. Some had their young women with them that they'd taken up with, but I never was much with them. I often wished I was at home again, and do now, but I can't think of going back in these rags; and I don't know if my father's dead or alive (his voice trembled), but I'd like to be there and have it over. I can't face meeting them in these rags, and I've seldom had better, I make so little money. I'm unhappy at times, but I get over it better than I used, as I get accustomed to this life. I never heard anything about home since I left. I have applied at the Marine Society here, but it's no use. If I could only get to sea, I'd be happy; and I'd be happy if I could get home, and would, but for the reasons I've told you."

The next was a boy with a quiet look, rather better dressed than most of the vagrant boys, and far more clean in his dress. He made the following statement:—

"I am now seventeen. My father was a cotton-spinner in Manchester, but has been dead ten years; and soon after that my mother went into the workhouse, leaving me with an aunt; and I had work in a cotton factory. As young as I was, I earned 2s 2d. a-week at first. I can read well, and can write a little. I worked at the factory two years, and was then earning 7s. a-week. I then ran away, for I had always a roving mind; but I should have stayed if my master hadn't knocked me about so. I thought I should make my fortune in London — I'd heard it was such a grand place. I had read in novels and romances, — halfpenny and penny books, — about such things, but I've met with nothing of the kind. I started without money, and begged my way from Manchester to London, saying I was going up to look for work. I wanted to see the place more than anything else. I suffered very much on the road, having to be out all night often; and the nights were cold, though it was summer. When I got to London all my hopes were blighted. I could get no further. I never tried for work in London, for I believe there are no cotton factories in it; besides, I wanted to see life. I begged, and slept in the unions. I got acquainted with plenty of boys like myself. We met at the casual wards, both in London and the country. I have now been five years at this life. We were merry enough in the wards, we boys, singing and telling stories. Song such as 'Paul Jones' was liked, while some sung very blackguard songs; but I never got hold of such songs, though I have sold lots of songs in Essex. Some told long stories, very interesting; some were not fit to be heard; but they made one laugh sometimes. I've read 'Jack Sheppard' through, in three volumes; and I used to tell stories out of that sometimes. We all told in our turns. We generally began. — 'Once upon a time, and a very good time it was, though it was neither in your time, nor my time nor nobody else's time' The best man in the story is always called Jack."

At my request, this youth told me a long story, and told it very readily, as if by rote. I give it for its peculiarity, as it is extravagant enough, without humour.

"A farmer hired Jack, and instructed him over-night. Jack was to do what he was required, or lose his head. 'Now, Jack,' said the farmer, [I give the conclusion in the boy's words,] 'what's my name?' 'Master, to be sure,' says Jack. 'No,' said he, 'you must call me Tom Per Cent.' He showed his bed next, and asked, 'What's this, Jack?' 'Why, the bed,' said Jack. 'No, you must call that, He's of Degree.' And so he bid Jack call his leather breeches 'forty cracks;' the cat, 'white-faced Simeon;' the fire, 'hot coleman;' the pump, the 'resurrection;' and the haystack, the 'little cock-a-mountain.' Jack was to remember these names or lose his head. At night the cat got under the grate, and burned herself, and a hot cinder struck her fur, and she ran under the haystack and set it on fire. Jack ran upstairs to his master, and said: —

> *'Tom Per Cent, arise out of he's of degree,*
> *Put on your forty cracks, come down and see;*
> *For the little white-faced Simeon*
> *Has run away with hot coleman*
> *Under the little cock-a-mountain,*
> *And without the aid of the resurrection*
> *We shall be damned and burnt to death.'*

So Jack remembered his lesson, and saved his head. That's the end. Blackguard stories were often told about women. There was plenty told, about Dick Turpin, Sixteen-string Jack, Oxford Blue, and such as them; as well as about Jack Sheppard; about Bamfylde Moore Carew, too, and his disguises. We very often had fighting and quarrelling among ourselves.

"Once, at Birmingham, we smashed all the windows, and did all the damage we could. I can't tell exactly why it was done, but we must all take part in it, or we should be marked. I believe some did it to get into prison, they were so badly off. They piled up the rugs; there was no straw; and some put their clothes on the rugs, and then the heap was set fire to. There was no fire, and no light, but somebody had a box of lucifers. We were all nearly suffocated before the people of the place could get to us. Seventeen of us had a month a-piece for it: I was one. The rugs were dirty and filthy, and not fit for any Christian to sleep under, and so I took part in the burning, as I thought it would cause something better. I've known wild Irishmen get into the wards with knives and sticks hidden about their persons, to be ready for a fight.

"I met two young men in Essex who had been well off — very well, — but they liked a tramper's life. Each had his young woman with him, living as man and wife. They often change their young women; but I never did travel with one, or keep company with any more than twelve hours or so. There used to be great numbers of girls in the casual wards in London. Any young man travelling

the country could get a mate among them, and can get mates —
partners they're often called — still. Some of them are very pretty
indeed; but among them are some horrid ugly — the most are ugly;
bad expressions and coarse faces, and lame, and disgusting to the
eye. It was disgusting, too, to hear them in their own company;
that is, among such as themselves; — beggars, you know. Almost
every word was an oath, and every blackguard word was said
plain out. I think the pretty ones were worst. Very few have
children. I knew two who had. One was seventeen, and her child
was nine months old; the other was twenty-one, and her child
was eighteen months. They were very good to their children. I've
heard of some having children, and saying they couldn't guess
at the fathers of them, but I never met with any such myself.
I didn't often hear them quarrel, — I mean the young men and
young women that went out as partners, — in the lodging-houses.

"Some boys of fifteen have their young women as partners, but
with young boys older women are generally partners — women
about twenty. They always pass as man and wife. All beggar-girls
are bad, I believe. I never heard but of one that was considered
virtuous, and she was always reading a prayer-book and a testament in her lodging-house. The last time I saw her was at Cambridge. She is about thirty, and has traces of beauty left. The
boys used to laugh at her, and say, 'Oh! how virtuous and righteous
we are! but you get your living by it.' I never knew her to get
anything by it. I don't see how she could, for she said nothing
about her being righteous when she was begging about, I believe.
If it wasn't for the casual wards, I couldn't get about. If two
partners goes to the same union, they have to be parted at night,
and join again the morning. Some of the young women are very
dirty, but some's as clean. A few, I think, can read and write.
Some boasts of their wickedness, and others tell them in derision
it's wrong to do that, and then a quarrel rages in the lodging-
house.

"I like a roving life, at first, being my own master. I was fond
of going to plays, and such-like, when I got money; but now I'm
getting tired of it, and wish for something else. I have tried for
work at cotton factories in Lancashire and Yorkshire, but never
could get any. I've been all over the country. I'm sure I could

347

settle now. I couldn't have done that two years ago, the roving spirit was so strong upon me and the company I kept got a strong hold on me. Two winters back, there was a regular gang of us boys in London. After sleeping at a union, we would fix where to meet at night to get into another union to sleep. There were thirty of us that way, all boys; besides forty young men, and thirty young women. Sometimes we walked the streets all night. We didn't rob, at least I never saw any robbing. We had pleasure in chaffing the policemen, and some of us got taken up. I always escaped. We got broken up in time, — some's dead, some's gone to sea, some into the country, some home, and some lagged. Among them were many lads very expert in reading, writing, and arithmetic. One young man — he was only twenty-five — could speak several languages: he had been to sea. He was then begging, though a strong man. I suppose he liked that life: some soon got tired of it.

"I often have suffered from cold and hunger. I never made more than 3*d.* a-day in money, take the year round, by begging; some make more than 6*d.*: but then, I've had meat and bread given, besides. I say nothing when I beg, but that I am a poor boy out of work and starving. I never stole anything in my life. I've often been asked to do so by my mates. I never would. The young women steal the most. I know, least, I did know, two that kept young men, their partners, going about the country with them, chiefly by their stealing. Some do so by their prostitution. Those that go as partners are all prostitutes. There is a great deal of sickness among the young men and women, but I never was ill these last seven years. Fevers, colds, and venereal diseases, are very common."

The last statement I took was that of a boy of thirteen. I can hardly say that he was clothed at all. He had no shirt, and no waistcoat; all his neck and a great part of his chest being bare. A ragged cloth jacket hung about him, and was tied, so as to keep it together, with bits of tape. What he had wrapped round for trousers did not cover one of his legs, while one of his thighs was bare. He wore two old shoes; one tied to his foot with an old ribbon, the other a woman's old boot. He had an old cloth cap. His features were distorted somewhat, through being swollen with the cold. "I was born," he said, "at a place called Hadley, in Kent. My father died when I was three days old, I've heard my mother say. He was married to her, I believe, but I don't know what he was. She had only me. My mother went about begging, sometimes taking me with her; at other times she left me at the lodging-house in Hadley. She went in the country, round about Tunbridge and there, begging. Sometimes she had a day's work. We had plenty to eat then, but I haven't had much lately. My mother died at Hadley a year ago. I didn't know how she was buried. She was ill a long time, and I was out begging; for she sent me out to beg for myself a good while before that, and when I got back to the lodging-house they told me she was dead. I had sixpence in my pocket, but I couldn't help crying to think I'd lost my mother. I cry about it still. I didn't wait to see her buried, but started on my own account. I met two navvies in Bromley, and they paid my first night's lodging; and there was a man passing, going to London with potatoes, and the navvies gave the man a pot of beer to take me up to London in the van, and they went that way with me.

"I came to London to beg, thinking I could get more there than anywhere else, hearing that London was such a good place. I begged; but sometimes wouldn't get a farhing in a day; often walking about the streets all night. I have been begging about all the time till now. I am very weak — starving to death. I never stole anything: I always kept my hands to myself. A boy wanted me to go with him to pick a gentleman's pocket. We was mates for two days, and then he asked me to go picking pockets; but I wouldn't I know it's wrong, though I can neither read nor write. The boy asked me to do it to get into prison, as that would be better than the streets. He picked pockets to get into prison. He was starving about the streets like me. I never slept in a bed since I've been in London: I am sure I haven't: I generally slept under the dry arches in West-street, where they're building houses — I mean the arches for the cellars. I begged chiefly from the Jews about Petticoat-lane, for they all give away bread that their children leave — pieces of crust and such-like. I would do anything to be out of this misery."

TWO FEMALE TRAMPS

THE FIRST — a young woman 20 years of age — gave me the following statement. Her face was what the vulgar would call "good-looking," as her cheeks were full and deep-coloured, and her eye tolerably bright, and her teeth good. She was very stout, too. Her dress was tolerably clean and good, but sat close about her, as if she had no under-clothing. She said: —

"I am a native of ——, where my father was a woolcomber. I was an only child. I can't remember my mother, she died when I was so young. My father died more than four years ago. I've heard as much since I left home. I was sent to the National School. I can read, but can't write. My father went to work at Wellington, in Somersetshire, taking me with him, when I was quite a little girl. He was a good father and very kind, and we had plenty to eat. I think of him sometimes: it makes me sorrowful. He would have been sadly distressed if he had seen me in this state. My father married again when I was 12, I suppose. He married a factory-woman. She was about 30. She wasn't good to me. She led me a dreadful life, always telling my father stories of me, — that I was away when I wasn't, and he grumbled at me. He never beat me, but my stepmother often beat me. She was very bad-tempered, and I am very bad-tempered, too — very passionate; but if I'm well treated my passion doesn't come out. She beat me with anything that came first to hand, as the hearth-brush, and she flung things at me. She disliked me, because she knew I hated my father marrying again. I was very happy before that, living with my father. I could cook dinner for him, young as I was, make his bed, and do all those sort of things, all but his washing. I had a bed to myself. My father was a good man. He came home drunk sometimes, but not often. It never made any difference in him, he was always kind. He seemed comfortable with my stepmother, but I wasn't. I used to tell my father how she used me, but he said it was nonsense.

"This went on till I was 15, when I ran away. I'm sure I had

351

been a good girl till then. I never slept out of my father's house up to that time, and didn't keep company with any young men. I could stand my stepmother's treatment no longer. If she had been kind I wouldn't have run away. I was almost as big then as I am now. I had 4s. or 5s. with me, I don't remember just how much, I started in such a passion; but it was money I had saved up from what my father had given me. I took no clothes with me but what I had on. I was tidily dressed. It was in the haymaking time, and I made straight away to London. I was so young and in such a rage, I couldn't think of nothing but getting away. When I cooled I began to think of my father, but at home I had heard of young girls being sent out to Australia and having done well, and I thought I could easily get sent out from London, and so I went on.

"I slept in lodging-houses. I was shocked the first night I got into Bridgwater, men, women, and boys, all sleeping in the same room. I slept with another young woman, a travelling-woman, but married. I couldn't think of going back. I couldn't humble myself before that stepmother. I thought anything would be better than that. I couldn't sleep at all the first night I was out. I never was in such a bed before.

"A young man who saw me there wanted me to live with him; he was a beggar, and I didn't like a beggar, and I wouldn't have nothing to say to him. He wasn't impudent; but he followed me to Bristol, all the time, wherever I met with him, teasing me to live with him. I lived on my money as long as I could, and then had to go and sleep in a union. I don't know where. It was a dreadful place. The rats ran over my head while I slept; and I prayed for daylight for I used to pray then. I don't now. I don't like the thoughts of it. At last I got to London. I was sitting in Hyde-park thinking where I should go – I know it was Hyde-park, for I was taken up from it since. The park-keeper took me up for making a noise – that's a disturbance – in the park; me and some other young women; we were only washing ourselves where the horses drink, near the canteen. In Hyde-park, while I was sitting, as I've told you, some girls and some young men, and some older men, passed me, carrying rakes. I was sitting with three other girls I'd got acquainted with on the road, all Irish girls. The people that passed me said, 'We are going half-way to Watford a-hay making. Go with us?' We all went. Each of those Irish girls soon took up with a mate. I think they had known each other before.

"I had a fortnight at haymaking. I had a mate at haymaking, and in a few days he ruined me. He told the master that I belonged to him. He didn't say I was his wife. They don't call us their wives. I continued with him a long time, living with him as his wife. We next went into Kent harvesting, then a-hopping, and I've been every summer since. He was kind to me, but we were both passionate — fire against fire — and we fought sometimes. He never beat me but once, for contradicting him. He wasn't jealous, and he had no reason to be so. I don't know that he was fond of me, or he wouldn't have run away. I liked him, and would have gone through trouble for him. I like him still. We never talked about marrying. I didn't care, for I didn't think about it. I lived with him, and was true to him, until he ran away in haymaking time in 1848. He ran away from me in Kent, where we were hopping. We hadn't quarrelled for some days before he started. I didn't think he was going, for he was kind to me just before. I left him once for a forthinght myself, through some quarrel, but he got me back again.

"I came up to London in a boat from Gravesend, with other hoppers. I lived on fifteen shillings I had saved up. I lived on that as long as it lasted — more than a week. I lodged near the Dials, and used to go drinking with other women I met with there, as I was fond of drink then. I don't like it so much now. We drank gin and beer. I kept to myself until my money was gone, and then I looked out for myself. I had no particular friends. The women I drank with were some bad and some good. I got acquainted with a young girl as I was walking along the Strand looking out for my living by prostitution — I couldn't starve. We walked together. We couldn't stay in the Strand where girls were well-dressed, and so we kept about the Dials. I didn't think much about the life I was leading, because I got hardened. I didn't like it, though. Still I thought I should never like to go home. I lodged in a back street near the Dials. I couldn't take anybody there. I didn't do well. I often wanted money to pay my lodgings, and food to eat, and had often to stay out all night perishing. Many a night out in the streets I never got a farthing, and had to walk about all day because I dursn't go back to my room without money. I never had a fancy man.

"There were all sorts in the lodging-house — thirty of them — pick-pockets, and beggars, and cadgers, and fancy men, and some that wanted to be fancy men, but I never saw one that I liked. I never picked pockets as other girls did; I was not nimble enough with my hands. Sometimes I had a sovereign in my pocket, but it was never there a day. I used to go out a-drinking, treating other women, and they would treat me. We helped one another now and then. I was badly off for clothes. I had no illness except colds. The common fellows in the streets were always jeering at me. Sometimes missionaries, I think they're called talked to me about the life I was leading, but I told them, 'You mind yourself, and I'll mind myself. What is it to you where I go when I die?' I don't steal anything. I swear sometimes now. When I was at home and good, I was shocked to hear such a thing. Me and the other girls used to think it clever to swear hard, and say bad words one to another or to anybody — we're not particular. If I went into the Magdalen, I know I could'nt stay there, I have not been there but I know I couldn't from what I've heard of it from the other girls, some of whom said they'd been; and I suppose they had, as there was no motive at all for them to tell lies about it. I have been in the casual wards at Holborn and Kennington when I was beat out. It was better than walking the streets. I think, by the life I lead — and without help I must lead it still, or starve — I sometimes get twenty shillings a week, sometimes not more than five shillings. I would like best to go to Australia, where nobody would know me. I'm sure I could behave myself there.

"There's no hope for me here: everybody that knows me despises me. I could take a service in Sydney. I could get rid of my swearing. I only swear now when I'm vexed — it comes out natural-like then. I could get rid of my love of drink. No one — no girl can carry on the life I do without drink. No girl's feelings would let her. I never met one but what said so, and I know they all told the truth in that I am strong and healthy, and could take a hard place with country work. That about Australia is the best wish I have. I'm sure I'm sick of this life. It has only drink and excitement to

recommend it. I haven't a friend in the world. I have been told
I was a fool not to pick pockets like other girls. I never begged but
once, and that was as I was coming to London, and a woman said,
'You look better than I do!' so I never begged again—that checked
me at once. But I've got tickets for the 'straw-yards' or the
'leather-houses', as some call them [asylums for the houseless].
The old women all say it was far better when they were young.
I think what a change it is from my country life; but when I get
sad, I go and get a glass of gin, if I have the money. I can get
a pennyworth in some houses. I can't do much at my needle. The
idleness of the life I lead is terrible. There is nothing to interest
me."

The next was a mere girl, who had lost all traces of feminine
beauty. There was an impudence in her expression that was
utterly repulsive; and even in her most serious moments it was
evident that she had the greatest difficulty to restrain her inward
levity. Her dress consisted principally of a ragged red and green
plaid shawl, pinned tight over her neck, and a torn straw-bonnet,
worn back upon her head.

"I have a father alive," she said; "I have got no mother. I have
been away these three years. I came away with a chap. I was
living, sir, when I was at home, with my father in Maidstone. My
father was a gardener, and I used to work at shirtmaking when
I was at home with my father. My mother has been dead eight
years, I think. I can't say how old I was then. I am twenty now.
My father, after my mother's death, married again. She was dead
seven years before he got another wife. He didn't marry again
while I was at home. My mother was a very good mother. I was
very fond of my mother, for she was a very good mother; but not
of my father, for he was a bad father. Why, sir, he used to treat
us three girls so ill, my biggest sisters was obliged to go to Australia
from him. My next sister was younger than me, and I don't know
whether she is at home now; but I don't believe that she can stop
at home, because I have been down as far as Maidstone since
I went away with my young man and I've heard that she's almost
dead between the pair of them. By the pair of them, I mean my
father and stepmother. My mother-in-law is the worst to my
sister. My father was bad before she came; he was such a drunkard.

"We went to school, where we paid nothing a week, in Maidstone; it's a free school. I can read. I can't write. All the money my father used to earn he used to drink, and leave us without any food. I went to the shirt-making when I was twelve years of age, and that used to bring me about 4*d*. a day, and with that I used to buy bread, for we never got a halfpenny from my father to keep us. My father used to work for a gentleman, and got pretty good wages. The young chap that I first took up with was a carpenter. He was apprenticed to the trade. He enticed me away. He told me if I'd come to London with him he'd do anything for me. I used to tell him how badly my father treated me, and he used to tell me not to stop at home. I have been knocking about three years, and I'm twenty now, so I leave you to say how old I was then. No, I can't say. I'm twenty now, and I've been away these three years, and I don't know how old that would make me. I never learnt any ciphering.

"My father used to beat us and knock us about when he came home drunk. I liked the young man that came a-courting on me very well. I thought all he said was true, and I thought he would make me much happier than I was at home." [Here she shook her head with apparent regret.] "Yes, sir, he promised he would marry me; but when I came over to London he ruined me, and then ran away and left me. I knew it was wrong to go away and live with him without being married; but I was wretched at home, and he told me he would make me his wife, and I believed him. He brought me up to London with him, into the Borough. He took me to a low lodging-house there. The charge was 6d. a night for the two of us. There were six sleeping in the same room beside us two. They were men and women. Some of 'em were married, and some were not.

"He had 4*s*. 6*d*. when he came up to London with me, and I had none. He stopped with me. He stopped with me in the same house a week. He was 22 years of age, or 23, I can't say which. While he was with me he was very kind to me: oh, yes, sir, much kinder than my father, and I loved him a great deal more, I'm sure. I hadn't any clothes when I left my father's home. I had nothing but what I stood upright in. I had no more clothes when I was at home. When my young man left me there was another young girl in the same lodging-house, who advised me to turn out upon the streets. I went and took her advice. I did like the life for a bit, because I see'd there was money getting by it. Sometimes I got 4s. or 5s. a-day, and sometimes more than that. I still kept at the same house.

"There were a lot of girls like me at the same place. It was not a bad house, but they encouraged us like. No tramps used to come there, only young chaps and gals that used to go out thieving. No, my young man didn't thieve, not while he was with me, but I did afterwards. I've seen young chaps brought in there by the girls merely to pay their lodging-money. The landlady told us to do that; she said I could do better than knocking about with a man. If I hadn't had enough to pay for my lodging. I couldn't have had a bed to lie on.

"We used to be all in the same room, chaps and girls, sometimes nine or ten couples in the same room—only little bits of girls and chaps. I have seen girls there 12 years of age. The boys was about 15 or 16. They used to swear dreadful. I fell out with the gal as first told me to go on the streets, and then I got with another at another house. I moved to Paddington. I lived at a little public-house there—a bad house; and I used to go out shoplifting with my pal. I used to take everything I could lay my hands on. We went one night, and I stole two dresses, at a linendraper's shop, and had two months a-piece for it. Yes, sir, I liked prison very well, because I had such bad clothes; and was glad to be out of the way. Some days we hardly had a bit to put in our mouths. Sometimes we used to get nothing shoplifting: the men, perhaps, would notice—the fly-men, as we called them. They used to be too wide-awake for us. Sometimes we used to make 5s. in the day; but then we used to spend it all in waste—why, spending it in anything. We'd buy fish, and meat, and baked potatoes, and pudding. No, sir, very little drink we had. We didn't care for gin, nor any liquor at all. There was none among us but one that cared for drink, and she used to pawn all her clothes for it.

"I dare say there was upwards of twelve of thirteen gals; the kitchen used to be full. The mistress used to treat us well if we paid her; but she used to holler at us if we didn't. The chaps used to serve her out so. They used to take the sheets, and blankets, and everything away from her. She was deaf. They was mostly all prigs that used to come to see us. They used to go out nailing — that's thieving. There was one that they used to call Fogerty was transported: another got seven months; and another got a twelve-month. I had one fancy-man. He was a shoplifter and a pick-pocket: he has got two years now. I went to see him once in quod; some calls it 'the Steel.' I cried a good deal when he got nailed sir: I loved him. A little time after he went away, I went down into the country; down into Essex. I saw I couldn't get him off, 'cause it was for a watch, and the gentleman went so hard against him. I was with him at the time he stole it, but I didn't know he'd got it till I saw him run. I got the man down by a sawmill; he was tipsy. He was a gentleman, and said he would give me five shillings if I would come along with him. My fancy-man always kept near to me whenever I went out of a night. I usen't to go out to take the men home; it was only to pick them up.

"My young man used to tell me how to rob the men. I'd get them up in a corner, and then I used to take out of their pockets whatever I could lay my hands on; and then I used to hand it over to him, and he used to take the things home and 'fence' them. We used to do a good deal this way sometimes: often we'd get enough to keep us two or three days. At last he got caught for the watch; and when I see'd I couldn't get him off, I went down into the country—down into Essex, sir. I travelled all parts, and slept at the unions on the road. I met a young girl down in Town Malling, in Kent. I met her, and then we used to go begging together, and tramp it from one union to another. At last we got so ragged and dirty, and our things all got so bad, that we made up our minds to go in for three months into prison, at Battle, down in Sussex. We used to meet a great many on the road boiling their kettle, and sometimes we used to stop and skipper with them of a night. Skippering is sleeping in barns or under hedges, if it's warm weather. They weren't gipsies.

"We usen't to stop to speak to the gipsies—not much—unless we went to fairs or horse-races. Then we used to sit with them for a little while, if they had their tent. We generally used to steal on the way. If we could see anything, we used to take it. At last, when our clothes got bad, I and the other girl—she still kept with me — determined to break the parson's windows at Battle. We broke one because the house was good for a cant — that's some food — bread or meat, and they wouldn't give it us, so we got savage, and broke all the glass in the windows. For that we got three months. After we got out, the parson sent word for us to come to his house, and he gave us half-a-crown a-piece to take us on our road. He would have given us some clothes — we had no shoes and stockings: we was very bad off; but his wife was in London.

"So we went on the road tramping again, and I have been tramping it about the country ever since. I was all last winter in Town Malling union with the fever, and when I got well I set off tramping again. I didn't have no more chaps since I left my fancy-man — I mean, I never took up with no others, not to keep their company. I have been about two years tramping altogether; out of that I had five months in prison for stealing and breaking windows. I like the tramping life well enough in the summer, 'cause there's plenty of victuals to be had then, but it's the winter that we can't stand. Then we generally come to London, but we can't call at house to house here as we do in the country, so we make but a poor thing of it. I never was so bad off as I am now, excepting when I was at Battle, for I had no shoes or stockings then.

"The police is too sharp for us in London. I'm very fond of going through the country in fine weather. Sometimes we don't make much freedom with the chaps in the union, and sometimes we do. They tells us to go along with them, for they knows good houses to call at. What you make is all according to whether you're in a lonesome road. I've travelled a day, and not seen a house that I could get anything at. Some days I've got a shilling given to me, and some days as much as half-a-crown. We can always get plenty of bread and meat, for countryfolks is very good.

"If I had some good things — that is, good boots — I should like to go into the country again. Sometimes we gets so much scran we sells it among ourselves. I should sell my lot to some travellers on the road. They gives us 3d. or 4d., but we must give them a good lot for that. I can't say which is the best of the unions now, for they are all shut up. They used to be good at one time, but the Irish ruined them; they came in such swarms, the people, I knew, would never stand it. We used often to say of a night that them Irish Greeks would ruin the business. They are much better beggars than we are, though they don't get as much as the English, because they go in such swarms up to the door. Now, down in Hawkhurst, there used to be a twopenny loaf allowed to everybody that called at the parson's house, little and big; it was allowed by a lady, till the pigs of Irish came in such lots, that they spoilt all the game. The parson won't give it to no one now, except eight travelling-men in the morning. I know all the good houses, and the tidy grubbikens, — that's the unions where there's little or nothing to do for the food we gets.

"We walk mostly eleven miles a-day. If it's hot we walk only six miles, and turn in under a hedge if we've got our things with us to make a tent. We go all right round the country, up to Yorkshire, and as far as Northumberland. We don't try Warwick gaol, because the shilling they used to give on being discharged is stopped, excepting to those that's not been there before, and there's very few of the trampers, boys or girls, that hasn't. Then there's the twopenny-house down in Highfield, in Kent. I'm blowed if they ain't been and stopped that! I can't tell what's come to the country of late. It's got very bad and scaly, there's no hospitality going on. I've been two years at the business, and I've seen it grow worse and worse, meaner and meaner, every day before my very eyes. I don't know, I'm sure, what poor trampers will do if it gets any worse. Some do talk of the good old times, when there was plenty of money-getting in them days. I shouldn't like to give it up just yet. I do like to be in the country in the summer-time. I like haymaking and hopping, because that's a good bit of fun.

"Still, I'm sick and tired of what I'm doing now. It's the winter that sickens me. I'm worn out now, and I often sits and thinks of the life that I've led. I think of my kind, dear mother, and how good I would have been if my father had taught me better. Still, if I'd clothes I'd not give up my present life. I'd be down in the country now. I do love roving about, and I'm wretched when I'm not at it. After my mother died I never liked to be at home. I've seen many an unhappy day since I've been away; still, I wouldn't go back to my home, because it's no home to me."